BUSINESS IN ISLAM:
Contextualizing Business and Mission in Muslim-Majority Nations

Robert J. Stefan

WIPF & STOCK · Eugene, Oregon

Book Five of the APTS Press Monograph Series

Wipf and Stock Publishers
199 W 8th Ave, Suite 3
Eugene, OR 97401

Business in Islam
Contextualizing Business and Mission in Muslim-Majority Nations
By Stefan, Robert J.
Copyright©2019 APTS Press
ISBN 13: 978-1-7252-5710-8
Publication date 11/3/2019
Previously published by APTS Press, 2019

Publishers Preface

We are pleased to offer this fifth title in our APTS Press Monograph Series. This is the publication of the author's doctoral dissertation done through the Concordia Theological Seminary in Fort Wayne, Indiana, USA. The purpose of this series is to give our readers broader access to good scholarship that would otherwise be unavailable outside of the academic community. This is part of our ongoing commitment to discipleship through publishing.

The other four titles in this series, *Theology in Context: A Case Study in the Philippines,* by Dave Johnson, *Leave a Legacy: Increasing Missionary Longevity*, by Russ Turney, *Understanding the Iglesia ni Cristo*, by Anne Harper, and *A Theology of Hope: Contextual Perspectives in Korean* Pentecostalism, by Sang Yun Lee, are all available at www.aptspress.org. If you have any questions, you can reach us through our website. We would be happy to hear from you.

We hope you enjoy this book. Please feel free to communicate with us through our website.

THE PUBLISHER

Dedication

To my wife, Marilyn, for her missions' heart, which brought us into new areas of service, for our long discussions about business and mission, her disregard for the riches of this world, and her constant encouragement.

and

To Glenn, my brother in Christ, who modeled business and mission (before it had a name), and without whose stewardship this work could never have been completed.

> "Behold, I am sending you out as sheep among wolves, so be wise as serpents and innocent as doves."

Matthew 10:16 (English Standard Version)

Contents

Publishers Preface	iii
Dedication	v
Preface	ix
Acknowledgments	xi
Abbreviations	xiv
Glossary of Terms	xv
Chapter 1 Introduction	1
Chapter 2 Business in the Quran	17
Chapter 3 Business in Sunnah	49
Chapter 4 Business in Thought and Law	87
Chapter 5 Business in Islamic History	129
Chapter 6 Business in Modern Islam	197
Chapter 7 Business and Christian Mission	263
Chapter 8 Contextualization, Research Findings, Approaches and Conclusion	287
Appendix One	323
Appendix Two	327
Appendix Three	335
Bibliography	336

Preface

In December 1993, the course of my life, along with the lives of my wife and our children, took a radical shift. At the age of 38, I retired from the investment banking firm of which I was a founding shareholder. My partners, associates and clients were respectful of my decision, but I could sense they questioned why I would leave my career at a time when my earning potential was at its peak. In short, my wife and I sensed the Lord had another plan for our lives. A number of years later, my wife and I were appointed as missionaries and traveled to a Muslim-majority nation to establish for-profit kingdom businesses, in partnership with national believers. Our ultimate goal was to assist local churches in becoming financially self-supporting.

My experience as a Wall Street investment banker and entrepreneur taught me many things about starting, financing and successfully operating businesses. However, building a business—that is also missional—in a foreign country (with the attendant hurdles of language, culture and corruption) required more preparation. I discovered that when the center of the mission is not a church, a Christian ministry or a mission base, but rather a for-profit business, the obstacles become greater. Mindful of the Biblical admonition about not being able to serve both God and mammon, missionaries engaged in business and mission strategies in Muslim-majority nations (MMNs) need to simultaneously be disciples of Christ and effective businesspeople in a Muslim society. Such business and mission workers will need to communicate the Gospel in ways that Muslims working in the marketplace can understand. Missionaries will need to establish stepping stones for Muslims doing business in Islam if they are to become followers of Jesus—doing business in Christ. I wrote my dissertation, and ultimately this book, in order to begin to address these needs.

Acknowledgments

I want to acknowledge two pastors whose ministries greatly impacted the trajectory of my life leading to this book. The first, is Pastor Robert Schmidgall who imparted a vision for world missions. The second, is Pastor Patrick Rusch who encouraged me, and gave me the opportunity, to use my business talents and training for the benefit of the Church and the Kingdom of God.

I would also like to acknowledge the members of the faculty of Asia Pacific Theological Seminary during the three years I spent there studying and teaching.

The seeds of thinking theologically and contextually about missions were sown during those years, both in the classroom and in the many times of fellowship that we shared.

I want to acknowledge the vision and support of Jerry Parsley and Dr. Mark Hausfeld for giving me the opportunity to plow new ground in business and mission. Dr. William Menzies also supported our work with many words of encouragement and prayer at our commissioning. In my mission's travels, many individuals have impacted my thoughts—too many to mention specifically. Dr. Don McCurry, however, provided insightful comments over a dinner in Cairo, where I shared with him the focus of my research. Specifically, he commented that my research could result in "stepping stones" to assist Muslim businesspeople in their understanding of the person and work of Christ, which subsequently influenced my approach to contextualization.

I also want to acknowledge Dr. Detlev Schulz. His encouragement and receptivity regarding the topic of my research greatly influenced my decision to pursue my studies at Concordia Theological Seminary. His kind words throughout the years were a tangible reminder of the importance of finishing the work God had prepared for me to do. Dr. Adam Francisco, both as my Dissertation Advisor and as a Professor of Islamic Studies, modeled what it means to engage in the study of Islam from an academic perspective. I also want to thank Dr. Carl Fickenscher for his willingness to be a reader despite his many responsibilities, both academically and outside the seminary.

Lastly, I would like to acknowledge the encouragement of two friends. Dr. Timothy Jenney would often send emails and call me to see how I was progressing, and to encourage me with advice as someone who had walked the Ph.D. path before me. Also, Melvin Ho shared his thoughts about ministry to Muslims along with books he was reading, which often proved timely. To Tim and Melvin, thank you both for extending your pastoral hearts to me.

Abbreviations

BAM	Business as mission
Bu	*Sahîh Al-Bukhâri*
Daw	*Sunan Abu Dawud*
Maj	*Sunan Ibn Mâjah*
MED	Micro-enterprise development
MMN	Muslim-majority nation
Mus	*Sahîh Muslim*
Muw	*Al-Muwatta of Imam Malik ibn Anas*
Nas	*Sunan An-Nasâ'i*
Tir	*Jāmi' At-Tirmidhi*

Glossary

ahadith—A single passage containing a saying, action, habit or event from the life of Muhammad.

alim—A scholar of Islam, one who is a guardian or interpreter of religious knowledge.

ayah—An individual verse of the Qur'an.

ayat—Plural form of *ayah*

dhimmi—A non-Muslim subject of the Islamic state who is required to pay a poll tax.

fatwa—A religious ruling by an Islamic law expert.

gharar—Refers to a situation, such as a business transaction, where there is excessive risk due to incomplete information or terms which greatly favor one party to a transaction over another.

hadith—Collections of Muhammad's sayings, actions, habits and events as codified by his companions or by later Muslims.

halal—Something allowed under Islamic law.

haram—Something prohibited under Islamic law.

hisbah—An institution in early Islamic history which regulated the actions of participants in the marketplace and provided necessary municipal services.

hiyal—Legal tricks or gimmicks designed to allow transactions, which would otherwise be prohibited, to meet the requirements of Islamic law.

ijara—An equipment or asset lease.

ijtihad—The application of personal effort (including study of the Qur'an and *hadith*) to gain wisdom and extend Islamic law to new situations.

khalifah—A trustee or one who exercises stewardship on behalf of another.

jihad—An effort or striving enjoined in the Qur'an and *hadith* with the purpose of advancing Islam.

jizya—A poll-tax levied on non-Muslims living in Muslim states.

mudarabah—Islamic partnership or contract where one partner provides capital and the other management skill. Profits are divided based on a percentage. Losses are borne by the provider of capital.

mufti—A public official who assists Islamic judges by supplying them with *fatwas*.

muhtasib—A Muslim official who supervises marketplaces.

murabaha—Installment sale contract which involves the lender buying an asset, marking it up, and receiving an agreed upon number of payments from the borrower.

musharakah—Joint venture contract constructed around a specific product or line of business.

riba—The increase or premium paid by a borrower to a lender, over and above the principal, as part of a loan agreement.

sadaqa—Charity given of a donor's free will.

sheikh—A wise elder; an Islamic scholar.

sira—Islamic biographical literature, commonly used to refer to writings about the life of Muhammad.

surah—A chapter of the Qur'an.

surat—The plural of *surah*.

tafsir—A commentary on the meaning of the Qur'an.

tawhid—A theological term referring to the oneness of Allah.

tijarah—Commercial activities, trade and trading.

ulema—The scholars, past and present, of all aspects of Islam.

ummah—The worldwide community of Muslims.

usufruct—The income or produce of an asset.

wakala—Warehouse used in transit trade, which frequently offered living accommodations for traders and space to display wares.

wakil—An agent or attorney of a merchant used in connection with long-distance trade.

waqf—Islamic charitable foundation used to channel the *usufruct* of assets for the benefit of the poor or the public.

zakat—An annual percentage tax on assets owned by Muslims for the benefit of the poor. The percentage of the tax varies depending on the type of asset.

CHAPTER 1

Introduction

Introduction

On a recent trip to Cairo, Egypt, I walked past several dozen tanks and armored personnel carriers, manned and at the ready, flanking a barbed-wire-covered pathway leading to the entrance of the Egyptian Museum. Overlooking the museum was the charred remains of former Egyptian President Mubarek's political headquarters building—a testimony to the national strife that had rocked the country and led to the election of President Morsi (supported by the Muslim Brotherhood) followed by a counter-takeover led by the Egyptian military. In Amman, Jordan, I walked past the offices of the Muslim Brotherhood, whose activities were being opposed by the king of Jordan.

Clearly, nations where Muslims are in the majority ("Muslim-majority nations" or "MMNs") are facing tumultuous times. Yet, the citizens of those nations are linked with the world through economic globalization, and there is no shortage of foreign-owned businesses operating in MMNs. These businesses, however, have frequently come under suspicion and even outright attack. It is common to read news accounts of Muslims coming into conflict with businesses and their owners as Muslims seek to force businesses (foreign- and locally-owned) to comply with certain aspects of *sharia*. For example, in Pakistan, a women's clothing store was bombed after Islamists warned it not to sell certain clothes, shoes, and bangles:[1] and armed Muslims attacked Christians to collect the *jizya* from Christian merchants.[2]

Notwithstanding these conflicts, many Christian mission organizations have enthusiastically embraced "business" as a means of entry for Christian workers who might not otherwise be able to get into these nations, especially MMNs. However, the embracing of business raises some immediate concerns. In light of existing tensions between business and Islam, won't missions-connected businesses be under the same cloud of conflict? More importantly, isn't the Gospel put under this cloud, thereby negatively impacting the spread of the kingdom of God? Also, if the business-and-mission companies' expatriate owners and employees are western (especially American) won't the conflicts inevitably intensify? And if so, are there ways such entities can be operated in order to minimize the conflict with Islamic sensitivities? This book will address these and other related questions.

Research Concern

Christians are commanded by Jesus to, "Go therefore and make disciples of all nations" (Matthew 28:19, ESV). The Great Commission has not changed—the Gospel is for all mankind. In the world at present, many nations, including those where the Gospel has either never been communicated or communicated only sparsely, have imposed numerous obstacles to the carrying out of Jesus' command. Depending on the nation, these obstacles take a

---

[1] *Jihad Watch*, "Sharia in action in Pakistan: Women's clothing store blown up after Islamic supremacists warned it not to sell women clothes, shoes, and bangles," http://www.jihadwatch.org/2012/08/sharia-in-action-in-pakistan-womens-clothing-store-blown-up-after-islamic-supremacists-warned-it-not.html (accessed August 24, 2012).

[2] *Jihad Watch*, "Pakistan: Armed Muslims attack Christians, collect *jizya* from Christian merchants," http://www.jihadwatch.org/2012/09/pakistan-armed-muslims-attack-christians-collect-jizya-from-christian-merchants.html (accessed September 3, 2012).

number of different forms, including severe limitations on entry of religious workers, restrictions on permitted religious activities, outright bans on religious proselytizing, and limitations on how long religious workers may reside in the nation. Such obstacles often block traditional methods of missionary work. How then are Christians to carry out the Great Commission in nations that have raised such obstacles?

In response to this challenge, various Christian mission strategies have arisen, including those that involve the establishment of businesses. Two models that have gained acceptance among Christians engaged in missions are "business as mission" (BAM) and various forms of micro-enterprise development (MED). Under BAM, for-profit businesses are established by believers in nations where there is a need to spread the Gospel. The BAM business is managed in order to make a profit while also being missional (i.e., allowing for, or promoting, the intentional spread of the Gospel). The BAM company also serves as the basis of a believer's entry visa application and increases the likelihood that the visa will be granted, since national authorities typically view business investment favorably. MED differs in that it seeks to lift the poor by helping them (primarily with financing) to establish small businesses. While each model may be attractive from a Great Commission standpoint (gaining entry into "all nations"), missionaries using these strategies find themselves engaging the host culture from an entirely new entry point—the marketplace—which, as discussed in the opening statement, is not without potential conflict.

The research concern addressed here is focused on contextualizing business when it is used as part of business-and-mission strategies in Muslim-majority nations in order to minimize potential conflicts. The book researches the Islamic view of business, with the goal of contextualizing the various business and mission models as practiced currently in Christian missions in MMNs.

Missiological Rationale for Research Concern

The need to contextualize business, as practiced in various business-and-mission strategies, with the Islamic view of business is missiologically important for three reasons. First, missionaries have learned the need to be sensitive cross-culturally to many factors as they seek to establish relationships in the setting where they are living and ministering. Those so engaged in business and mission will be working in the local marketplace for much of their time. Thus, they need to be able to articulate their business, and their activities, in ways that can be understood and accepted within the host culture. They need to be able to answer the question, "Why are you here?" with integrity and convincingly. The "simple" answers (e.g., "To build a successful business," "To help people out of poverty," or "To make a profit") are insufficient and confusing, if not offensive, to non-Western minds. An effective answer to the basic question must travel over cultural bridges into the host culture's religious, historical, and intellectual traditions. Where business-and-mission projects are located in MMNs, the cultural bridges must take into account not only the Qur'an and the example of the Prophet Muhammad as described in the traditions (*hadith*) and life of Muhammad (*sira*), but also Islamic theology, law, and the commercial history and practice of Muslim societies. Such cultural sensitivity may lead to a greater longevity of the business-and-mission company in the host country (along with those missionaries associated with the company). The longevity issue is becoming a central concern among mission organizations, since the permissible length of stay in many MMNs seems to be shortening substantially.

Second, many of the MMNs where business-and-mission strategies may be of the greatest use are in nations where there exists a high degree of suspicion (if not outright antagonism) toward ideas and people from the West. This is especially so of businesses operated by foreigners, since, in the minds of many local people, such businesses are more or less linked with globalism, which is commonly viewed as being exploitive. Given that business-and-mission companies are ultimately missional, it would be optimal if their structure and manner of operation do not rely exclusively on Western business management and economic development theory to explain their existence and operation. Rather, their structure and operations should be sensitive to their host Islamic contexts.

Third, by establishing culturally accepted business-and-mission company models, the missionaries are advancing a sustainable form of economic activity for the community at large. Local Muslim converts to Christianity (in addition to being spiritually discipled in the normal fashion) would see an economic model that allows them to remain in their local communities while engaging in acceptable forms of employment and trade. Ultimately, local businesses owned by local believers have proven to be highly beneficial in establishing a strong financial base for the church. Providing for local financial support is especially important in cultures where any form of outside financial assistance is viewed as simply "buying souls." Such a view is not uncommon in MMNs.

Relevant Literature

In researching the topic of "Business in Islam," it is appropriate to begin with the Qur'an and the commonly accepted *hadith* traditions; English translations of these texts are readily available. Aside from these primary sources, there are also topical indexes and digital versions that can be searched to direct the reader to those specific topics that shed light on the Islamic understanding of business. Relating to the Qur'an, there are a variety of widely accepted *tafsirs*, which seek to explain the Qur'an's teachings. Since the life of Muhammad is also regarded as authoritative for Muslims, biographical and other works on his life also constitute relevant literature. Although written many years after Muhammad's death, several Muslim scholars and jurists (including Ibn Taymiya, Ibn Khaldun, and Imam Malik ibn Anas) wrote works that address numerous Islamic business and financial practices. These works provide useful insights into the interpretation of Qur'anic verses and *hadith* passages that relate to business.

There has also been much written, primarily by Muslim authors, on how business and economics should be structured and conducted in a society that seeks (or should seek) to be Islamic. The bulk of it was written following the collapse of colonialism in the aftermath of World War II. Some of these authors grounded their arguments by repeatedly quoting the Qur'an and various *ahadith* of Muhammad that they deemed pertinent. Others have taken a more political and economic approach to set forth an Islamic economic system (derived from Islamic principles but with far fewer references to the Qur'an or *hadith*), which they then compare and contrast with other economic systems, such as capitalism, socialism, and communism.

Another grouping of relevant literature is centered on the subject of "*sharia*-compliant" business and finance. This literature is derived from a fundamentalist understanding of the Qur'an and *hadith* traditions, which rose in popularity among many Muslims in the 20th century. One example of this is the notoriety of Sayyid Qutb, an Egyptian writer and early member of the Muslim Brotherhood, whose commentary on the Qur'an is widely cited. Authors who ascribe to this fundamentalist interpretation of Islam advocate for structuring all business transactions, particularly banking (in order to eliminate interest) in a manner that is *sharia*-compliant. While Muslim authors write most of the *sharia*-compliant literature, there are a significant number of Western authors who interpret *sharia*-compliant business for Western readers and, in many cases, advocate for it—although their motives appear more financial than Islamic.

Another grouping of relevant literature consists of historical accounts of the business and economic practices found in Islamic societies at various times and places. This literature serves a useful purpose, because it illustrates how the various verses and passages from the Qur'an and *hadith* that pertain to business (along with the ideas of respected Islamic thinkers) were actually implemented and practiced.

The linkage of business with Christian mission has a long history that is well documented. The history of Christian missions contains numerous examples of missionaries who were sent by various mission societies and groups to plant churches and who were expected to support themselves through their skills in a trade or craft. The mission strategies of BAM and MED, which involve starting businesses cross-culturally with the intention of evangelization and church planting, are relatively new. The literature pertaining to these types of business-and-mission projects generally date from the 1980s. It is relevant because it provides a basis upon which contextualization strategies can be applied.

While there is a significant amount of literature with titles akin to "Doing Business in X," where X represents any number of host countries, these works tend to give scant attention to contextualizing the form of business itself to the local (including the Islamic) context. The authors seem to assume that business principles are universal and that Western business forms most correctly and efficiently embody such practices. Although the Christian literature on business-and-mission does emphasize the cross-cultural aspects of such work, it pays little attention to how the business itself is perceived by the local community, or to how the Christian owners/managers should articulate their businesses in order to build bridges of understanding.

Christian literature on contextualization generally focuses on how the Gospel message can be made understandable in another cultural setting. Such literature is applicable, but when the center of the mission is a business in a MMN, many of the recipients of the Gospel message will be from a unique group within the culture—i.e., Muslim business people and other people connected with the marketplace. There are also recent works that highlight certain biblical patterns for contextualization, yet such patterns do not specifically address the case where a business is used as a platform for spreading the Gospel. These works can, however, provide useful guidelines when researching how business might be contextualized within Islamic cultures.

Research Design

Research Problem

The research problem is to determine how for-profit businesses situated in Muslim-majority nations, as part of Christian mission strategies, can be organized and operated in such a manner as to help ensure that those businesses will be religiously and culturally accepted in their host environments. Addressing this research problem involves answering a number of questions.

Research Questions

The central question of the research is: "What is the Islamic view of business?" Also, to be answered is this complementary question: "What is the Islamic view of possessions?" The two are related, since business cannot be conducted without assets and capital, which are obtained through the accumulation of possessions. These are complex questions due to Islam's varied geographical, cultural, and historical settings. A reasonable starting point, however, would be to focus on Islam's founding document—the Qur'an—and ask the two questions above. While the Qur'an is at the core of Islam, it is interpreted through the life and example of the prophet Muhammad. The same questions, therefore, would also need to be asked with reference to the various *hadith* traditions and the Islamic theological, philosophical, and *sharia* interpretations relating to business.

Once an Islamic view of business has been developed from the core documents of Islam, a survey of the commercial and trade practices throughout Islamic history is a valid check on the answers derived from Islam's core documents. The questions to be answered here are these: "How did Muslims conduct business over time in the various places where Islam gained ascendancy?" and, "How were Islam's holy texts interpreted by merchants and traders in actual practice?" A corollary question is, "What accounts for the differences?" (e.g., influences of particular Islamic scholars).

Particular attention should also be paid to recent Islamic views of business and commerce, since such ideas and practices would have the most impact on Christian businesses involved in missions currently. Some key questions here would be: "What is the Islamic view of modern capitalism?" "Are there aspects of modern businesses that are particularly troublesome to Muslims?" and, "What underlies the call for shariah-compliant finance?"

The next set of questions to be answered relates to how "business" is conducted in Christian missions. Businesses vary widely in terms of their size, products and services, types of operation engaged in (raw materials procurement, manufacturing, assembly, distribution, etc.), and how they are owned and financed (privately, as public companies, through grants and donations, via government-affiliation, etc.). Questions to be asked include, "What are the types of businesses most commonly used in missions?" and, "What are the key characteristics of such businesses?" The answers should narrow the scope of "business" enough so that a meaningful attempt at contextualizing such businesses to the Islamic setting can be set forth.

The final set of questions involves drawing certain inferences from the Islamic view of business to how businesses are to be formed and operated as part of Christian missions. Following are questions that should be addressed at this stage: "Are certain business structures favored under Islam?" "Are there restrictions Islam places on the conduct of businesses that may impact Christian business and mission companies?" "Are there business strategies that enable Christians to share the gospel message while minimizing possible conflicts with Islam?" "Are there forms of business that Christians have not typically used in missions but that would be more acceptable in MMNs?" and, "What impact will the trend toward *shariah*-compliant business have on Christian business and missions?"

Research Methodology

The research will be conducted using two methodologies. The primary one is exegetical in nature and will focus on the core documents of Islam—the Qur'an and the *hadith*. The exegesis will be divided into topical categories derived inductively from verses in the Qur'an and passages from the *hadith* traditions. The categories will relate to various aspects of doing business in Islam. It should be noted that, while the Qur'an and *hadith* address other economic matters (e.g., taxation, including the *zakat* or poor tax), the funding and administration of the public treasury, support of the poor, and treatment and taxation of non-

Muslims, these matters will not be addressed in detail in this publication. The reason is that the research questions are focused on business from a micro-economic standpoint as opposed to the above macro-economic matters. Although the treatment and taxation of non-Muslims living in Muslim societies could be relevant to Christians doing business in MMNs, this topic only becomes operative when Muslim nations are governed exclusively by *shariah,* and where non-Muslims are treated as *dhimmis*—a situation not often found.

The Qur'an will be covered in Chapter 2 and the *hadith* in Chapter 3. While the Qur'an can be read in its entirety with categories developed directly from the reading, the various *hadith* traditions will be analyzed topically using *hadith* indexes and searchable electronic texts. Various *tafsirs* on the Qur'an will also be examined as part of the development and analysis of the topics. Chapter 4 will extend the exegetical analysis of the topics by viewing them from the perspective of the writings of key Islamic thinkers and jurists from the mid- to high-Middle Ages (often viewed as the "classical period of Islam").

The research methodology will shift in Chapter 5 and Chapter 6 to a historiographical approach. This shift is warranted because a historical examination tests the coherence of Islamic teachings in the Qur'an and *hadith* with actual practice. Combining an understanding of business derived inductively from Islamic history with a deductive understanding of business derived from the Qur'an and *hadith* will result in a full-orbed understanding of business in Islam. Chapter 5 will focus on selected societies where Islam achieved dominance. The assumption is that during such times of Islamic hegemony, the Islamic approach to business would be most observable. Three such times and places will be examined: 1) Arabia during the period from Muhammad and the early caliphs through the Abbasid period, 2) Egypt during the Fatimid period, and 3) Egypt during the Middle Ages and the period of Ottoman rule. Egyptian society is highlighted because it has served as a principal seedbed for modern Islamist thought and action to reform Islamic society, including the manner in which Islamic business is conducted. Chapter 6 examines these reformist ideas, focusing primarily on developments in the 20th century and the increasing emphasis on *sharia*-compliant Islamic business and finance.

Chapter 7 and Chapter 8 will focus on applying the insights gained from the exegetical and historical analysis of business in Islam to the conduct of business in Christian missions in MMNs. Chapter 7 will present the current state of business as it commonly exists in Christian missions. The methodology will be historiographical, focusing on a survey of the literature on the topic. Chapter 8 will be a missiological reflection, resulting in a series of recommendations as to how businesses (and their personnel) engaged in mission to Muslims and operating in MMNs, can be contextualized so as to minimize tensions and provide a culturally acceptable business platform in the host countries while at the same time preserving their Christian witness.

Chapter 9 will summarize the findings and present areas for potential additional research.

Special Notes

The translation of the Qur'an used in this book will be that of M.A.S. Abdel Haleem.[3] Due to extensive references to Qur'anic passages in Chapter 2, along with numerous references to Qur'anic passages in other chapters, footnotes referring to Haleem's translation of the Qur'an will be in the

---

[3] *The Qur'an*, trans. by M.A.S. Abdel Haleem (Oxford, UK: Oxford University, 2005).

form of inline citations providing the *surah* and *ayah* (or *ayat*) separated by a colon. In the event that a translation other than Haleem's is used, the footnote will appear at the bottom of the page.

References to *ahadith* in Chapter 3 and following will be in the form of inline citations providing a three-letter abbreviation of the specific *hadith* tradition (as set forth in Abbreviations), the book, chapter, and *hadith* number with the three numbers separated by colons. Complete bibliographic data on each *hadith* tradition used are provided in the bibliography. Quotations from the Bible will also be followed by inline citations providing the Bible book name, chapter, and verse (separated by a colon), and the name of the translation.

The order of the 114 *surat* contained in the Qur'an is not chronological. When researching the Qur'an topically, it is important to take into consideration (as much as possible) the particulars of each *surah* when drawing conclusions on the teachings of the Qur'an about a given topic. The dating of a *surah*, which unlocks information as to its background, has been the topic of much academic research, and numerous chronological lists of the *surat* are available. A detailed discussion of the chronology of the *surat* is well beyond the scope of this publication. In preparing Appendix 1, "Topical Analysis of Business in the Qur'an," the author has relied upon the chronological order prepared by scholars at Al-Azhar, Cairo, Egypt, who are also responsible for the Arabic Cairo edition of the Qur'an. A copy of this chronological listing of *surat* can be found in *Bell's Introduction to the Qur'an*.[4]

The *hadith* traditions used here will be limited to those that have been translated into the English language. These will include *Sahih Al-Bukhari, Sahih Muslim, Sunan Abu*

---

[4] W. Montgomery Watt, *Bell's Introduction to the Qur'an* (Edinburgh, Scotland: Edinburgh University, 1970), 205-213.

Dawud, Sunan Ibn Majah, Sunan An-Nasai, and *Jami At-Tirmidhi.*

In order to enhance readability for Western readers, this publication seeks to minimize the use of specialized grammatical symbols. Quotations, however, will retain the symbols and markings of the original text. In Islamic literature, whenever the Prophet Muhammad's name is written, it is typically accompanied by a blessing formula. When literature containing such a blessing is quoted, that blessing formula has been omitted in order to reduce the length of the quotation and to make reading easier.

CHAPTER 2

Business in the Qur'an

The Qur'an's treatment of topics related to business is divided into two sections. The first section focuses on *ayat* related to possessions and wealth, the second on *ayat* related to trade and commerce. This breakdown is warranted since almost every business requires tangible assets to operate (e.g., money, land, buildings, equipment, tools, vehicles). Even in technology-driven businesses where less tangible assets are required, money is still needed to hire people, rent office space, purchase computers, etc. While the Qur'an obviously does not discuss business assets in the same sense as they are thought of currently, it has much to say about the nature, acquisition, and proper use of possessions and wealth, which certainly encompasses such assets. Building on the following discussion of *ayat* related to possessions and wealth, this chapter will then proceed to an examination of *ayat* related to trade and commerce.[1]

---

[1] As other Islamic texts are examined, such as the *hadith* traditions, the same organizational arrangement will be utilized—wealth and possessions examined first, followed by trade and commerce.

Possessions and Wealth in the Qur'an

The Role of Allah

Allah is the Creator and Owner

The Qur'an makes clear that Allah is the creator of everything. Allah is given credit for building and spreading out the sun, moon, sky, and earth (91:1-5). Allah's creation was "sound and well-proportioned upon the correct nature."[2] The Qur'an also states that Allah "created the heavens, the earth, and everything between, in six Days without tiring" (50:38). Allah's creation of the earth includes "firm mountains and rivers" and "two of every kind of fruit" (13:3), along with "all the pairs of things that the earth produces" (36:36). The fact that parts of the earth are productive and other parts barren does not disprove Allah's creation. Such variation only "indicates the existence of the Creator Who does what He wills."[3] Allah is also identified as having created man from a "drop of sperm,"[4] along with livestock (16:5). In addition, Allah is credited with making "mates for you from among yourselves—and for the animals too—so that you may multiply" (42:11).

Far from being aloof from his creation, the Qur'an maintains that Allah has "established Himself on the Throne, governing everything" (10:3). Even when man thinks he is in control, it is only illusory and temporary. Speaking of Allah, the Qur'an states emphatically— "God, holder of all control, You give control to whoever You will and remove it from whoever You will" (3:26). Allah's control and power over everything is a major theme in the Qur'an. "Exalted is He who holds all control in His hands; who has power over all things" (67:1). Another *ayah* states, "Do you [Prophet] not know that

---

[2] *Tafsir Ibn Kathir*, abr. ed. (Riyadh, Saudi Arabia: Darussalam, 2003), 10:496.
[3] Ibid., 5:236.
[4] Ibid., 5:431.

God has power over everything? Do you not know that control of the heavens and the earth belongs to Him?" (2:106-107). The Qur'an repeats this theme to almost the last *surah* (number 112 of 114), when it states, "Control of the heavens and earth and everything in them belongs to God: He has power over all things" (5:120).

Allah is the Sustainer

The Qur'an also portrays Allah as exercising, on an ongoing basis, His ownership and power over creation. The Arabic term *rabb* is associated with Allah when He is described as the "Lord [*rabb*] of the Worlds" (1:2). The translator notes that the word used in the *ayah* "has connotations of caring and nurturing in addition to lordship."[5] Another translator renders *rabb* as "Sustainer," since *rabb* "comprises the ideas of having a just claim to the possession of anything and, consequently, authority over it, as well as of rearing, sustaining. and fostering anything from its inception to its final completion."[6] Still another translator, while using "Lord" to translate *rabb,* employs a cluster of English words to give the reader a fuller understanding of the term, his list includes: "Creator, Owner, Organizer, Provider, Master, Planner, Sustainer, Cherisher, and Giver of security."[7]

This extension of Allah's role from that of creator and owner to sustainer is supported in numerous *ayat.* For example, Allah sends winds and rain to "revive a dead land" and provide "drink to many animals and people" (25:48-49). In a similar vein, "It is God who sends the winds, bearing good news of His coming grace; and when they have gathered up

---

[5]*The Qur'an,* translated by M.A.S. Abdel Haleem (Oxford, UK: Oxford University, 2005), 3.

[6]Muhammad Asad, *The Message of The Qur'ān* (London, UK: The Book Foundation, 2003), 5.

[7]Muhammad Taqi-ud-Din Al-Hilali and Muhammad Muhsin Khan, *Interpretation of the Meanings of The Noble Qur'ān in the English Language* (Riyadh, Saudi Arabia: Darussalam, 2000), 1:29-30.

the heavy clouds, We drive them to a dead land where We cause rain to fall" (7:57). Allah's objective in regard to sustaining the earth is to make "everything grow there in due balance" (15:19). One commentator stresses that, regarding "due balance," Allah makes "everything grow in due proportion . . . by a known amount."[8]

The produce of agriculture is often described as coming from Allah, who "put gardens of date palms and grapes in the earth, and . . . made springs of water gush out of it so that they could eat its fruit" (36:34-35). Expanding on this theme, the Qur'an notes that, "It is He who produces both trellised and untrellised gardens, date palms, crops of diverse flavours, the olive, the pomegranate, alike yet different" (6:141). Adding to the list of agricultural produce ascribed to Allah, the Qur'an states, "Let man consider the food he eats! We pour down abundant water and cause the soil to split open. We make grain grow, and vines, fresh vegetation, olive trees, date palms, luscious gardens, fruits, and fodder" (80:24-31).

In addition to food, the Qur'an makes clear that other necessities of life are also attributable to Allah. "Consider the water you drink—was it you who brought it down from the rain-cloud or We? If We wanted, We could make it bitter: will you not be thankful? Consider the fire you kindle—is it you who make the wood for it grow [sic] or We?" (56:68-72).

In regard to Allah's ability to sustain the creation, the Qur'an asserts, "He knows all that goes into the earth and all that comes out of it; He knows all that comes down from the heavens and all that goes up to them" (34:2). After creating the earth, the sky, and the seven heavens, the Qur'an reminds the reader, "It is He who has knowledge of all things" (2:29). Allah's knowledge extends even to "the number of

---

[8] Jalalu'd-Din Al-Mahalli and Jalalu'd-Din As-Suyuti, *Tafsir Al-Jalalayn*, translated by Aisha Bewley (London, UK: Dar Al Taqwa, 2007), 549.

raindrops that sink into the depths of the earth, and the seeds that have been sown."⁹

Allah is the Provider

The Qur'an moves from describing Allah as the one who brings forth the means of sustenance from the earth to the one who provides each individual with possessions and wealth. Allah's role as provider is set forth in numerous passages. "God is the Provider, the Lord of Power, the Ever Mighty" (51:58). Mankind is not in a position to provide possessions and wealth for themselves, since "God is the source of wealth and you are the needy ones" (47:38). If man thinks otherwise (i.e., that he is self-sufficient), it "exceeds all bounds" (96:6-7). Muhammad is told that, "All grace is in God's hands; He grants it to whoever He will—He is all embracing, all knowing—and He singles out for His mercy whoever He will" (3:73-74). By way of metaphor, the Qur'an affirms Allah as provider when it describes Him as possessing "the keys of the heavens and the earth" (42:12). One commentator writes, "He knows not only what every human being 'deserves,' but also what is intrinsically—though not always perceptibly—good and necessary in the context of His plan of creation."¹⁰ Even Mary is quoted as affirming the personal provision of Allah in her life. "Whenever Zachariah went in to see her in her sanctuary, he found her supplied with provisions. He said, 'Mary, how is it you have these provisions?' and she said, 'They are from God'" (3:37).

Apart from Allah, there is no other source of provision, the Qur'an stating, "There is not a thing whose storehouses are not with Us" (15:21). The Qur'an warns those who place their trust in anything but Allah—"What you worship instead of God are mere idols; what you invent is nothing but

---

⁹*Tafsir Ibn Kathir*, 8:61.
¹⁰Asad, 838.

falsehood. Those you serve instead of God have no power to give you provisions, so seek provisions from God" (29:17). Not only is Allah the only source of provision, but the Qur'an maintains that, "No one can withhold the blessing God opens up for people, nor can anyone but Him release whatever He withholds" (35:2).

The Qur'an specifies in some detail the types of things Allah provides. Included in the list of provisions are: wealth and sons (74:12-13); adornments of various kinds (7:32); seeds for planting, rain, and wood for fire (56:63, 68, 71-72); livestock, gardens, and springs of water (26:133-134); homes and furnishings for shelter, along with animal skins, wool, fur, and hair to make garments of various types fit for travel and war (16:80-81).

The extent of Allah's earthly provision is also spoken of in the Qur'an, which states that God provides not begrudgingly or with a tight fist, but with hands opened wide (5:64). His provision is described as being "according to a well-defined measure" (15:21), yet abundant (29:62), immeasurable (2:212), never ending (38:54), and limitless (24:38). According to one commentary, the "well-defined measure" spoken of in 15:21 carries with it the notion of a predetermined amount.[11] This is supported by another *ayah* that states the wealth people have in this world amounts to "their preordained share" (7:37). (As will be discussed later in this chapter, predetermination of provision becomes a source of contention as it relates to the Qur'an's position on work and success.) The Qur'an also presents Allah as providing for individuals in special situations, including orphans (93:6), parents of children (17:31), husbands and wives after they have divorced (4:130), as well as those who are single and desire the means to enter into marriage (24:32-33). Allah's provision also extends to the next world (4:134).

---

[11] *Tafsir Ibn Kathir*, 5:386.

Allah is the Decider

There are numerous passages in the Qur'an that portray Allah as the sole decider with regard to how wealth and possessions are distributed on earth. The Qur'an states, "Your Lord [Allah] gives abundantly to whoever He will, and sparingly to whoever He will; He knows and observes His servants thoroughly" (17:30). The next *surah* (chronologically) applies the same theme to bounty when it states, "If God inflicts harm on you, no one can remove it but Him, and if He intends good for you, no one can turn His bounty away; He grants His bounty to any of His servants He will" (10:107). It is significant to note that the Islamic term "bounty" is, according to one Islamic author, synonymous in the Qur'an with earned income.[12] *Surah* 10:107 makes clear that, even though man works, the fruits of his labor are still determined by Allah.

In maintaining Allah's absolute control over the distribution of wealth and possessions, the Qur'an also acknowledges in numerous *ayat* that the resulting inequalities are also a matter of Allah's will. For example, the Qur'an asks, "Do they not know that God provides abundantly for anyone He will and gives sparingly to anyone He will?" (39:52). In a later *surah*, the Qur'an asks almost the same question— "Do they not see that God gives abundantly to whoever He will and sparingly [to whoever He will]?" (30:37). The Qur'an emphasizes this point when it states matter of factly, "God has given some of you more provision than others" (16:71). The disparity in wealth is mirrored in social standing in that Allah "raises some of you above others in rank" (6:165). In responding to unequal distribution of wealth and possessions, Allah cautions man to "not gaze

---

[12] Nik Mohamed Affandi bin Nik Yusoff, *Islam and Wealth: The Balanced Approach to Wealth Creation, Accumulation and Distribution* (Selangor, Malaysia: Pelanduk, 2001), 7.

longingly at what We have given some of them to enjoy, the finery of this present life" (20:131) and not to covet others' portions (4:32).

The role of Allah as sole decider of how wealth and possessions are distributed raises some difficult issues of interpretation, since there are many other *ayat* (discussed in the next section) that seem to link material possessions with certain actions that are carried out by man. The scope of this issue goes far beyond possessions and wealth. Ultimately, it is a question of whether or not Islam teaches predestination or free will. Although such a question is beyond the scope of this book, after reading the previous *ayat*, it would be hard not to side with one western theologian who states, "There is a very strong predestinarian strain in the Qur'an."[13]

The Role of Man

Piety Is Rewarded

Although Allah is clearly the source of provision, numerous *ayat* appear to teach that the piety of a believer, or community of believers, determines how Allah allocates wealth and possessions. From the earliest *surat*, prosperity is linked to piety. For example, it is said in the second *surah* of the Qur'an chronologically, "There will be Gardens of bliss for those who are mindful of God" (68:34). The eighth *surah* states, "Prosperous are those who purify themselves" (87:14). The Qur'an also quotes Moses as advising the Jews, "Turn to God for help and be steadfast: the earth belongs to God—He gives it as their own to whichever of His servants He chooses—and the happy future belongs to those who are mindful of Him" (7:128). The Qur'an lists some characteristics of the pious in the following passage:

---

[13] James R. White, *What Every Christian Needs to Know About the Qur'an* (Bloomington, MN: Bethany House, 2013), 150.

> This is the Scripture in which there is no doubt, containing guidance for those who are mindful of God, who believe in the unseen, keep up the prayer, and give out of what We have provided for them; those who believe in the revelation sent down to you [Muhammad], and in what was sent before you, those who have firm faith in the Hereafter. Such people are following their Lord's guidance and it is they who will prosper (2:2-5).

In order to be efficacious, however, the piety of believers must also find expression in works. "It is all recorded in a clear Record so that He can reward those who believe and do good deeds; they will have forgiveness and generous provision" (34:3-4). This promise of reward is available to both men and women and is based "according to the best of their actions" (16:97). The good deed of giving to Allah receives special commendation— "Who will give God a good loan, which He will increase for him many times over?" (2:245). Another verse even specifies the return for giving to Allah's cause—"Who will make God a good loan? He will double it for him and reward him generously" (57:11). The Qur'an also maintains that Allah "will replace whatever you give in alms" (34:39). Provision for believers, however, is conditioned on continued thankfulness— "Remember that He promised, 'If you are thankful, I will give you more; but if you are thankless, My punishment is terrible indeed'" (14:7). The Qur'an also extends the pious' provisions into eternity— "This is a lesson. The devout will have a good place to return to: Gardens of lasting bliss with gates wide open" (38:50-51).

If Allah rewards the pious, what becomes of those who do not believe in Allah or are evil? The Qur'an gives a firm answer to this question:

> Have you considered the man who rejects our revelation, who says, "I will certainly be given wealth

and children"? Has he penetrated the unknown or received a pledge to that effect from the Lord of Mercy? No! We shall certainly record what he says and prolong his punishment: We shall inherit from him all that he speaks of and he will come to Us all alone (19:77-80).

Allah will "repay those who do evil according to their deeds" (53:31) and punish those who reject the truth (7:96).

While evil is punished, the Qur'an does acknowledge that some unbelievers will possess wealth. In such cases, the Qur'an counsels believers to "not look longingly at the good things we have given some to enjoy. Do not grieve over the [disbelievers]" (15:88). Even if some have wealth, they cannot be assured of retaining it if they disbelieve. For example, in a lengthy parable of two gardens, the impious owner of the larger garden boasted that his wealth would not leave him. The pious owner of the smaller garden rebuked the impious boaster with the following assertion:

> "Although you see I have less wealth and offspring than you, my Lord may well give me something better than your garden, and send thunderbolts on your garden from the sky, so that it becomes a heap of barren dust; or its water may sink so deep into the ground that you will never be able to reach it again." And so it was: his fruit was completely destroyed, and there he was, wringing his hands . . . (18:39-42).

The Qur'an even quotes Allah as telling Jesus, after having provided a feast for him, that "anyone who disbelieves after this will be punished with a punishment that I will not inflict on anyone else in the world" (5:115).

Man is Responsible for Possessions and Wealth

While the Qur'an teaches that possessions and wealth are owned by Allah, the Qur'an also teaches that "the Creator has transferred to mankind the right of possession (*usufruct*). Thus, true ownership and the right of possession are clearly demarcated."[14] There are numerous *surat* (discussed below) that indicate possession of many kinds of property were given to individuals who could control them as they saw fit. This is consistent with the modern legal concept of "private property."

It should be noted at the outset that, with respect to land, there is an ongoing debate among Muslims as to whether the Qur'an teaches that land can be owned by individuals or whether it should remain under the ownership and control of the Islamic state. One modern Muslim scholar notes, "The Qur'ān does not make any direct or indirect allusion to private ownership of land."[15] Other scholars, however, argue that there are numerous references in the Qur'an that establish property rights—including land.[16] The interpretation of the *ayat* discussed below and the resulting legal frameworks will thus vary among Muslim-majority nations.

In the Qur'an, the case for private possession and use of property is clearly seen with regard to movable goods. For example, it is said of Allah that "[He gave you] livestock, as beasts of burden and as food. So eat what God has provided for you" (6:142). The Qur'an further states, "Can they not see how, among the things made by Our hands, We have created livestock they control" (36:71). Even David acknowledges the unfairness of one partner taking an ewe from the [private]

---

[14]Murat Çizakça, *Islamic Capitalism and Finance: Origins, Evolution and the Future* (Cheltenham, UK: Edward Elgar, 2011), 14.

[15]S.M. Hasanuz Zaman, *Economic Functions of an Islamic State: The Early Experience*, Rev. ed. (Leicester, UK: The Islamic Foundation, 1991), 31.

[16]Siraj Sait and Hilary Lim, *Land, Law & Islam: Property and Human Rights in the Muslim World* (London, UK: Zed Books, 2006), 10.

flock of his partner (38:24). Goods that are traded are also included in the category of private property when it is said, "You who believe, do not wrongfully consume each other's wealth but trade by mutual consent" (4:29). In perhaps the ultimate illustration that property, even if it is movable, has a rightful owner, the Qur'an also prescribes the cutting off of the hands of thieves (5:38).

Numerous *ayat* indicate that homes were regarded as private property. Considering that, during the years *surat* were being dictated to Muhammad, many Muslims were nomadic, the following *ayah* would have been quite apropos—"It is God who has given you a place of rest in your homes and from the skins of animals made you homes that you find light [to handle] when you travel and when you set up camp; furnishings and comfort for a while from their wool, fur, and hair" (16:80). Alternatively, for those who lived in villages, this *ayah* would have been meaningful—"Believers, do not enter other people's houses until you have asked permission to do so and greeted those inside" (24:27). There is also an *ayah* making it clear that extended family members often owned their own houses—complete with entrance keys (24:61).

The Qur'an also references several "special situations" that affirm the notion of private property. One such situation involves the property of orphaned children. The Qur'an gives the following admonition—"Do not go near the orphan's property, except with the best [intentions], until he reaches the age of maturity" (17:34). Another is the command to not commingle the funds of orphans—"It is good to set things right for them. If you combine their affairs with yours, remember they are your brothers and sisters. God knows those who spoil things and those who improve them" (2:220). The Qur'an also sets forth specific guidelines for inheritances of property among family members (4:176); such detailed commands would only be necessary if property was within the purview of the individual to possess and manage, thus private property.

The payment of booty to warriors engaged in *jihad* is another special situation that further affirms the notion of private property in the Qur'an. *Surah* 8, which pertains to the distribution of spoils after the battle of Badr, addresses the subject in the first *ayah*—"They ask you [Prophet] about [distributing] the battle gains" (8:1). This question arose because, in Bedouin society, plunder had been an accepted means of providing for life's necessities. and there had been accepted customs for sharing movable booty.[17] Later in the *surah,* Allah replies "that one-fifth of your battle gains belongs to God and the Messenger, to close relatives and orphans, to the needy and travellers" (8:41). The remainder would be distributed to the warriors for their personal possession and use.

Another special situation relates to the distribution of property after death. The Qur'an affirms private property in that it allows two-thirds of an individual's property to be distributed to lineal descendants and to near family relations in varying proportions (4:11-12, 176). This represents an abrogation from 8:73, where Muhammad gave priority to the spiritual ties between the Emigrants from Mecca and the Ansar in Medina, thus allowing inheritances between individuals in these groups.[18] An individual can also leave bequests of property as long as there are two witnesses to attest to the bequests (5:106).

Man's Use of Property Will be Tested

The Qur'an describes possessions and wealth both positively and negatively. In the positive sense, one Islamic

---

[17] *The Encyclopaedia of Islam,* CD-ROM ed. (Leiden, Netherlands: E. J. Brill, 2002), s.v. "Ghanīma."

[18] Robert Roberts, *The Social Laws of the Qorân,* (London, UK: Curzon, 1971), 63-64.

scholar notes that, "Islam does not castigate worldly wealth nor man's application to economic pursuits; the Qur'an sometimes terms wealth as *khayr* (virtue), *fadl* (honour), *rahma* (blessing), and regards it as Allah's bounty."[19] The Qur'an states forthrightly that, "The love of desirable things is made alluring for men—women, children, gold and silver treasures piled up high, horses with fine markings, livestock, and farmland" (3:14). However, the Qur'an warns that such things constitute "merely [temporary] gratification and vanity" (28:60) and a "fleeting enjoyment of this world" (42:36). Wealth can "distract you from remembering God" (63:9) and "bar people from the path of God" (8:36).

Due to the double-edged nature of wealth and possessions, the Qur'an portrays them as a test of man's piety. For example, the Qur'an provides almost identical counsel in 8:28 and 64:15 when it is stated, "Be aware that your possessions and your children are only a test, and that there is a tremendous reward with God" (8:28). There are graphic warnings to those with wealth who do not heed the Prophet. "Just because he has wealth and sons, when our revelations are recited to him, he says, 'These are just ancient fables.' We shall brand him on the snout!" (68:14-16). Not only is the abundance of possessions a test, but so is the lack of possessions and their loss, Allah stating, "We shall certainly test you with fear and hunger, and loss of property, lives, and crops" (2:155).

How then should man handle possessions and wealth? What is his proper role? According to one Muslim scholar, the solution lies in recognizing that

> according to Islam, man is a vicegerent of Allah, the Creator, the Sustainer, and the Sole Sovereign of this universe. Allah has appointed him as His deputy on this earth to carry out His will, indicated His will in

---

[19] Zaman, 40.

the form of the *Shari'ah*, which was finally revealed through Muhammad.[20]

The Qur'anic support for this statement is found in 2:30, which states, "Behold, thy Lord said to the angels: 'I will create a vicegerent on earth.'"[21] Ali notes that this vicegerent has "the power of will or choosing. . . . The perfect vicegerent is he who has the power of initiative himself, but whose independent action always reflects perfectly the will of his Principal."[22]

A term that is often used instead of vicegerent is *khalifah*. In describing what it means to be a *khalifah*, one Muslim scholar notes that he is the '[representative] of Allah, perfect in form, and endowed with all that is necessary to fulfill the divine will."[23] Another *ayah* portrays man as a trustee when it states, "We offered the Trust to the heavens, the earth, and the mountains, yet they refused to undertake it and were afraid of it; mankind undertook it" (33:72). Since the Qur'an describes the heavens and the earth as being "afraid" to take on the role of *khalifah*, it comes as no surprise when the Qur'an predicts that man will have a difficult time. "The true believers are the ones who have faith in God and His Messenger and leave all doubt behind, the ones who have struggled with their possessions and their persons in God's way" (49:15).

---

[20]Muhammad Akram Khan, *Economic Teachings of Prophet Muhammad: A Select Anthology of Hadith Literature on Economics* (New Delhi, India: Oriental Publications, 1989), 2.

[21]ʿAbdullah Yūsuf ʿAlī, *The Meaning of the Holy Qurʾān*, 10th ed. (Beltsville, MD: Amana, 1999), 24.

[22]Ibid., 24, note 47.

[23]Mark Durie, *The Third Choice: Islam, Dhimmitude and Freedom* (n.p.: Deror Books, 2010), 20.

Possessions and Wealth are to be Used Rightly

The "struggle" mentioned in 49:15 above involves using possessions and wealth in a right manner and forsaking wrong uses. The Qur'an contains many admonitions as to what constitutes these right and wrong uses.

One of the foremost duties of every Muslim is the payment of *zakat*. The word *zakat* is mentioned 30 times in the Qur'an.... It is generally accepted that every free and sane Muslim adult... is ordained to pay the zakat."[24] Essentially, the *zakat* payment amounts to a certain percentage of one's income, and there are many conditions that enter into the calculation of that payment:

> First, the property or cash subject to *zakat* must be clearly in the possession of the person liable to pay. Second, the taxable wealth or property should be able to yield revenue. Third, a minimum amount of property, *nisab*, should be possessed. Until a person accumulates this minimum amount, he/she would not be responsible to pay the *zakat*. Fourth, *zakat* is due only after the primary needs have been satisfied. Fifth, before its due *zakat* is paid [sic], an asset must be legally possessed for a full year.[25]

The percentage rate of *zakat* varies by the type of asset(s) used to generate the income. One scholar summarized the *zakat* rates as follows:

> (1) Two and a half per cent on all the accumulated wealth and business capital, (2) five or ten per cent (depending on the quality of land in question) on all agricultural produce, (3) twenty per cent on mines and treasures found underneath the earth, and (4) a

---

[24]Çizakça, 55.
[25]Ibid., 55-56.

specified percentage (the rate differs for different kinds of animals) on livestock.[26]

Those who are eligible to receive *zakat* are limited to "the poor, the needy, those who administer them, those whose hearts need winning over, to free slaves and help those in debt, for God's cause, and for travellers in need" (9:60).

There are many other forms of obligatory and non-obligatory payments and institutions within Islam that have their basis in the Qur'an. A detailed discussion of these—or even a listing of them—is beyond the scope of this book. However, it is important to note that, for Muslim businesspeople, Allah does seem to promise them a prosperous business in exchange for their giving. The Qur'an states, "Those who recite God's scripture, keep up the prayer, give secretly and openly from what We have provided for them may hope for a trade that will never decline: He will repay them in full and give them extra from His bounty" (35:29-30). One commentator drives home the financial implications of these *ayat*, noting that Allah "may give them a reward for what they have done and multiply it by adding more, such as has never occurred to them."[27] Giving also is a way of "purifying" wealth. The Qur'an states that Allah will be "well pleased" with the pious "who gives his wealth away as self-purification, not to return a favour to anyone but for the sake of his Lord the Most High" (92:18-20).

Apart from giving, the Qur'an commands that possessions and wealth not be squandered and that Muslims should "not be tight-fisted nor so open-handed that you end up blamed and overwhelmed with regret" (17:26-29). In addition, the Qur'an wants wealth to be spread out in the community "so that [it does] not just circulate among those

---

[26]Mushtāq Ahmad, "Business Ethics in the Qur'an: A Synthetic Exposition of the Qur'anic Teachings Pertaining to Business" (Ph.D. dissertation, Temple University, 1984), 122.

[27]*Tafsir Ibn Kathir*, 8:146.

of you who are rich" (59:7). For those who are miserly, the Qur'an warns. "Whatever they meanly withhold will be hung around their necks on the Day of Resurrection" (3:180).

A case for conspicuous consumption can even be made from the Qur'an. One Muslim writer observes that Allah allows for "generous consumption . . . [of] good food, beautiful clothing, spacious houses . . . reasonable and proper adornments and beautification."[28] However, there does appear to be a limit as to how far a Muslim's spending can be justified. "Children of Adam, dress well whenever you are at worship, and eat and drink [as We have permitted] but do not be extravagant; God does not like extravagant people" (7:31). Muslims are also warned not to overindulge in luxury (56:45). The key is for a Muslim to be "neither wasteful nor niggardly when they spend, but keep to a just balance" (25:67).

Trade and Commerce in the Qur'an

Work and Success

In order for any business to survive, let alone succeed, a substantial number of hours must be devoted to it consistently over months and years. It is therefore appropriate to begin an analysis of the Qur'an's view of trade and commerce with this question— "How does the Qur'an view work?" The Arabic term often translated as "work" is *amal*. The term is broad and can be used to describe spiritual or religious works, moral actions, judicial actions, or labor in an economic sense.[29] Focusing only on its economic use, the Qur'an has much to say about *amal*. The emphasis on work is understandable since, in the view of one Muslim writer, Islam is "a whole way of life covering both the needs to prepare for the Hereafter as well as the worldly needs to

---

[28] Yusoff, *Islam and Wealth*, 117.
[29] *The Encyclopaedia of Islam*, s.v. "amal."

enable mankind to live a secure and comfortable life in this world."[30]

Allah is credited with having prepared the earth for man to work in it. According to the Qur'an, Allah "has subjected all that is in the heavens and the earth for your [man's] benefit, as a gift from Him" (45:13). The Qur'an even specifies that Allah "sent iron with its mighty strength and many uses for mankind" (57:25), along with molten brass and wind to facilitate journeys (34:12). Man is, therefore, to manage the earth, "travel its regions, [and] eat His provision" (67:15). The Qur'an also states that the various livelihoods on earth are bestowed on man by Allah (43:32).

Given Allah's preparations, man is thereby ordained to work while on earth. Allah states, "We have created man for toil and trial" (90:4). Work is for everyone, there being no exemption for certain individuals or classes of people. The Qur'an maintains "that no soul shall bear the burden of another, that man will only have what he has worked towards, that his labour will be seen, and that in the end he will be repaid in full for it" (53:38-41).

One of the important goals of work is obtaining the "bounty of Allah," a frequent Qur'anic theme. This "bounty" includes both material rewards on earth as well as rewards to be received after death. "If anyone strives for the rewards of this world, We will give him some of them. If anyone strives for the rewards of the Hereafter, We will give him some of them" (3:145). Allah's bounty can be earned by both men and women (4:32), as well as by those on pilgrimage to Mecca (2:197). In the view of one Islamic scholar,

> The Qur'an wants that every able-bodied person must work in order to earn his living for himself. Nobody is allowed, in ordinary circumstances, to

---

[30]Nik Mohamed Affandi bin Nik Yusoff, *Islam and Business*, ed. Ismail Noor (Selangor, Malaysia: Pelanduk, 2002), 13.

resort to begging, or, to become a liability on one's relatives or the state. The Qur'an has highly praised those persons who strive in order to seek the "Bounty of Allah."[31]

Although work and striving are key ingredients to obtaining Allah's bounty, the Qur'an also links piety with Allah's bounty, commanding that Muslims, after "prayer has ended, [to] disperse in the land and seek out God's bounty. Remember God often so that you may prosper" (62:10).

Merchants and Trading

Although the word "business" does not appear in the Qur'an, a closely related word, *tijarah* from the root T-J-R, is used nine times.[32] *Tijarah* is defined as "commerce, merchandise, trading, [and] trade."[33] Based on the nine uses of the term, *tijarah* should be profitable (2:16, 24:37, 35:29, 61:10), carefully managed (2:283), and done by mutual consent (4:29). However, *tijarah* can distract a person from Allah (9:24, 24:37, 62:11). In addition to the term *tijarah*, one scholar notes that the Qur'an contains within it an extensive

> *business atmosphere* [which] shows itself most plainly and characteristically. On almost every page we meet with . . . words elsewhere used to express some familiar commercial idea, here transferred to the relations between God and man. . . . These words, belonging to some twenty different stems, occur in the Koran about 370 times.[34]

---

[31] Ahmad, 17.

[32] The root T-J-R is found in 2:16; 2:282; 4:29; 9:24; 24:37; 35:29; 61:10; and twice in 62:11. Hanna E. Kassis, *A Concordance of the Qur'an* (Berkeley, CA: University of California, 1983), s.v. "tijārah."

[33] Ibid.

[34] Charles Cutler Torrey, *The Commercial-Theological Terms in the Koran* (Leiden, Netherlands: E. J. Brill, 1892; reprint, n.p.: Kessinger, n.d.), 3.

An example of this type of usage is found in an *ayah* where the context is clearly the Day of Judgment, but where a business term—bargaining— is used. "You who believe, give from what We have provided for you, before the Day comes when there is no bargaining, no friendship, and no intercession" (2:254). One writer provides the following partial list of such expressions:

> Although the most commonly used business terms in the Qur'an are measure and weight, profit, loss, sell, price, gain, account, credit, and loan, other business terms such as investment, contract, liability, and capital sums, are also found. The most commonly used terms are account (about 90 times), profit (about 65 times), measure and weight (about 35 times).[35]

The frequency of business language in the Qur'an is not serendipitous. According to one Islamic scholar, "Economic activity has great significance in the Islamic system of life . . . Muslims are enjoined, instigated, and mobilized in different ways to strive for the economic benefits of this life."[36] The fact that business and spiritual matters are often linked is also significant:

> Islam is *ad-Deen*, i.e., it is a whole way of life covering both the needs to prepare for the Hereafter as well as all the worldly needs to enable mankind to live a secure and comfortable life in this world . . . The concept of *ad-Deen* not only provides for both the material and spiritual pursuits of mankind but also renders the two aspects inseparable.[37]

---

[35]Yusoff, *Islam and Business*, 11.

[36]Muhammad Junaid Navdi, "Understanding Economic Philosophy of the Holy Qur'ān," *Hamdard Islamicus* 29, no. 3 (July-September 2006): 42-43.

[37]Yusoff, *Islam and Business*, 13.

In addition to the many *ayat* that support business (albeit indirectly), there are many *ayat* that directly address the activity of trading and the role of the merchant. One of the clearest affirmations of trading occurs when the Qur'an confronts the argument that trade and usury (i.e., receiving interest) are the same. To this, the Qur'an states, "God has allowed trade and forbidden usury" (2:276). One scholar even notes that a "capitalistic covenant"[38] is contained in the following *ayah* of the Qur'an—"Those who recite God's scripture, keep up the prayer, give secretly and openly from what We have provided for them, may hope for a trade that will never decline (i.e., will enjoy unfailing profit from commerce)" (35:29). The merchant is also given a high status in the Qur'an, one *surah* linking those "traveling through the land seeking God's bounty" with "others fighting in God's cause" (73:20). In doing so, one Islamic scholar concludes that, "Islam assigns an honest merchant struggling to earn and enlarge his assets legitimately the highest social status. Indeed, it is believed that such a merchant/businessman/ entrepreneur will be exalted and shall join the ranks of the prophets and the martyrs."[39]

It is particularly interesting, in light of the cross-cultural nature of many Christian business- and-mission projects, to note the Qur'an's many affirmations of traveling long distances to conduct business. There are at least 12 passages that speak of ships engaged in trade—all of those passages portraying trade in a favorable light.[40] For example, one such *surah* speaks of seeing ships in both fresh and salty bodies of water "ploughing their course so that you [merchants] may seek God's bounty and be grateful" (35:12). For those engaged in overland trade, similar encouragement can be found. There are at least eight passages that encourage trade by

---

[38] Gene W. Heck, *Charlemagne, Muhammad, and the Arab Roots of Capitalism* (Berlin, Germany: Walter de Gruyter, 2006), 322.
[39] Çizakça, 267.
[40] The twelve are: 2:164; 10:22; 14:32-34; 16:14; 17:66-70; 22:65; 23:21; 30:46; 31:31; 35:12; 40:79; and 45:12-13.

land.⁴¹ One of those passages seamlessly links trade, travel, and eternity. "It is He who has made the earth manageable for you—travel its regions; eat His provision—and to Him you will be resurrected" (67:15).

Marketplace Ethics

Marketplace ethics in Islam encompasses numerous concepts contained in the Qur'an. A good beginning point would be to understand what is lawful and what is unlawful. As one Islamic scholar noted in outlining the features of an economy, "The most important characteristic of a system based on a divine creed and revealed ethics [such as Islam] is the concept of good and bad, virtuous and vicious, and lawful (*ḥalāl*) and unlawful (*ḥarām*)."⁴² In Islam, it is Muhammad "who commands them to do right and forbids them to do wrong, who makes good things lawful to them and bad things unlawful" (7:157). Regarding *haram* (unlawful) activities, an Islamic scholar has compiled the following list:

> Acquisition [of wealth and possessions] through theft (5:39), plunder (5:33), interest (2:275-9), and gambling (2:219; 5:90, 91). Practices which cause indecency and immorality are prohibited. These include earnings through obscene professions (2:268; 7:33; 24:33), wine (2:219; 5:90), misleading pastimes (31:6) and prostitution (24:33). Defrauding others is sinful. This covers earnings through under-weighing and under-measurement (55:9; 83:3), breach of trust (3:161), misappropriation (2:188), embezzle-ment (3:161), deluding publicity and advertisement, getting a favourable court decree to obtain other's property

---

⁴¹The eight are: 2:184; 2:273; 10:22; 16:7, 14; 23:21; 40:79; and 67:15.
⁴²Zaman, 34.

wrongfully through bribe (2:188) and tampering with documents of business or debt (2:282).[43]

In addition to activities that are regarded as *haram*, the Qur'an contains other ethical concepts equally as important, one of which is *adl*. "*Adl*, the substantive, means justice; as an adjective, it means rectilinear, just, well balanced; it thus applies both to beings and to things."[44] It is appropriate to note that when an abbreviated form of *adl* was stamped on coins, it meant that the coins "have the just weight and are current."[45] One Islamic scholar asserts that *adl* lies at the core of the Qur'anic teaching and that "the Qur'an itself asserts that the purpose of its revelation is to establish justice and equity."[46] Allah, for example, "commands justice, doing good, and generosity towards relatives, and He forbids what is shameful, blameworthy, and oppressive" (16:90). Allah also states, "We sent Our messengers with clear signs, the Scripture and the Balance, so that people could uphold justice" (57:25).

There are many *ayat* in the Qur'an that apply these concepts to marketplace ethics. The five sections that follow summarize selected *ayat* related to certain key areas of business ethics.

Individual Responsibility for Actions

The prerequisite for the various imperatives and guidelines contained in the Qur'an is the Muslim's individual responsibility for personal actions. While there are many *ayat* that could be cited in this regard, the following *ayah* summarizes the Qur'anic words and phrases used in many other *ayat*— "Each soul is responsible for its own actions; no

---

[43] Ibid., 35-36.
[44] *The Encyclopaedia of Islam*, s.v. "adl."
[45] Ibid.
[46] Ahmad, 161.

soul will bear the burden of another. You will all return to your Lord in the end, and He will tell you the truth about your differences" (6:164). The goal, according to one writer, is for every Muslim "to have a 'balanced good sense' to know what is good and bad for them."[47]

Honesty and Mutual Consent in Business Transactions

Numerous *ayat* call for Muslims to give full measure in their business transactions. The Qur'an pronounces woe upon "those who give short measure, who demand of other people full measure for themselves, but give less than they should when it is they who weigh or measure for others!" (83:1-3). There are also several *ayat* where Shu'ayb (identified as Moses' father-in-law, Jethro)[48] advises the people of Midian to "Give full measure: do not sell others short. Weigh with correct scales: do not deprive people of what is theirs" (26:181-183).

Aside from specific transactions, the Qur'an also issues the following imperatives designed to enhance the believers' trustworthiness (*amana*)—"Believers, do not betray God and the Messenger, or knowingly betray [other people's] trust in you" (8:27), and "God commands you [people] to return things entrusted to you to their rightful owners, and, if you judge between people, to do so with justice" (4:58).

Honesty in court proceedings or judicial matters is also commended in the Qur'an:

> You who believe, uphold justice and bear witness to God, even if it is against yourselves, your parents, or your close relatives. Whether the person is rich or poor, God can best take care of both. Refrain from following your own desire, so that you can act justly—

---

[47] Yusoff, *Islam and Wealth*, 93.
[48] Asad, 246.

if you distort or neglect justice, God is fully aware of what you do (4:135).

One Muslim author notes that business transactions should be conducted in such a fashion that "both the buyer and seller achieve mutual benefit and satisfaction."[49] This is affirmed in the Qur'an when Muslims are commanded to not "wrongfully consume each other's wealth but trade by mutual consent" (4:29).

Keeping Oaths and Honoring Contracts

The Qur'an makes clear in numerous *ayat* that oaths and promises made in God's name are not to be broken. "Fulfill any pledge you make in God's name and do not break oaths after you have sworn them, for you have made God your surety: God knows everything you do" (16:91). A Muslim should also keep his oath even if economic gain must be sacrificed. "God loves those who keep their pledges and are mindful of Him, but those who sell out God's covenant and their own oaths for a small price will have no share in the life to come" (3:76-77). The Qur'an does, however, allow for the breaking of a "thoughtless" oath—although a payment or act of atonement is required (5:89).

Written contracts are also supported in the Qur'an. With reference to recording a debt, the Qur'an prescribes, "Do not disdain to write the debt down, be it small or large, along with the time it falls due: this way is more equitable in God's eyes, more reliable as testimony, and more likely to prevent doubts arising between you" (2:282). The use of two male witnesses is also commended—although if only one male witness can be found, two females can be substituted for the missing man "so that if one of the two women should forget, the other can remind her" (2:282).

---

[49] Yusoff, *Islam and Business*, 87.

Relationships with Employees

The hiring of workers or laborers is supported in the Qur'an. In an *ayah* describing how Allah provides man with livelihoods, it is stated that Allah has "raised some of them above others in rank, so that some may take others into service" (43:32). The Qur'an even affirms the hiring of Moses by Jethro. "When Moses came to him and told him his story, the old man [Jethro] said, 'Do not be afraid, you are safe now from people who do wrong.' One of the women said, 'Father, hire him: a strong, trustworthy man is the best to hire'" (28:25-26).

However, there are certain conditions that the Qur'an places upon those employing workers. They are to be paid for their labors. Moses is quoted as telling a laborer who repaired a wall that, "If you had wished you could have taken payment for doing that" (18:77). Workers are also to be paid promptly. For example, in the context of an agricultural harvest, laborers are to be paid "what is due on the day of harvest" (6:141). There is also a sense that workers should be treated respectfully, the Qur'an stating that Muslims should "conduct their affairs by mutual consultation" (42:38)—presumably this would include employees.

Competing in the Marketplace

Since many of the products traded in the time of Muhammad were agricultural and not distinguishable to any great degree, competition between traders would inevitably be highly personal. The Qur'an uses *ihsan*, along with other forms of the root H-S-N, to describe what is good, beautiful, kind, and upright.[50] In describing the moral fiber of the early Islamic state, one scholar defines *ihsan* as encompassing "benevolence, fineness, proficiency, or magnanimity in

---

[50]Kassis, s.v. "Ḥ-S-N."

dealing with others.... It implies a more liberal treatment [of others] than what justice requires. It begins where the precincts of *'adl* end."[51]

Character traits inconsistent with *ihsan* are prohibited in the Qur'an, one example being "unjustified aggression" (7:33). In a similar vein, the Qur'an regards as evil those who "strut arrogantly about the earth" (17:37-38). While the moral applications contained in the aforementioned verses are not specifically addressed to the marketplace, they certainly shed light on the type of behavior one could expect to see in early adherents of Islam.

Finance and Ownership

While the Qur'an has much to say about possessions and wealth, and their use in trade and commerce, it is appropriate to ask whether the Qur'an addresses how trade and commerce is to be financed, and how it is to be organized and owned. On those subjects, the Qur'an is largely silent. However, one area that the Qur'an does address in detail is the prohibition of *ribā*, which one scholarly source defines as

> any unjustified increase of capital for which no compensation is given. The exact meaning of *ribā* is unknown, but it entailed, evidently, a condemnation, from a moral point of view, of those who grew rich through the misery of others, without the loan granted helping the borrower in any way to retrieve his fortunes, such as lending dates to a starving man, etc.[52]

---

[51] Zaman, 39.
[52] *The Encyclopaedia of Islam*, s.v. "ribā."

The key passage in the Qur'an addressing the prohibition of *riba* is found in *Surah* 2:

> But those who take usury will rise up on the Day of Resurrection like someone tormented by Satan's touch. That is because they say, "Trade and usury are the same," but God has allowed trade and forbidden usury. Whoever, on receiving God's warning, stops taking usury may keep his past gains—God will be his judge—but whoever goes back to usury will be an inhabitant of the Fire, there to remain. God blights usury.... Give up any outstanding dues from usury if you are true believers. If you do not, then be warned of war from God and His Messenger. You shall have your capital if you repent, and without suffering loss or causing others to suffer loss (2:275-279).

There is an ongoing debate among Muslim scholars as to whether *riba* should be interpreted as interest or usury, with the later term defined as "excessive interest." Clearly, in the translation quoted above, Haleem views *riba* as usury. With the rise of the "*sharia*-compliant finance movement", this debate has taken on new importance and will be addressed in greater detail in Chapter 6: Business in Modern Islam.

While *riba* is prohibited in the Qur'an, it is important to note that the Qur'an permits Muslims to incur debts, which in modern terms can be viewed as analogous to trade credit. The key Qur'anic passage in this regard is only a few *ayat* after the passage on *riba:*

> You who believe, when you contract a debt for a stated term, put it down in writing: have a scribe write it down justly between you. No scribe should refuse to write: let him write as God has taught him, let the debtor dictate, and let him fear God, his Lord, and not diminish [the debt] at all.... Do not disdain

to write the debt down, be it small or large, along with the time it falls due: this way is more equitable in God's eyes, more reliable as testimony, and more likely to prevent doubts arising between you (2:282).

The Qur'an does not address the topic of business ownership or the matter of partnerships among traders, although there is an oblique reference to "partners" made by David (38:24). However, the *hadith* literature, which will be examined in the next chapter, does address these topics.

CHAPTER 3

Business in the *Sunnah*

The *Sunnah* is comprised of the life of the Prophet Muhammad *(sira)* and the accumulated traditions and sayings of Muhammad *(hadith)*. While the *ayat* of the Qur'an generally do not have specific dates and historical backgrounds associated with them, the *sira* and *hadith* have a historical context, since they consist of events in his life. Although scholars take a variety of positions related to the historicity of Muhammad and these events, this book adopts a traditional viewpoint, accepting his history as set forth in the biography written by Ibn Ishaq.[1]

The first section of this chapter deals with business in the *Sira*. It will highlight aspects of Muhammad's life as relating to business, along with background information on the trade and commercial practices in the Hijaz (the place where he was born and lived). The goal here is to provide a foundation for understanding the various statements and traditions of Muhammad, which are the focus of the chapter's second section, which deals with business in the *Hadith*.

---

[1] Ibn Ishaq, *The Life of Muhammad: A Translation of Isḥāq's Sīrat Rasūl Allāh*, trans. Alfred Guillaume (Karachi, Pakistan: Oxford University, 1967).

Business in the *Sira*

Life in the Hijaz

Located in western Arabia, Hijaz means "barrier." According to one scholar, the Hijaz "is so called because it is, in fact, barren country standing like a barrier between the uplands of Najd and the low coastal region called Tihamah (lowland)."[2] The two places mentioned most frequently in the life of Muhammad—Mecca and Medina—are both situated in the Hijaz. In describing life in the Hijaz, two natural groups will be discussed. Originally described by Ibn Khaldun, these two consisted of the sedentary peoples and the desert nomads (the Bedouins).[3]

Bedouin Culture

Arabs in pre-Islamic Arabia lived in "tents of hair and wool, or houses of wood, clay or stone."[4] A key component of the Bedouin's life was the one-humped camel, which dates to the third millennium BC.[5] Phillip Hitti captures the importance of the camel for Bedouins thusly:

> The dowry of the bride, the price of blood, the profit of *maysir* (gambling), the wealth of a sheikh, are all computed in terms of camels. It is the Bedouin's constant companion, his *alter ego*, his foster parent. He drinks its milk instead of water (which he spares for the cattle); he feasts on its flesh; he covers himself

---

[2] Irving M. Zeitlin, *The Historical Muhammad* (Cambridge, UK: Polity, 2007), 33.
[3] Ibn Khaldûn, *The Muqaddimah: An Introduction to History*, abr. ed. Bollingen Series, ed. N. J. Dawood, trans. Franz Rosenthal (Princeton, NJ: Princeton University, 2005), 91.
[4] Zeitlin, 16-17.
[5] Robert G. Hoyland, *Arabia and the Arabs: From the Bronze Age to the Coming of Islam* (Oxon, Canada: Routledge, 2001), 90.

with its skin; he makes his tent of its hair. Its dung he uses as fuel, and its urine as a hair tonic and medicine. To him the camel is more than "the ship of the desert;" it is the special gift of Allah.[6]

The centrality of the camel is also signified by the fact that, "The Arabic language is said to include some one thousand names for the camel in its numerous breeds and stages of growth, a number rivaled only by the number of synonyms used for the sword."[7] The camel allowed the Bedouins to travel far into the interior of Arabia because it "can go without water for up to a month in the wintertime and for a number of days even in the height of summer, and can subsist on parched grass and desiccated shrubs it is able to survive under the least favourable of watering and pasturing conditions."[8] In addition, "The camel was also a great beast of burden: it was unrivalled, except by the elephant."[9]

Bedouin culture was also characterized by inter-tribal raiding. One scholar notes:

> Among the contemporary Arab tribes, the traditional method of self-enrichment was attack on another tribe and seizure of its animals and other possessions. . . . The Arabic word *ghazwa* (raid) meant a sudden attack on a caravan or another tribe for the purpose of seizing property and women and thereby easing the hard task of survival in Arabia.[10]

---

[6] Philip K. Hitti, *History of the Arabs: From the Earliest Times to the Present*, rvd. tenth ed. (Hampshire, UK: Palgrave Macmillan, 2002), 21-22.

[7] Hitti, 22.

[8] Hoyland, 91.

[9] Marshall G. S. Hodgson, *The Venture of Islam: Conscience and History in a World Civilization*, vol. 1, *The Classical Age of Islam* (Chicago, IL: University of Chicago, 1974), 148.

[10] 'Ali Dashti, *Twenty-Three Years: A Study of the Prophetic Career of Mohammad*, trans. F. R. C. Bagley (Costa Mesa, CA: Mazda, 1994), 86.

In the Bedouin mind, he regarded himself as a warrior, and the only occupations worthy of a man were hunting and fishing—along with raiding.[11] In reality, however, Bedouins were interdependent upon others in the Hijaz engaged in crop growing and animal husbandry.[12]

Settled Culture

While the Hijaz had no rivers, there was a network of wadis and oases that were fed seasonally by floodwaters and underground springs. The most common crop grown in these fertile areas was the date palm. As the camel was foundational to Bedouin life, the date palm played the same role for those who lived in settled areas of the Hijaz. One writer notes, "The fruit of the date palm (*tamr*), together with the milk of camels and goats, is the chief food of the Bedouin . . . Except for the flesh of a camel slaughtered for food when its useful life was at an end, the date fruit was the Bedouin's only solid food."[13] In addition to the date palm's use as food, "Its fermented beverage is the much-sought *nabīdh*. Its crushed stones furnish the cakes which are the everyday meal of the camel. To possess 'the two black ones' (*al-aswadān*), i.e., water and dates, is the dream of every Bedouin."[14] Medina and Khaybar were both date-growing agricultural settlements with large Jewish agricultural colonies in each.[15]

The settlement of Taif, located in the mountains above Mecca, developed somewhat differently due to its better water supply. One writer paints a word picture of Taif this way:

---

[11]Zeitlin, 27.
[12]W. Montgomery Watt, *Muhammad at Mecca* (London, UK: Oxford University, 1960), 2.
[13]Richard A. Gabriel, *Muhammad: Islam's First Great General* (Norman, OK: University of Oklahoma, 2007), 7.
[14]Hitti, 19.
[15]Watt, *Mecca*, 2.

> Situated at an altitude of 6,000 feet, and rich in shady trees and a variety of succulent fruits, [Taif] was a summer resort for the Meccan elite. The products of this settlement included honey, watermelons, bananas, figs, grapes, almonds, peaches, and pomegranates. Its roses were known for the attar from which some Meccans produced perfume.[16]

Between the Bedouins and the date-growers were a variety of others, ranging from those "growing field crops such as wheat, barley and lentils on the arable plains, and raising sheep and goats on the stubble fields and on nearby mountain slopes and desert pastures" to those engaged in "the seasonal movement of people and animals in search of grazing land...between winter pastures in the lowlands and summer pastures in the cooler highlands."[17]

Trade in the Hijaz

Trade in the Hijaz was both local and long-distance. Most of the inhabitants of Arabia would have participated in local trade. For example,

> pastoralists bartered their surplus of animals and animal products (milk, clarified butter, wool, hides, skins, etc.) for the goods of agricultural communities (grain, oil, clothing, wine, arms, etc.). This could go on informally at any time; otherwise one could attend one or more of the grand markets staged at fixed times of the year in different parts of Arabia.[18]

---

[16]Zeitlin, 33.
[17]Hoyland, 89.
[18]Ibid., 109.

The desert Bedouins would also have participated in local trade since "the mobile life [is not] compatible with developed craft specialization, and a visit to the town will often be necessary for vital manufactures: metal utensils, weapons, clothing, and so on."[19] The residents of Taif, for example, were known for their skill in leather working.[20]

The long-distance overland camel trade routes on the western edge of Arabia had long been established. One reason for this is that the roughly parallel Red Sea shipping route was difficult to navigate. One scholar summarizes the difficulties as follows:

> It [the Red Sea] is flanked on both sides by hundreds of miles of waterless desert. Immense coral reefs skirt both coasts and in places extend far out into the sea... Good harbors are almost wanting here, so that there was no safe refuge from the dangers of storms or pirates. The northward passage was especially hard to early seafarers, because northerly winds blow down this part of the sea the whole year round.[21]

The extent of the trade, the products that were traded, and control of the trade routes have been the subject of much debate. The traditional view, stated by a scholar writing in the early 1960s, is that, at the time of Muhammad, "Much of the transit trade between the Indian Ocean and the Mediterranean basin was passing through Arabian overland routes."[22] According to this traditional view, the composition of this trade was mostly spices, luxury items, and incense. However, there are numerous objections to that view. One

---

[19] Ibid., 98.
[20] Watt, *Mecca*, 4.
[21] George F. Hourani, *Arab Seafaring: In the Indian Ocean in Ancient and Early Medieval Times*, rvd. exp. ed., ed. John Carswell (Princeton, NJ: Princeton University, 1995), 5.
[22] Hodgson, *Venture*, vol. 1, 153.

scholar, focusing on the supply side of the trade, noted that the Ptolemies of Egypt and the Romans after them had begun to navigate the Red Sea from the Nile, using various canal and land routes across Egypt, which directly competed against the Arabian land routes. In that scholar's view, "The entry of the Roman shipping into the Indian Ocean sounded the knell of South Arabian prosperity."[23] Another scholar, focusing on the demand side of the trade, argued that, because of the rise of Christianity in the Roman Empire, the market for frankincense and other ostentatious luxury items had ceased to thrive.[24]

Even if the Indian Ocean spice/luxuries/incense trade was omitted, there are still reasons to accept that the overland trade routes in the Hijaz were yet functioning and valuable. Even the Islamic scholar whose criticisms of the traditional view noted above acknowledges that large-scale export of "leather in various forms" can be trusted to have occurred, as well as the export of "clothing, animals, [and] miscellaneous foodstuffs," including raisins, wine, and slaves.[25]

There also appears to have been more than 1,000 sites in western Arabia where substantial gold and silver mining operations occurred, which (through Carbon 14 analysis) can be dated to the period of Muhammad and classical Islam.[26] Furthermore, a 1st century A.D. Roman document, the *Periplus of the Red Sea*, gives an account of Muza (a port in Yemen) where "the whole place is crowded with Arab ship owners and seafaring men and is busy with the affairs of commerce."[27] While the *Periplus* focuses on Muza's trade

---

[23] Hitti, 60.
[24] Patricia Crone, *Meccan Trade and the Rise of Islam* (Piscataway, NJ: Gorgias, 2004), 27.
[25] Ibid., 87.
[26] Gene W. Heck, "Gold Mining in Arabia and the Rise of the Islamic State," *Journal of the Economic and Social History of the Orient* 42, no. 3 (1999): 365.
[27] Hourani, 32.

with the east African coastal cities, it is also likely that goods from Muza were transported inland to the Hijaz.

Trade in Mecca

Mecca's Competitive Advantage

By the time of Muhammad, Mecca had become the primary trading center in the Hijaz, two factors accounting for its primacy. The first was its location at the intersection of two trade routes. "One [route] went south and north, through the mountainous Ḥijâz from the Yemen and the Indian Ocean lands to Syria and the Mediterranean lands; the other, of less importance, went east and west from the Iraq, Iran, and the central Eurasian lands to Abyssinia and eastern Africa."[28]

The second was its status as a sacred territory, one Muslim scholar crediting that status to the water from the well Zamzam.[29] He writes, "Water was so dear in that environment that the territory around Mecca was held to be sacred; thus a *haram* area grew with a sacred enclave called the Ka'ba."[30] By mutual consent of the tribes, the Meccans established their own lunar calendar.[31] "During three consecutive months (the last two of one year and the first of the following) and during the seventh month (Rajab), war was by the mutual consent of the tribes suspended."[32] The seventh month of each year was also important for trade in that a cooperative trade fair was held in Mecca, which "provided ample opportunity for the exhibition of native wares, and for trade and exchange of commodities."[33]

---

[28] Hodgson, *Venture*, vol. 1, 154.
[29] Mahmood Ibrahim, *Merchant Capital and Islam* (Austin, TX: University of Texas, 1990), 34.
[30] Ibid.
[31] Hodgson, *Venture*, vol. 1, 155.
[32] Zeitlin, 44.
[33] Hitti, 94.

The Tribes of Mecca

The city of Mecca (and Bedouin society more generally) was comprised of a number of clans where "members of the same clan consider each other as of one blood, submit to the authority of but one chief— the senior member of the clan— and use one battle-cry. 'Banu' (children of) was the title with which they prefixed their joint name."[34] Related clans were referred to as a "tribe." The power exercised by clans and tribes was directly related to their wealth. With respect to individual members of clans and tribes, one scholar noted,

> Inherited wealth and business connexions [sic] could give a man a start, but in the end his influence depended chiefly on his personal qualities—his commercial and financial shrewdness, his diplomacy in dealing with other clans and tribes and with the representatives of the great powers, and his ability to get his equals in the clan and in wider circles to follow his lead.[35]

In Mecca, one tribe achieved dominance—the Quraysh, of which Muhammad was a part. Its dominance came in stages. "First, they sold protection to caravans. Then they began to offer wares for sale along the overland routes leading through their territory. Finally, they entered the large markets located outside their area."[36] According to Muslim sources, the member of the Quraysh tribe most responsible for its success was Hashim, who traveled to Syria and negotiated favorable trade agreements with the Byzantine

---

[34] Ibid., 26.
[35] Watt, *Mecca*, 9.
[36] Eric R. Wolf, "The Social Organization of Mecca and the Origins of Islam," *Southwestern Journal of Anthropology* 7, no. 4 (Winter, 1951): 332.

merchants there as well as with various tribes along the trading route.[37]

The Merchant Capitalists of Mecca

Trade and capitalism characterized the Meccan society into which Muhammad was born and raised. "The inhabitants of Mecca, belonging to the tribe of Quraysh, caused their capital to fructify through trade and loans. . . . By buying and selling commodities they simply sought to increase their capital, which took the form of money."[38] Mecca sent two large caravans each year that either traveled to "Damascus or Aila on the Gulf of Aqaba, the latter ultimately bound for Gaza and Egypt, or traveled northeast across the desert to Hira in Iraq and the towns along the Persian Gulf."[39] In addition, smaller caravans traveled to Yemen in the winter months.[40]

Besides being a trading center, Mecca had also become a financial center, due to the large amount of capital invested in each caravan. One scholar estimates that "Caravans comprised up to 2,500 camels and were valued . . . [at] the equivalent of 2,250 kg of gold."[41] In order to successfully organize these ventures, the leaders of the tribes during the time of Muhammad "were above all financiers, skillful in the manipulation of credit, shrewd in their speculations, and interested in any potentialities of lucrative investment from Aden to Gaza or Damascus."[42] Such ventures also required the financial participation of most Meccans, following the pattern of set forth by Hashim the Qurayshite, who "argued

---

[37]Ibrahim, 42.
[38]Maxime Rodinson, *Islam and Capitalism*, trans. Brian Pearce (London, UK: Saqi, 2007), 57-8.
[39]Gabriel, 12.
[40]Haleem, *The Qur'an*, 464, note b.
[41]Wolf, 333.
[42]Watt, *Mecca*, 3.

that the weak and the poor should be allowed to invest in the caravans."[43]

It should be noted that there were many residents of Mecca who did not benefit from the caravan trade. There had been a steady inflow of settlers to Mecca who were poor or cut off from their tribes. "In Mecca, they were known as *al-mustad'afun* . . . Most often, they had the status of a slave or at best a *mawla*."[44] These individuals would join the ranks of daily wage laborers as well as professions such as "tailors, carpenters, smiths, arrow makers, veterinarians, and various other shopkeepers. Other professions catered specifically to the caravan economy, such as porters, herders, guides, guards, entertainers, and servants . . . [as well as] those who prepared food and sold it in the streets of Mecca."[45]

These divisions resulted in class distinctions where the leading tribes of Mecca and the leading men of those tribes—who were also the leading merchants—occupied the top class. As capital became more concentrated among these merchants, [They] began to use their excess capital in another form of banking practice: moneylending. *Riba* (usury) played a significant role in maintaining a diversified social and economic structure . . . those who had no original capital were encouraged to borrow from those who did, the merchants.[46]

All these factors combined to shape Muhammad's work experience and were the ground into which the *surat* and *hadith* were sown.

---

[43] Ibrahim, 41.
[44] Ibid., 77.
[45] Ibid., 62.
[46] Ibid., 61.

Muhammad, Merchants, and the Marketplace

Muhammad's Work Experience

Although Muhammad was born into the leading Meccan tribe of Quraysh, his clan was not particularly wealthy:

> The fortunes of 'Abd al-Muṭṭalib [Muhammad's grandfather] had waned during the last part of his life, and what he left at his death amounted to no more than a small legacy for each of his sons.... Abū Ṭālib [Muhammad's guardian uncle] was poor, and his nephew felt obliged to do what he could to earn his own livelihood.[47]

According to one source, Muhammad herded sheep and goats at times, which "at his age [was] a humiliating task generally given to slaves and girls."[48]

Muhammad was also attracted to the caravan trade. When his uncle, Abu Talib, was about ready to leave for Syria in a merchant caravan, Muhammad (being either age 9 or 12) "attached himself closely to him [Abu Talib] so that he took pity on him and said that he would take him with him."[49] It is also recorded that Muhammad accompanied another of his uncles, Zubair, to Yemen.[50] It is likely that Muhammad showed skill as a trader since, in his early 20s, "he was asked to take charge of the goods of a merchant who was unable to travel himself, and his success in this capacity led to other similar engagements. He was thus able to earn a better livelihood, and marriage became a possibility."[51]

---

[47] Martin Lings, *Muhammad: His Life Based on the Earliest Sources* (Rochester, VT: Inner Traditions, 2006), 29.
[48] Émile Dermenghem, *The Life of Mahomet*, trans. Arabella York (New York, NY: Lincoln MacVeagh, 1930), 44.
[49] Ishaq, 79.
[50] Dermenghem, 44.
[51] Lings, 33.

Muhammad's marriage to Khadijah, when he was age 25, began as a business relationship. She, a 40-year-old widow who had been married twice, "was a merchant woman of dignity and wealth. She used to hire men to carry merchandise outside the country on a profit-sharing basis."[52] The reports from other merchants who had entrusted Muhammad with their merchandise were that he was "al-Amīn, the Reliable, the Trustworthy, the Honest."[53] Based on these comments, along with good reports from her family (also belonging to the Quraysh tribe), "One day she sent word to him, asking him to take some of her merchandise to Syria. His fee would be the double of the highest she had ever paid to a man of Quraysh."[54]

After Muhammad married Khadijah, he "had now set his foot on at least the lowest rung of the ladder of worldly success" and had "sufficient capital to take a moderate share in trading enterprises."[55] For example, it was recorded that he had entered a partnership and traded in leather goods.[56] In later years, after he began to speak as a prophet of Allah, Muhammad was criticized as having been a man of the marketplace. "What sort of messenger is this? He eats food and walks about in the marketplaces!" (25:7). It appears that he was regarded as one of the most promising youths of the clan and, in subsequent years, was able to arrange marriages for his daughters with members of some of the prominent clans of the tribe.[57]

---

[52]Ishaq, 82.
[53]Lings, 34.
[54]Ibid.
[55]Watt, *Mecca*, 38.
[56]Crone, 98.
[57]Watt, *Mecca*, 39.

Muhammad Versus the Merchants of Mecca

The prosperity of the elite merchant class did not lift all the residents of Mecca from economic peril. There were many who lived day-to-day as laborers. The wealthier of the Meccan merchants "engaged in money-lending at usurious rates (*riba*)."[58] Those who encountered severe financial losses were often "forced to practice ritual suicide *(i'tifad)*. A merchant who lost his wealth was forced to separate himself and his family from the rest of the clan and to starve to death."[59] Even when suicide was not forced, the consequences were severe, as Muhammad would have seen firsthand. His uncle, Abu Talib, borrowed 10,000 dirhams from his brother, Al Abbas. When Abu Talib couldn't repay the loan on time, Al Abbas took away certain offices and privileges that Abu Talib had held.[60]

One Islamic historian summarized the economic situation as follows:

> With the development of Mecca as a commercial and financial centre, the moral standards of Bedouin society no longer served well. Though the Quraysh seem to have kept the dangerous custom of feuding under control at least within Mecca, a type of economic inequality had arisen between man and man which threatened tribal solidarity and in any case undermined the Bedouin ideal of generous manliness in which wealth was a welcome but relatively transient distinction. In Mecca, as the individual began to act more freely in his own private interest, the tribal expectations came to fit less well. Particularly those who were disadvantaged in the new, more individualistic pattern welcomed a moral

---

[58] Ibrahim, 46.
[59] Ibid., 41.
[60] Ibid., 61.

conception which could restore something of the older moral security in a form adapted to individualistic, commercial life.[61]

Into this economic milieu, Muhammad began his work as a prophet at the age of 40. "Consecrated and fired by the new task which he felt called upon to perform as the messenger (*rasūl*) of Allah, Muhammad now went among his own people teaching, preaching, delivering the new message."[62] The messages of the 90 Meccan *surat* "are mostly short, incisive, fiery, impassioned in style and replete with prophetic feeling. In them the oneness of Allah, His attributes, the ethical duties of man, and the coming retribution constitute the favourite themes."[63] A Muslim scholar characterized the Meccan *surat* as being

> full of his displeasure at the state of affairs in Mecca. Meccans were asked to moderate their social relations, especially those with the poor, the orphans, the widows, and all those who were weak and in need of aid. Wealth might have been the "pleasure of this world," but wealth based on the deprivation of a sizable sector of the society would be meaningless once the individual was called to account before God.[64]

Muhammad's message "found a public capable of responding to it."[65] It also generated opposition from the Quraysh leadership, which could not afford to have pilgrims to Mecca "hear their gods insulted by Muhammad and his followers, and . . . be urged to forsake the religion of their

---

[61] Hodgson, *Venture*, vol. 1, 167.
[62] Hitti, 113.
[63] Ibid., 124.
[64] Ibrahim, 82.
[65] Hodgson, *Venture*, vol. 1, 167.

forefathers and to adopt a new religion."⁶⁶ Such speech from a member of their tribe could also have led to the ouster of the Quraysh from their leadership of Mecca, which had happened to other tribes before them.⁶⁷ For all the Quraysh knew, Muhammad's agitation might also be "connected with some Roman plot to control the Ḥijâz trade through a local puppet, such as the Quraysh had had to resist before."⁶⁸ Although the other clans of the Quraysh boycotted Muhammad's clan,⁶⁹ they could not physically attack or kill him due to the protection afforded him by his clan's leader, Abu Talib. However, when both Khadijah and Abu Talib died, he was now clearly at risk, which set the stage for him and his followers to emigrate to Medina.

Muhammad Versus the Merchants of Medina

At Medina, Muhammad escalated his attacks on the Quraysh and on Meccan trade while also taking steps to control the trade of Medina. One historian notes his changed approach as follows: "Leaving the city of his birth as a despised prophet, he entered the city of his adoption as an honoured chief. The seer in him now recedes into the background and the practical man of politics comes to the fore."⁷⁰

Not long after arriving in Medina, Muhammad began to raid Meccan caravans, which gave the Muslims an "independent economic position at Medina, without which the life and social order of the new community there must remain artificial."⁷¹ The emigrants were also heavily involved in Medina's marketplaces.⁷² The most significant step taken

---

⁶⁶Lings, 55.
⁶⁷Ibid.
⁶⁸Hodgson, *Venture*, vol. 1, 161.
⁶⁹Ibid., 171.
⁷⁰Hitti, 116.
⁷¹Hodgson, *Venture*, vol. 1, 175.
⁷²W. Montgomery Watt, *Muhammad at Medina* (London, UK: Oxford University, 1956), 250-251.

by Muhammad, "which secured the economic base and strengthened the prestige of the Moslems was their seizure of the property of the Jews of Yathreb [Medina]."[73] Although the circumstances varied, the economic results were the same. After besieging each tribe, the Jews' moveable property was confiscated and distributed to Muhammad's followers, as were the Jews' agricultural lands and date plantations.[74] Outside of Medina, he altered his tactics with respect to the Jews, but the outcome was similar. "The Jews of Khaybar, a strongly fortified oasis north of al-Madīnah, surrendered in 628 and paid tribute."[75] While private possession of property was affirmed in the Qur'an, Muhammad's early actions in Medina were a sign of things to come—his authority was absolute, the right of possession was not.

During this period of time in Medina, Islam became more than a religion. "Hitherto it had been a religion within a state; in al-Madīnah; after Badr, it passed into something more than a state religion—it itself became the state. Then and there Islam came to be what the world has ever since recognized it to be—a militant polity."[76] The "state" aspect of Islam was reflected in the Medinan *surat*. These *surat*, which comprise about one-third of the Qur'an, "are rich in legislative material" governing a wide range of areas, including

> public prayer, fasting, pilgrimage and the sacred months, laws prohibiting wine, pork, and gambling; fiscal and military ordinances relating to alms-giving *(zakāh)* and holy war *(jihād)*; civil and criminal laws regarding homicide, retaliation, theft, usury,

---

[73] Dashti, 87.
[74] Ibid., 89-90.
[75] Hitti, 117.
[76] Ibid.

marriage and divorce, adultery, inheritance, and the freeing of slaves.[77]

Muhammad's Merchants and Marketplace

The traditional view of Muhammad's relationship with merchants and the marketplace is summarized by respected Islamic scholar W. Montgomery Watt, who writes, "In Muhammad himself there seems to have been no intention of hindering legitimate trade or of revolutionizing the financial practices of Mecca."[78] As it relates to the Qur'an's view of trade, Watt goes on to state, "There is hardly anything that could be called reform in the other rules of the Qur'ān dealing with commerce and finance. They exhort to upright dealing, and in certain cases prescribe that the matter should be put in writing."[79] With due respect to such an eminent scholar, on the matter of Muhammad's intentions regarding trade and commerce, there are a number of actions he had undertaken that had the effect of overthrowing the traditional authority structure of the Hijaz and giving himself (and future caliphs) control of trade and commerce wherever it was conducted under Islamic rule.

Muhammad undermined the authority of tribal and clan leaders (who also controlled most of the capital used for trade in the Hijaz) by elevating the *ummah* above tribal affiliations. "The primacy of Islam over all old customs was asserted; in effect, no bond or tie of pagan society need hold in the Islamic community, unless explicitly acknowledged anew within Islam . . . the Ummah of Islam was proclaimed wholly independent."[80] Another historian described the overthrow as follows: "By one stroke the most vital bond of Arab relationship, that of tribal kinship, was replaced by a

---

[77]Ibid., 124.
[78]Watt, *Medina*, 298.
[79]Ibid.
[80]Hodgson, *Venture*, vol. 1, 175-6.

new bond, that of faith; a sort of Pax Islamica was instituted for Arabia."[81]

Muhammad also placed himself at the center of all activities that generated booty or income. For example, raiding (a traditional source of income for the tribes) was outlawed in Islam unless it was directed at non-Muslims.[82] Muhammad took control of a fifth of the booty from such activities, unless it was acquired by intimidation or agreement without fighting—in which case he took total control of it all.[83] While some might argue that Muhammad's control of one-fifth of the booty was less onerous (perhaps even magnanimous) than the one-quarter share traditionally taken by tribal leaders, it must be noted that his fifth came out of a much larger amount of booty, since the united armies of Islam were attacking neighboring empires versus a handful of raiders attacking isolated caravans or herds. Further, "Under the old ways, individuals kept whatever booty they had captured. Muhammad required that all booty be turned in to the common pool where it was shared equally among all combatants."[84] But its distribution was still under Muhammad's control. Apart from the initial booty, he also levied annual taxes against subjugated non-Muslims for "protection"—a tax that was later known as *jizya*.

Even capital that was privately owned by Muslims was subject to indirect control and taxation. "Definite proportions of property or income to be paid as 'alms' to Muhammad or one of his agents are mentioned in some of the treaties from the last two years or so of his life."[85] Later, these became mandatory—the *zakat* tax. When the operators of lucrative mining operations in the Hijaz tried to pay the relatively low *zakat* tax of 2.5%, Muhammad intervened and they were

---

[81]Hitti, 120-1.
[82]Gabriel, 19.
[83]Watt, *Medina*, 256.
[84]Gabriel, xxiv-xxv.
[85]Watt, *Medina*, 253.

assessed a 20% mineral tax.[86] Upon a Muslim's death, inheritances were limited to immediate family members and could not be diffused throughout the clan.[87]

While merchants were still free to trade, they came under increasing controls. For example, Muhammad placed a high priority upon agricultural development. To this end

> [he] encouraged the hiring of labor to help in the agricultural development of Medina. Some traditions even imply the extension of workdays to include evening hours. Furthermore, Muhammad asked that those landlords who could not develop their land because they lacked time or expertise hire workers who might have both but own no land. At one point, he asked those landlords to give up the land for the benefit of those who could develop it.[88]

Muhammad also reorganized the market system in Medina, the existing markets generally being small and localized.[89] He personally visited several potential locations and chose one particular location where he established a new tax-free market.[90] One can only speculate as to how long the other markets could have remained viable, competing both against a tax-free market and against Muslims who received the prime locations in the new market.

Muhammad also regulated all activities that involved buying and selling products in any place but the marketplace. A list of some of these prohibited transactions is as follows:

---

[86]Heck, *Gold*, 383.
[87]Hodgson, *Venture*, vol. 1, 181.
[88]Ibrahim, 88.
[89]Ibid.
[90]M. J. Kister, "The Market of the Prophet," *Journal of Economic and Social History of the Orient* 8 (1965): 276.

Mukhadara (the selling of green wheat before it was harvested in exchange for already harvested wheat). Also discouraged were the practices of *m'awama* (selling the crop several years in advance), *kira'* (the buying of a crop before it was ripe or harvested in exchange for another crop), and *muzabana* (the selling of grapes in exchange for raisins or wheat in exchange for prepared food). Finally, Muhammad discouraged merchants from meeting caravans before they reached the market to buy up their merchandise.[91]

While Muhammad's relationship with merchants and markets can be viewed from a number of perspectives, it is certainly reasonable to draw the conclusion, based upon his life and actions, that he was not opposed to trade and commerce nor did he revolutionize trade in the Hijaz.

As one Islamic scholar noted,

> Mohammed was *not original*... What made him the founder of a new era was not that he was able to provide a philosophical system for the Arab merchants and marauders, but that he understood his own people and knew how to build up what was *Arabic*, even with materials obtained from other nations.[92]

Muhammad did, however, succeed in controlling the trade and commerce of the Hijaz and channel income from it into the further expansion of Islam. It is through this lens that the various *ahadith* related to business should be viewed.

---

[91] Ibrahim, 87.
[92] Torrey, 49-50.

Business in the *Hadith*

Possessions and Wealth in the *Hadith*

While there are numerous passages in the Qur'an that establish Allah's role in the creation and distribution of possessions and wealth, the *hadith* are far more concerned with man's use of possessions and wealth. According to Muhammad, "You should not be extremists [in religious practices] but try to be near to perfection and receive the good tidings that you will be rewarded" (Bu 2:29:39). This is accomplished by conforming one's actions (the practical side of life) to the requirements set forth in the Qur'an and the *hadith*.[93]

Despite this difference in emphasis, there are *ahadith* that speak to Allah's role in possessions and wealth. For example, "O Allah! . . . You are the Maintainer of the heavens and the earth. All the praises are for You; You are the *Rabb* (Lord) of the heavens and the earth and whatever is therein" (Bu 97:35:7499). Allah is also credited with bringing forth crops by directing rainfall to cropland (not on houses or livestock) in response to wherever the Prophet moved his hand (Bu 15:24:1033). Muhammad also urges reliance upon Allah because "He would provide for you just as the bird is provided for; it goes out in the morning empty and returns full" (Tir 34:33:2344). In one *hadith,* Allah seems to have miraculously increased a debtor's supply of dates as Muhammad paid off the creditors (Bu 43:18:2405).

Also, there are differences between the Qur'an and *hadith* with regard to Allah's role in possessions and wealth. For example, the Qur'an makes it clear that Allah is the sole decider of who receives possessions; but in one *hadith* Muhammad seems to take on this role when he states, "I have only been appointed as a *Qâsim* (distributor); I

---

[93]Maulana Muhammad Ali, *A Manual of Hadith*, 2d ed. (Lahore, Pakistan: Ahmadiyya Ishaat Islam, 2001), 14.

distribute among you" (Mu 38:5:5592). As to Allah's unequal distribution of property, the Qur'an counsels those who have received less not to envy those who have received more; whereas in the *hadith,* the pious poor are given added encouragement since, "The poor *Muhājirīn* will enter Paradise before the rich among them by five hundred years" (Tir 34:37:2351).

In the matter of private property, one Islamic scholar has noted that the *Sunnah* does not challenge this concept.[94] In fact, it even seems to extend private ownership to land, a matter that is left unclear in the Qur'an, since Muhammad "allotted large tracts of land to a number of Companions."[95] The rights of landowners are expanded upon in numerous *ahadith*. For example, "Whoever farms a people's land without their permission, then nothing he farms belongs to him, and its finances are due to him [the owner]" (Tir 13.29.1366). There are even *ahadith* that clarify the rights of joint owners of land. Muhammad "allocated partners the right of pre-emption in property which had not been divided up. When boundaries had been fixed between them, then there was no right of pre-emption" (Muw 35.1.1).

Moveable private property is also protected in the *hadith*. While the following *hadith* addresses primarily the ownership of animals, by analogy it also speaks to stores of goods:

> An animal should not be milked without the permission of its owner. Does any of you like that somebody comes to his store and breaks his container and takes away his food? The udders of the animals are the stores of their owners where their provision is kept, so nobody should milk the animals

---

[94] Rodinson, 43.
[95] Zaman, 32.

of somebody else, without the permission of its owner (Bu 45.8.2435).

Owners of property are also entitled to take back their property, even if it has been sold to someone else. "If anyone finds his very property with a man, he is more entitled to it (than anyone else), and the buyer should pursue the one who sold it" (Daw 17:1325:3524). Thieves were dealt with severely, as Aisha (Muhammad's wife) affirmed when she said, "The Prophet used to cut off a thief's hand for a quarter of a dīnār and upwards (Daw 33:1615:4370). Those finding property should make an attempt to return it. Muhammad commanded a Bedouin who had picked up a lost item, "Make public announcement about it for one year. Remember the description of its container and the string with which it is tied; and if somebody comes and claims it and describes it correctly (give it to him); otherwise, utilize it" (Bu 45:2:2427). Perhaps the strongest affirmation of private property is given when Muhammad stated,"Whoever is killed while protecting his property, then he is a martyr" (Bu 46.33.2480).

There are many *ahadith* that address the right and wrong uses of possessions and wealth. Prominent among the list of right uses are matters of giving, specifically *zakat* and *sadaqah*. Muhammad does not mince words on these topics, "'You have to pay the *Zakāt*.' The man asked, 'Is there anything other than the *Zakāt* for me to pay?' Allah's Messenger replied, 'No, unless you want to give alms of your own [*sadaqah*]'" (Bu 2:34:46).

Likewise, many *ahadith* prohibit the wrong use of possessions and wealth in various ways. For example, Muslims should limit their expenditures on furniture. Muhammad drove home this point when he said, "A bed for the man, a bed for his wife, a third for the guest, and the fourth is for the *Shaitân* [Satan]" (Mu 37:8:5452). Clothing should not be ostentatious, and silks are forbidden. When a follower commented that a certain striped silk garment would be appropriate for Muhammad for Friday prayers at the mosque and for meeting delegations, he replied, "This is only worn by one who has no share in the Hereafter" (Mu 37:1:5401). Another *hadith* prohibits wearing clothing that was dyed with a red dye made from safflowers (Tir 22:5:1725).

Also, limited are the types of possessions that a Muslim could acquire, one example being vessels made from silver. "The one who drinks from a vessel of silver is gulping the fire of Hell into his belly" (Mu 37:1:5385). And the amount of a Muslim's eternal reward was reduced for each day that the individual owned a dog—except if the dog was used for hunting or to guard livestock (Tir 16:17:1487). Artwork that contained certain images like humans, animals, and birds are prohibited. "The angels do not enter a house in which there is a dog or an image" (Maj 32:44:3649).

Muhammad stressed that possessions and wealth were all temporal. "The likeness of this world in comparison to the Hereafter is that of anyone of you dipping his finger into the sea: let him see what he brings forth" (Maj 37:3:4108). True riches are not measured externally. "Richness is not abundance of (worldly) goods, rather richness is richness of the heart" (Mu 12:40:2420). In the final analysis, according to Muhammad, "Allah does not look at your forms or your wealth, rather He looks at your deeds and your hearts" (Maj 37:9:4143).

Trade and Commerce in the *Hadith*

Work and Success in the *Hadith*

In a *hadith* entitled "Divine Preordainment," it is said that, prior to man's soul being breathed into him, "Allah sends an angel and orders him to write . . . is provision, his stated term to die (age), and whether he will be of the wretched or the blessed" (Bu 82:1:6594). Another *hadith* lists the things written as deeds, livelihood, date of death, and whether the person will be blessed or wretched in eternity (Bu 59:6:3208). Allah thus appears to decide a man's work and income before birth. Perhaps for this reason, Muhammad urges, "O people, fear Allah and be moderate in seeking a living, for no soul will die until it has received all its provision, even if it is slow in coming" (Maj 12:2:2144). Whenever a man begins to succeed at earning a living, Muhammad counsels, "Let him stick with it" (Maj 12:4:2147). He also urged his followers to work and not beg saying: "By Him in Whose Hand my life is, it is better for anyone of you to take a rope and cut the wood (from the forest) and carry it over his back and sell it (as a means of earning his living), rather than to ask a person for something and that person may or may not give him" (Bu 24:50:1470).

Not all work, however, is good. Several *ahadith* state that Allah's blessings are possible only when one gives to charity out of earnings from good work. "Whoever gives *sadaqa* from good earnings—and Allah only accepts the good—it is as if he placed it in the palm of the Merciful to raise it, as one of you might raise his foal or young camel until it is like the mountain" (Muw 58.1.1). One type of work clearly not acceptable is *Ghulûl.* "Allâh, the Mighty and Sublime, does not accept prayer without purification or charity from *Ghulûl*' (Nas 23:48:2525). *Ghulûl* is defined as "goods pilfered from the spoils of war prior to them being presented to the commander for proper distribution. It may also refer to wealth amassed unlawfully" (Nas 23:48:2525, note 1). Engaging others to cultivate land on your behalf is also unacceptable, Muhammad's counsel is quite terse, "Cultivate it (yourself) or give it to your brother" (Nas 36:45:3893).

On the other hand, certain kinds of work are highly commended in the *hadith*. "The Prophet said, 'Nobody has ever eaten a better meal than that which one has earned by working with one's own hands. The Prophet of Allâh, Dāwūd

(David) used to eat from the earnings of his manual labour'" (Bu 34:15:2072), Muhammad himself having engaged in manual labor. One *hadith* refers to him sleeping in a room where there were "some hides hanging . . . and some grass for tanning" (Bu 77:31:5843)—perhaps in connection with his leather trade.

The work of a man's children is also credited to him as good. "The Messenger of Allah said: 'The best (most pure) food that a man eats is that which he has earned himself, and a man's child (and his child's wealth) is part of his earnings'" (Nas 44:1:4454). Although a child's income from work belongs to the father, spending on one's family is highly rewarded since, "What a man spends on himself, his wife, his child and his servant, then it is charity" (Maj 12:1:2138).

Merchants and Trading in the *Hadith*

Various *ahadith* are quite favorable to merchants and trading. In fact, based on the following one, a merchant can be highly esteemed, "The trustworthy, honest Muslim merchant will be with the martyrs on the Day of Resurrection" (Maj 12:1:2139), Muhammad himself having been a trader. A future caliph, Umar, also stated that "I used to be busy trading in markets, i.e., going out for trading" (Bu 34:9:2062). Another *hadith* affirms the practice of trading while on pilgrimage and makes reference to the *ayah* in the Qur'an that approved such activities (Bu 65:34:4519).

Despite favorable *ahadith,* there are *ahadith* that present an entirely different view of merchants and trading. Muhammad is quoted as saying, "The most beloved land to Allah, may He be exalted, is the *Masâjid* [site of a mosque]; and the most hated of land to Allâh is the marketplaces" (Mu 5:52:1528). Muhammad also referred to the marketplace as "the battleground of the *Shaiṭân* [Satan] where he sets up his banner" (Mu 44:16:6315). Another *hadith* relates how Muhammad had gone into the marketplace early in the morning, called out to the merchants and said, "The merchants will be raised on the Day of Resurrection as immoral people, apart from those who fear Allah and act righteously and speak the truth (i.e., those who are honest)" (Maj 12:3:2146).

Reconciling these opposing traditions becomes easier if viewed through the premise presented earlier—i.e., Muhammad was not opposed to trading *per se*, but he did need to defeat his adversaries (the traders from the Quraysh tribe who constituted the marketplace establishment) and then harness the income of the marketplace to finance the advance of Islam. Consistent with this premise, Muhammad offers traders ways to redeem their occupation, one such way being through giving. "Indeed, the *Shaiṭân* and sin are present in the sale, so mix your sales with charity" (Tir 12:4:1208). Another way is attending morning prayers. "Whoever goes to the Morning prayer first thing in the morning, he goes out with the banner of faith; but whoever goes out to the marketplace first thing in the morning, he goes out under the banner of *Iblis* [Satan]" (Maj 12:40:2234). Those who enter the marketplace proclaiming the praise of Allah will find that Allah "shall record a million good deeds for him, wipe a million evil deeds away from him, and raise a million ranks for him" (Tir 45:36:3428).

When the Quraysh were overthrown and Islam was established in the Hijaz, it is clear from many *ahadith* that Muhammad desired to see the markets and the caravan trade function as efficiently as possible, which (by the way) would also increase the flow of funds into the coffers of the Islamic caliphate. For example, numerous *ahadith* prohibit the purchase of goods before they arrived at the marketplace. "We used to go ahead to meet the caravan and used to buy foodstuff *[sic]* from them. The Prophet forbade us to sell it till the foodstuff has reached the market" (Bu 34:72:2166). The effect of this *hadith* would be to increase the prices in the market and thus the incomes of the traders.

Allowing products to be siphoned from the market would result in "black markets," which, from Muhammad's viewpoint as the head of the Islamic state, would be harder to control and tax.

Sales transactions in the marketplace should not be undone. "Do not urge somebody to return what he has already bought . . . from another seller so as to sell him your own goods" (Bu 34:58:2139). This *hadith* would have the effect of maintaining a higher level of turnover in the marketplace than would exist if trust were undermined through broken trades. The importance of trust in the functioning of markets was also likely a factor in Muhammad's repeated demands that goods be weighed at the time they were bought. The following *hadith* emphasizes the importance he placed on this practice: "I saw people being beaten (in punishment) at the time of the Messenger of Allâh for buying food unmeasured and selling it before bringing it to their own camp" (Nas 44:57:4612).

There is also a nexus of *ahadith* that connect speculation, transactions involving chance *(gharar)*, and usury *(riba)*. Muhammad forbade them all, the traditional explanation for these prohibitions are summarized as follows:

> Prohibitions directed against various practices have been seen as laying fetters upon the free working of a liberal economy. Thus, any speculation in foodstuffs, and especially the cornering of them, is forbidden. Above all, however, what is involved is prohibition of any selling in which there is an element of uncertainty. For instance, sale by auction, since the seller does not know what price he will get for the object being sold, or any sale in which the merchandise is not precisely, numerically defined (e.g. the fruits growing on a palm-tree) although the price is expressed in definite terms, etc . . . Some traditions, however, seem to make *gharar* (chance) a

special case—for instance, the sale of a slave or an animal that has run away, of an animal still in its mother's womb, etc. As usual, there are many disagreements among the learned over details, but the principle is accepted by all.[96]

In light of the circumstances of Muhammad's rise to prophethood (and power), these prohibitions likely had less to do with unfettering the marketplace than with insuring that the same factors leading to the rise of the merchant capital class in Mecca did not occur in Islam. The Meccan trading class employed their capital to speculate, lend money at high interest rates, and buy crops using futures contracts. All of these activities augmented the merchants' private capital through which they gained increasing power. By prohibiting such activities in many *ahadith*, Muhammad was preventing this rival power base from rising again.

Another traditional Bedouin practice of gaining wealth—and one that Muhammad employed to great effect in his rise to power—was raiding other clans. In the *hadith*, this was forbidden. In response to complaints from two visitors about the prevalence of robberies, Muhammad said, "There will shortly come a time when a caravan will go to Makkah (from Al-Madīna) without any guard" (Bu 24:9:1413). What was tolerated and honored, however, were raids against non-Muslims, as will be discussed further in Chapter 5, Business in Islamic History.

Marketplace Ethics in the *Hadith*

The *hadith* contains an extensive list of actions that are either approved or deemed unlawful by the words and actions of Muhammad. One historian summarized Islamic ethics as follows:

---

[96]Rodinson, 45-6.

Muhammad insisted on the moral responsibility of human beings. Life was no matter of play, it called for sober alertness; men dare not relax, secure in their wealth and their good family and their numerous sons—all these things would avail nothing at the Judgment, when a person's own personal worth would be weighed; humans must live in constant fear and awe of God, before whom they were accountable for every least deed.[97]

While many of these ethical requirements are focused on matters of religious observance and topics that have little relevance to business, there are certain ethical categories that have relevance for the conduct of business. Four such categories are highlighted here.

Competition, Prices, and Profits

The first concerns competition, prices, and profits in the marketplace. While Islam establishes control over many areas in the lives of Muslims, Muhammad did not seek to control prices in the marketplace, the following *hadith* explains his position:

> The people said: Apostle of Allah, prices have shot up, so fix prices for us. Thereupon the Apostle of Allah said: Allah is the one Who fixes prices, Who withholds, gives lavishly and provides; and I hope that when I meet Allah, none of you will have any claim on me for an injustice regarding blood or property (Daw 17:1296:3444).

The supply of products into the marketplace, however, was not to be manipulated. For example, hoarding was

---

[97]Hodgson, *Venture*, vol. 1, 164.

prohibited—especially for food items. "No one withholds goods till their price rises but a sinner" (Daw 1294:3440). The activities of middlemen were also restricted. To avoid speculation, middlemen were required to physically take possession of, and store, the products before they could be sold (Mu 21:8:3841). Competitive auctions for goods were allowed. "Malik said, 'There is no harm, however, in more than one person bidding against each other over goods put up for sale'" (Muw 31:45:96). However, bid rigging, where false bids are voiced with the goal of trying to manipulate the price (known in Arabic as *An-Najsh*), is prohibited (Tir 12:65:1304).

Drawing upon Arabic and Turkish sources, one Islamic scholar noted that, "There are also *ahadith* reporting that the Prophet approved of profits exceeding even 100 per cent providing they were made through permissible, *halal*, means. It has also been reported that some individuals were blessed by the Prophet and consequently made huge profits in the market."[98] He concluded that, "Islam does not impose a maximum profit rate, and freely functioning market mechanism is the accepted norm by classical Islamic capitalism."[99]

Cheating in the marketplace

A second category concerns cheating in the marketplace. Muhammad spared no words on this matter: "A person came to the Prophet and told him that he was always betrayed in purchasing. The Prophet told him to say at the time of buying, 'No cheating'" (Bu 34:48:2117). A similar *hadith* is found in Malik's *Muwatta*, except that Muhammad advises the man to say, "No trickery" (Muw 31.46.98). Such forbidden practices as tying with string the udders of an animal that is to be sold in order to keep "the milk in the udder . . . artificially inflating

---

[98] Çizakça, 13.
[99] Ibid.

prices" (Nas 44:16:4496) were likely the kind of trickery he had in mind.

A chapter in one collection of *hadith* is devoted to the need for goods sold in the market to be measured by the seller (Bu 34:51). The punishment for non-compliance could be quite severe. "I saw the people at the time of the Messenger of Allâh being beaten if they bought food without measure then sold it on the spot, unless they took it to their own places" (Mu 21:8:3847). The goal was for real buyers and sellers (not speculators) to engage in honest and transparent transactions. "If both the parties spoke the truth and described the defects and qualities (of the goods), then they would be blessed in their transaction; and if they told lies or hid something, then the blessings of their transaction would be lost" (Bu 34:19:2079).

Employees

A third category concerns the treatment of those hired to do work. The *hadith* affirm hiring for wages even those who are not Muslims. For example, Muhammad and Abu Bakr hired a pagan guide on their emigration to Medina (Bu 37:4:2264). Another *hadith* tells of a man who had employees and was admitted to Paradise by Allah (Bu 34:17:2077). In all cases, employees must be paid for their labor, Muhammad stating that, on the Resurrection Day, Allah will oppose "one who employs a labourer and takes full work from him but does not pay him for his labour" (Bu 37:10:2270). Even a slave "is entitled to his food and clothing, and he should not be burdened except with that which he can bear" (Mu 27:10:4316). Indeed, according to Muhammad, "Your slaves are your brethren upon whom Allâh has given you authority" (Bu 49:15:2545).

Bribery and Corruption

The fourth category concerns bribery and corruption. Again, Muhammad is unequivocal— "The Apostle of Allah cursed the one who bribes and the one who takes bribe" (Daw 18:1341:3573). He also warns state administrators that they will be judged on every gift they receive. "O people, if any of you is put in an administrative post on our behalf and conceals from us a needle or more, he is acting unfaithfully and will bring it on the Day of Resurrection" (Daw 18:1342:3574). Tax officials are to act "with sincerity and fairness . . . like one who goes out to fight for the sake of Allâh, until he returns to his house" (Maj 8:14:1809). They are not to be over zealous. In one *hadith*, Umar criticizes certain tax collectors for taking "from the Muslims those of their animals which are the best food-producers" (Muw 17:16:28). There are also numerous *ahadith* pertaining to judges. A judge is able to enter Paradise only if he "knows what is right and gives judgment accordingly" (Daw 18:1339:3566). Judges must never "make haste in decision" (Daw 18:1340:3570), but are to wait to hear both sides of a case (Daw 18:1343:3575).

Finance and Ownership in the *Hadith*

The *hadith* maintains the strong prohibition of *riba* (usury) that was begun in the Qur'an. In the Qur'an, the person receiving usury was likened to an insane person being led about by Satan (2:275). In the *hadith*, the condemnation of those receiving *riba* continues. For example, Muhammad tells of a dream where

> two men came and took me to a sacred land whence we proceeded on till we reached a river of blood, and in it (its middle) there was a man, and on its bank was standing another man with stones in his hands. The man in the middle of the river tried to come out, but

the other threw a stone in his mouth and forced him to go back to his original place ... I asked, "Who is this?" I was told, "The person in the river was a *Ribā*-eater" (Bu 34:24:2085).

There are also *hadith* linking usury to any form of transaction that does not involve an immediate physical exchange of money for goods. The following *hadith* specifically connects usury with trading in depository receipts:

> People bought and sold the receipts among themselves before they took delivery of the goods ... Marwan! [a seller of such receipts] do you make usury *halal?*" He said, "I seek refuge with Allah! What is that?" He said, "These receipts which people buy and sell before they take delivery of the goods." Marwan therefore sent guards to follow them and to take them from people's hands and return them to their owners (Muw 31.19.44).

Even when there is a physical exchange, the *hadith* prohibit exchanges of like items unless the exchange was for equal amounts (Nas 44:50:4583). This prohibition eliminates the possibility of a usurious increase:

> Despite concern in the *hadith* about usury, Muhammad clearly favors a monetary economy. To that end, he separates money exchange from *riba* when he states, "There is no *Ribā* (usury) (in money exchange) except when it is not done from hand to hand (i.e., when there is delay in payment)" (Bu 34:79:2178,2179). Muhammad also prohibits barter transactions in favor of monetary exchange. In a *hadith* focused on how dates of different quality are traded in the agricultural market of Khaibar, he

comments, "Are all the dates of Khaibar like this?" He said: "No, (by Allâh, O Messenger of Allâh.) We take a *Ṣâ'* of these for two for three *Ṣâ's* (of other types of dates)." The Messenger of Allah said, "Do not do that. Sell the mixed dates for *Dirhams* then buy the *Janîb* dates with the *Dirhams* (Nas 44:41:4557).

With a monetary economy, however, comes the temptation to debase the currency by removing small amounts of gold or silver from each coin. The *hadith* directly confronts such practices, stating, "Clipping gold and silver is part of working corruption in the land" (Muw 31.16.37).

One of the advantages of a monetary economy is the increased level of trade facilitated by the extension of trade credit and other types of debt. The *hadith* permit the lending of money and the extension of trade credit for a set time period. Ibn 'Umar said, concerning loans for a fixed time, "There is no objection to it, even if the debtor gives more than he owes if the creditor has not stipulated it." 'Aṭā' and 'Amr bin Dīnār said, "The lender has no right to demand his money before the due time of payment" (Bu 43:17:2404).

The *hadith* even approve of a transaction involving three parties that was facilitated through, essentially, a letter of credit (Muw 31.20.48). Property was also allowed to be pawned and the holder of the property was commanded to "not forfeit items held in pledge" (Maj 16:3:2441).

The permissiveness of the *hadith* as it relates to debt is consistent with Muhammad's actions. One *hadith* relates how he purchased food grains from a Jew on credit and mortgaged his iron armour to him (Bu 34:14:2068). He also financed the battle of Hunain by borrowing 90,000 dirhams, which he subsequently repaid through the spoils of battle.[100]

---

[100] Ibrahim, 94.

Numerous *ahadith* provide evidence that various types of partnerships and profit-sharing arrangements were common at the time of Muhammad and were approved. Such partnership agreements and the various business practices were much debated by the various Islamic law schools that emerged in the early centuries after Muhammad. These business refinements and developments are the subject of the next chapter.

CHAPTER 4

Business in Islamic Thought and Law

In this chapter, business is addressed first from the standpoint of Islamic thought and then from the standpoint of Islamic law. The term "Islamic thought" is used here as opposed to Islamic theology or Islamic philosophy since, in early Islam, the various disciplines were not demarcated.[1] The term "Islamic law" is used here instead of *"sharia"* since the later term has sharply different meanings, depending upon the context. For many Muslims, *sharia* stands for the perfect law of Islam as expressed in the Qur'an and *Sunnah*.[2] Since the focus of this chapter is on actual legal practice, the more generic "Islamic law" is appropriate. Islamic thought and law also overlap since many Islamic scholars were also jurists. Islamic scholarship and law were also impacted by many of the same factors. An overview covering both areas will precede the detailed examination of business from each standpoint.

Intellectual and Legal Landscape of Early Islam

After Muhammad, Muslims were left with passages of revelation given to him by Allah, which were ultimately collected and compiled into what we know as the Qur'an.

---

[1] W. Montgomery Watt, *The Formative Period of Islamic Thought* (Oxford, UK: Oneworld, 1998), 1.

[2] Knut Vikør, *Between God and the Sultan: A History of Islamic Law* (Oxford, UK: Oxford University, 2005), 2.

According to one scholar, there are about 500 verses in the Qur'an that have legal content.[3] There were also Muhammad's sayings and deeds along with those of some of his companions and the early caliphs after Muhammad, which were collected in various *hadith* traditions. The Qur'an and the *hadith* formed the basis of Islamic law. Problems arose, however, since some of the Qur'an's verses and various *ahadith* conflicted with other parts of the texts. To resolve those conflicts, various methodologies were employed. One such method—the theory of abrogation—came about to "[interpret] away or [cancel] out, the effect of those verses that were deemed inconsistent with other verses more in line with prevailing customs."[4] Another scholar notes that, because of the "conflicting statements in each of his primary sources . . . the concept of *naskh* [abrogation] was the Muslim's ingenious response to the stimulus of embarrassment."[5]

A third source of Islamic law emerged from the Muslim conquests. This source was comprised of "the administrative and legal practices then prevailing in the newly occupied lands...[which] continued to be applied with regard to many matters that were brought before the Umayyad rulers."[6] In the view of some scholars, the Qur'an and the *hadith*, when combined with the general practice of the Muslim community, provided the solution for any problem. The knowledge obtained from these elements and the manner in which that knowledge was processed can be described as follows:

---

[3] Wael B. Hallaq, *A History of Islamic Legal Theories: An Introduction to Sunnī Uṣūl al-Fiqh* (Cambridge, UK: Cambridge University, 1997), 3.
[4] Ibid., 9.
[5] John Burton, *The Sources of Islamic Law: Islamic Theories of Abrogation* (Edinburgh, UK: Edinburgh University, 1990), 4.
[6] Hallaq, 13.

> *'Ilm* came to signify knowledge of the Quran and the Sunna. Its binary opposite was *ra'y*, that is, considered opinion. An opinion arrived at on the basis of *'ilm* amounted to *ijtihād*, a term that was used ordinarily in conjunction with the word *ra'y*. *Ijtihād al-ra'y* thus meant the intellectual activity or the reasoning of the legal scholar whose sources of knowledge are materials endowed with religious (or quasi-religious) authority.[7]

Another scholar notes, "By *ra'y* was meant 'sound practice' or 'what is commonly done' based on local *sunna*."[8]

While the Qur'an and the traditions were central, one Islamic scholar noted that Islamic law was not immutable and that "Even in the early period of Islam, political and economic institutions had to be developed beyond the usage of primitive Islam."[9] Early Islamic scholars and jurists were guided by a "'living tradition' expressed in the consensus of the scholars."[10] This consensus was "the ultimate sanctioning authority which guaranteed the infallibility of those positive legal rulings and methodological principles that are universally agreed upon by Sunnī scholars."[11] Thus, Islamic law essentially became ...

> the work of the *muftī* or jurisconsult who gave his formal opinion *(fatwā)* upon the legal issues involved in a factual situation. Such *responsa* [replies from religious scholars on legal matters] formed the vital

---

[7] Ibid., 15.

[8] Vikør, 23.

[9] Ignaz Goldziher, *Introduction to Islamic Theology and Law*, trans. by Andras and Ruth Hamori (Princeton, NJ: Princeton University, 1981), 233.

[10] Joseph Schacht, *The Origins of Muhammadan Jurisprudence* (Oxford, UK: Clarendon Press, 1953), 98.

[11] Hallaq, 75.

link between the academic theories of pure scholarship and the influences of practical life.[12]

This living tradition, however, gave rise to a "maze of conflicting traditions from the Prophet, the Companions, and other authorities."[13] One jurist, Abu Shafi'i, was opposed to the multiplicity of sources of tradition. He argued . . .

> that nothing can override the authority of the Prophet, even if it be attested only by an isolated tradition, and that every well-authenticated tradition going back to the Prophet has precedence over the opinions of his Companions, their Successors, and later authorities.[14]

The view of Shafi'i was but one of many; and already by the early reign of the Abbasids, four legal schools had formed—each named after its founder. One scholar summarized the schools along with their views on economics as follows:

1. The first legal school was founded in Baghdad by Abu Hanifa (699-767), who emphasized human values and personal reasoning, with a special concern for the poor and the weak.
2. The Medinian school, whose champion was Malik Ibn Anas (712-96), stressed the idea of social utility (*maslaha*) . . .
3. The third school was founded by Abu Shafi'i (767-820), who may be called a theological fundamentalist. This school focused its attention on the economic responsibilities of the

---

[12] N.J. Coulson, *A History of Islamic Law* (Edinburgh, UK: Edinburgh University, 1964), 142.
[13] Schacht, 13.
[14] Ibid., 11.

rulers and on the canons of an equitable system of taxation (*Kitab al-kharaj*).

4. The fourth great school, initiated by Ahmad Ibn Hanbal (780-855), was a traditionalist reaction against speculative innovations, like the emphasis on pure rationalism and on analogical deduction under the influence of Greek [logic]. The Hanbalites rejected analogical reasoning in the most radical way. In economic matters the Hanbalites professed a moderate mercantilism and discussed more deeply than the other schools the necessary harmonization between individual and social welfare and utility.[15]

The fact that jurists and the various law schools were involved in economic matters is understandable since, according to one study, 75% of all jurists and religious scholars were businesspeople.[16] In addition, the education of jurists and merchants overlapped, as exemplified by the fact that scholars needed to study "mathematics at a level needed to become a competent merchant."[17]

The relationship between jurists and merchants was ongoing due to the need to adapt Islamic doctrine with economic reality:[18]

> This situation gave rise to a special branch of legal writings, the *ḥiyal* (legal devices) literature, in which the lawyers attempted to narrow down the area in which actions would be in violation of the law by

---

[15] Louis Baeck, *The Mediterranean Tradition in Economic Thought* (London, UK: Routledge, 1994), 100.

[16] Timur Kuran, *The Long Divergence: How Islamic Law Held Back the Middle East* (Princeton, NJ: Princeton University, 2011), 49.

[17] Ibid.

[18] Coulson, 139.

making them conform to the law formally while in reality circumventing it.[19]

For example, in the *hadith*, neighbors were given the preemptive right to buy adjacent property. This right, however, was circumvented when some jurists accepted the idea that a tiny sliver of land (perhaps only an inch wide) could be gifted to a party other than the neighbor, thereby allowing the owner of the land to sell the original property to the highest bidder, since the neighbor was no longer a neighbor by reason of the sliver of land being owned by another.[20] Such devices were also used in connection with the payment of *riba* and the operation of partnerships. The use of *hiyal* was denounced by several of the law schools, particularly by the Hanbal jurist and scholar Ibn Taymiyya,[21] whose views on business will be discussed below.

At the same time that the legal and religious debates were taking place among Muslim jurists, Islam was expanding into all of the Arabian Peninsula, Syria, Persia, and lands beyond. As Muslims came into contact with a variety of cultures, additional streams of thought were interjected into Islam. For example, during the Abbasid's ascendancy to power, Persians and Aramaeans, who had supported the Abbasid revolt, came to exercise much influence, especially after the caliphate's capital was moved to Baghdad.[22] Under Persian influence, a whole genre of literature—Mirrors for Princes—was developed to instruct the caliphs in managing the Islamic state.

Greek intellectual concepts posed an even greater challenge to Islam. As one scholar noted, "A system of Hellenistic education had been established in Iraq under the

---

[19]Abraham L. Udovitch, *Partnership and Profit in Medieval Islam* (Princeton, NJ: Princeton University, 1970), 11.
[20]Coulson, 139.
[21]Ibid., 141.
[22]W. Montgomery Watt, *Islamic Philosophy and Theology: An Extended Survey*, 2d ed. (Edinburgh, UK: Edinburgh University, 1985), 33.

Sasanians and was continued under the Muslims. The main subject of instruction was probably medicine; but philosophy and other 'Greek sciences' were always taught as well."[23] Initially, the Greek ideas were attractive to Muslims for practical reasons. "The caliphs were concerned for their own health and that of those around them, and believed that the practitioners of Greek medical science could do something to help them."[24]

The Hellenistic tradition's emphasis on the use of reason, however, would prove divisive for Muslims, both theologically and legally. On the one hand, even apart from Hellenistic education, one scholar notes that Iraqi converts to Islam "had a natural penchant towards the use of reason," and the legal school located in Baghdad (founded by Abu Hanifa) "favoured rational forms of argument."[25]

A political movement known as the Mutazilites formed which championed reason and the Qur'an concurrently rejecting most of the traditions of Muhammad. According to one author,

> The Mu'tazilites trusted that God is guided by the rationality of the universe He created. Their cosmology rested upon the trinity of God as reason, creation as a manifestation of that reason, and man's gift of reason as the means by which to apprehend God through His creation and, then, through His revelation.[26]

Some of their efforts to rationalize Islamic theology had implications for business in Islam. For example, the

---

[23] Ibid., 37.
[24] Ibid., 41.
[25] Ibid., 42.
[26] Robert R. Reilly, *The Closing of the Muslim Mind: How Intellectual Suicide Created the Modern Islamist Crisis* (Wilmington, DE: ISI Books, 2010), 26.

Mutazilites limited the Islamic concept of *rizq* (or sustenance) to what was lawfully owned by the individual. Prior interpretations of *rizq* included stolen property; but this, in the view of the Mutazilites, would "attribute evil to God."[27] Certainly, this view had the effect of strengthening private property rights.

The Mutazilites were opposed by the Asharites, who asserted that "The primacy of revelation over reason rises from the very nature of what is revealed: God as pure will and power. The response to this God is submission, not interrogation."[28] Two of the scholars, whose views on business are discussed below, represent the polar opposites of this issue, with Al-Ghazali championing the use of reason and Ibn Taymiyya rejecting it. The third scholar, Ibn Khaldun, was an Asharite who used reason within boundaries.

The Asharite view ultimately prevailed in Islam, and the permissible uses of reason were severely circumscribed, the result being that "In the tenth century, the law was cast in a rigid mould from which it did not really emerge until the twentieth century."[29] After the "'door of independent reasoning' was closed.... all future legal activity was relegated to commentary, explanation, and interpretation of the existing legal doctrine."[30] Across the entire field of Islamic law, compilations of the muftis' fatwas "came to have an authority as works of legal reference complementary to that of the standard Sharī'a manuals."[31] Two of these compilations will be referenced below to highlight Islamic law as it pertains to selected business topics.

---

[27]Watt, *Thought*, 233.
[28]Reilly, 48.
[29]Coulson, 5.
[30]Udovitch, 13.
[31]Coulson, 143.

Business in Islamic Thought

Islamic thought on economic and business matters is interwoven in a variety of literature. As one scholar noted,

> Economics has never been regarded as a separate discipline in Islamic writings. The Muslim conception of the economy has been deeply embedded in visions of a social ideal and economic questions have been viewed in terms of their importance to the present and the future of the community of believers.[32]

There are two types of literature that will be summarized in this section. The first type were manuals of instruction written by administrators and jurists of the early Islamic state. While much of the material in these manuals relates to public finance (i.e., the collection of various taxes) and to the administration of Islamic religious law (both of which are beyond the scope of this book), there are areas of instruction that do relate to the marketplace and to the setting of prices that warrant consideration.

The second type consists of the writings of Islamic scholars. Only the works of Al-Ghazali, Ibn Taymiyya, and Ibn Khaldun will be discussed. The first two were selected because of their historical stature and their current relevance. In the words of one Islamic scholar,

> For orthodox Islam, since the twelfth century, Ghazālī has been the final authority. In their literary struggles against the Meccan orthodoxy—which have not halted to this day—the Wahhābīs advance against Ghazālī the doctrines of the man whom the ruling

---

[32]M. Yassine Essid, *"Islamic Economic Thought"* in *Pre-Classical Economic Thought: From the Greeks to the Scottish Enlightenment,* ed. S. Todd Lowry (Boston, MA: Kluwer Academic, 1987), 78.

theology rejected: Ibn Taymīya. The names of Ghazālī and Ibn Taymīya have been the rallying cries in this struggle.[33]

Ibn Khaldun was selected due to the uniqueness of his economic ideas, as presented in his sociological history, *The Muqaddimah*.

Manuals of Instruction

Origin and Nature of the Manuals

In early Islam after Muhammad, the state and its institutions revolved around the caliphate. One scholar likened the early Islamic political, social, and economic order as an "octagon of justice," which was described as follows:

1. The world is a garden.
2. [The garden] wall is the state.
3. The state is a sovereign who is glorified by the Law.
4. The law is a government at whose head is the prince.
5. The army is composed of auxiliaries maintained by money.
6. Money is the means of subsistence supplied by the subjects.
7. The subjects are slaves, who are subjugated by justice.
8. Justice is the link by which the equilibrium of the world is maintained.[34]

---

[33]Goldziher, 245.
[34]Yassine Essid, *A Critique of the Origins of Islamic Economic Thought* (Leiden, Netherlands: E. J. Brill, 1995), 56-7.

Despite this neatly organized worldview, with Islam's rapid expansion, "Little imagination is needed to appreciate the tremendous problems of administrative organization that faced the Arab rulers as a result of the military conquests and the social and economic upheavals that followed in their wake."[35]

In response, Arabs began to write books of Islamic administrative ethics and finance. Some of these books were modeled after Persian manuals, known as "Mirrors for Princes" because they "*reflect* an ideal of government by which the people would wish to be ruled, at the same time leading the prince and the governing classes to *reflect* and meditate upon a body of rules of conduct which are judged appropriate for accomplishing this ideal."[36] The Mirrors dealt only tangentially with economic matters since the assumption was that "Good economy, the means and processes which make well-being and prosperity possible, is the same as good government *(sawāb al-tadbīr)*, which is the administration, supervision, organization, and control of the kingdom's subjects."[37]

It was during the reign of the Abbasids that Islamic jurists began to write books dealing specifically with economic matters. Abu Yusuf (731-798 AD) wrote *Kitab al-Kharaj*, which was the first such manual:

> His emphasis on the economic responsibilities of the ruler towards need fulfilment of his people and development of his realm, the need for justice and equity in taxation, and the ruler's duty to regard public money as a trust and be accountable for its

---

[35] Coulson, 21.
[36] Essid, 19-20.
[37] Ibid., 45.

expenditure are themes that recur in all future writings on the subject.³⁸

One of the more comprehensive works dealing with public finance in early Islam is Abu Ubayd's *Kitab Al-Amwal* (The Book of Finance).³⁹ "Abū 'Ubayd was a *mujtahid* (a jurist entitled to develop and form independent opinion) of high 99aliber."⁴⁰ Most of his book focuses on matters of taxation relating to various categories of assets and activities mentioned in the Qur'an.⁴¹

From the 9th to the 11th century AD, the manuals of instruction began to include topics related to the marketplace:

> The development of Muslim cities and the increasing complexity of the exchange process gave rise, on the one hand, to a specialized literature, the *ḥisba* handbooks, and, on the other, to the appointment of an official, the *muḥtasib*, exclusively in charge of supervising markets.⁴²

The name *hisbah* carried with it the Qur'anic idea of doing good, along with "the Islamic state's concern for justice, embracing all aspects of a Muslim's existence."⁴³ An example of this shift is al-Mawardi's *Al-Ahkam As-Sultaniyyah* (The Laws of Islamic Governance). While 19 of the 20 chapters consist of well-established instructions relating to the ruler's duties, taxation, and land administration, the final chapter is

---

³⁸Muhammad Nejatullah Siddiqi, "Islamic Economic Thought: Foundations, Evolution and Needed Direction," in *Readings in Islamic Economic Thought*, ed. Abul Hasan M. Sadeq and Aidit Ghazali (Dhaka, Bangladesh: Islamic Foundation Press, 2006), 31-32.
³⁹Ibid., 33.
⁴⁰Abu 'Ubayd, *The Book of Finance*, trans. Noor Mohammad Ghiffari (New Delhi, India: Adam Publishers, 2012), xvii.
⁴¹Ibid., xxii-xxiii.
⁴²Essid, *Islamic Economic Thought*, 79.
⁴³Essid, *Critique*, 137.

titled "Public Order (*hisbah*)," which describes the duties and responsibilities of the *muhtasib*.[44]

One scholar notes that *hisbah* handbooks ("Handbooks") were . . .

> produced by jurists and civil servants who wrote on the basis of their experience as market sherifs or chairmen of the commercial court, and who thereby completed and made explicit the simple norms contained in the *Qur'ān*. . . . Its volume is enormous. Also, different traditions developed in the various cities of the Islamic world: Damascus, Baghdad, Aleppo, Cairo, Kairouan and Cordoba.[45]

The scope of instruction provided in the Handbooks includes both religious and economic activities in the marketplace. The latter are discussed below.

Instructions Concerning the Marketplace

The Handbooks contain two areas of marketplace instruction that provide insight into how business was conducted during the classical period of Islam. The first area relates to the prescribed duties of the *muhtasib*, while the second revolves around how prices in the marketplace should be determined.

The economy in early Islam relied upon the marketplace in each city and town to distribute products. The management of these markets evolved over time. The Byzantines had appointed a market inspector, or *agoronomos*.[46] Under the Umayyads,

---

[44] Abu'l-Hasan al-Mawardi, *Al-Ahkam As-Sultaniyyah: The Laws of Islamic Governance*, trans. Asadullah Yate (London, UK: Ta-Ha Publishers, 1966), 337-8.
[45] Baeck, 102.
[46] Coulson, 28.

each city had one or even several market sherifs who were supposed to keep watch over commercial transactions. The sherif, who was nominated by the government, carried the title of *sahib al-suq* or, literally, master of the market and the merchants' guild. This was an Islamicization of the Byzantine market office (*agoranomos*).[47]

In the Handbooks, "the *muhtasib* became an impressive figure upon whom depended the entire city's welfare."[48] It should be noted that some Islamic scholars reject as "orientalist" any connection between the *muhtasib* and the Byzantine *agoronomos*, since the former evolved from injunctions in the Qur'an and had a much wider scope.[49]

The *muhtasib's* list of duties as it pertained to the marketplace included inspecting the quality of products sold, certifying accurate weights and measures, checking the quality of coins being exchanged, preventing usury, and, in general, "to assure good faith dealings in the market and to protect the customer from being cheated."[50] In addition, he supervised the delivery of city services, such as elementary education, water distribution, street upkeep and cleanliness, and the safety of public thoroughfares.[51] The *muhtasib's* authority exceeded that of the judiciary in that he could independently investigate matters and enforce his rulings so long as the force was not excessive.[52]

The Handbooks were also concerned about the manner in which prices were set in the marketplace. The concern "was with the problem of *tas'īr*, a word that means not the price itself but the action of evaluating by assigning a price

---

[47] Baeck, 101.
[48] Essid, *Critique*, 137.
[49] Muhammad Akram Khan, "*Al-Ḥisba* and the Islamic Economy," appendix in *Public Duties in Islam: The Institution of the Ḥisba,*" Ibn Taymiya, trans. Muhtar Holland (Leicester, UK: The Islamic Foundation, 1982), 139.
[50] Essid, *Islamic Economic Thought*, 80.
[51] Essid, *Critique*, 140-1.
[52] Al-Mawardi, 340.

to goods ... (with the goal being) to determine whether prices should be fixed by juridical or public intervention."[53] The Handbooks thus contained many prohibitions that concerned "hindrances to the free play of the market (for example, a merchant who is selling at a loss must raise his prices or leave the market), or opposing the purchase of goods before they have reached the market place."[54] Whenever supply and demand is distorted, it is referred to as *talaqqi*, which is prohibited in the Handbooks.[55] In line with the Qur'an, the Handbooks also prohibited hoarding and stated that such individuals "will be counted among the assassins"[56] on the day of judgment:

> The goal of all such prohibitions was to provide ... an ideal framework within which there must be perfect competition among the candidates to an exchange, ensuring the transparency of a transaction in which the supply-demand relation can be achieved only by the physical presence of both the goods and the vendors and buyers, the only means by which the "will of Allah" can act, by allowing the "fair" price (*si'r al-sūq si'r l-nās*) to reveal itself.[57]

In the event that prices for a product were deemed unlawful, the *muhtasib* was empowered to restore the product's "normal price." This was done either by calling the market participants together and cajoling them to "accept freely the price he has set" or by calculating the production cost of the product and adding a reasonable profit.[58]

---

[53] Essid, *Islamic Economic Thought*, 80.
[54] Essid, *Critique*, 154.
[55] Ibid., 156.
[56] Ibid., 155.
[57] Ibid., 157.
[58] Ibid., 161-2.

Reconciling the various marketplace regulations and the activities of the *muhtasib* with the Qur'an and the hadith was the subject of ongoing reflection and writing by Islamic scholars and jurists. The views of three key Islamic scholars on these subjects will be addressed below.

Economic Ideas of Selected Islamic Scholars

Al-Ghazali

Muhammad al-Tusi al-Ghazali was born in 1058 in the city of Hūs in northern Iran.[59] His scholarship extended across a number of subjects, including philosophy, sufism, theology, and jurisprudence.[60] Al-Ghazali's willingness to engage Greek philosophical categories was unique in the 11th and early 12th centuries:

> For over two centuries the religious scholars had kept all Greek learning at arm's length as something foreign and dangerous, or had tried to attack it without an adequate understanding of the problems and had thereby incurred the ridicule of the philosophers. Al-Ghazālī set about his task with an open mind, ready to follow the argument wherever it led him, but he was also trying to discover how far the results of the Greek sciences are compatible with the beliefs of Muslims.[61]

As it relates to business and economic pursuits, al-Ghazali linked spiritual success (the "straight path" or "middle way") with worldly involvement. "According to al-

---

[59] *The Encyclopaedia of Islam*, s.v. "al-Ghazali."
[60] Abul Hasan M. Sadeq, "Al-Ghazali on Economic Issues and Some Ethico-Juristic Matters Having Implications for Economic Behavior," in *Readings in Islamic Economic Thought*, ed. Abul Hasan M. Sadeq (Dhaka, Bangladesh: Islamic Foundation Press, 2006), 139.
[61] Watt, *Philosophy*, 89.

Ghazali, one cannot attain the stage of [the] straight path unless he follows the straight path in the seeking of livelihood."[62] His call for Muslims to follow the straight path was radical since, in the 11th century, "anyone conducting commerce in accordance with the law was looked upon as ridiculous by all other merchants."[63] He also maintained that a "basic knowledge of Islamic economics is compulsory on every economically active Muslim to the extent of basic Islamic legal norms relevant for his activity."[64] Among the areas he regarded as obligatory are "*bai'* (trade and commerce), *riba* (interest, usury), *salam* (forward buying), *ijarah* (renting), *musharakah* (partnership), and *mudarabah* (sleeping [silent] partnership for profit sharing)."[65]

Al-Ghazali displayed a more sophisticated understanding of economic matters than did the authors of the *hisbah* literature. For example, he realized that markets needed to be supported by transportation and storage centers,[66] and he recognized that money's primary function is as a medium of exchange, which overcomes problems associated with barter exchange.[67] While Sadeq draws a comparison between al-Ghazali and Adam Smith,[68] the two had very different views since al-Ghazali supported comprehensive market controls as contained in the *hisbah* literature and the role of the *muhtasib*,[69] as opposed to Adam Smith's "invisible hand." Furthermore, "al-Ghazali emphasized the need to supervise the expenditure pattern and consumer behaviour of the people to control wastage and

---

[62]Sadeq, 140.
[63]Udovitch, 7.
[64]Sadeq, 143.
[65]Ibid.
[66]Ibid., 149.
[67]Ibid., 147.
[68]Ibid., 150.
[69]Ibid., 156.

extravagance,"[70] which Adam Smith's laissez-faire approach to consumer choice would not have advocated.

Ibn Taymiyya

Ibn Taymiyya was born in 1263 in the city of Harran (in modern Turkey). When he was five, his family fled to Damascus due to the Mongol invasions.[71] His father, uncle, and grandfather were all Hanbali scholars, thus his studies included "all the disciplines of jurisprudence, traditions of the Prophet, and commentaries of the Qur'an, mathematics and philosophy."[72] According to one scholar, "From a socio-political and economic point of view, Ibn Taymiyyah (1263-1328) is without doubt the most influential Hanbalite jurist."[73] Despite being raised in a family of jurists, he became a reformer. As another scholar notes,

> The career of Ibn-Taymiyya is best understood when his primary problem is seen to be the same as that of al-Ghazālī, namely, the corruption of the ulema or religious scholars. As a class they were nearly all mainly interested in their own promotion in their academic or judicial career; and, since promotion was in the hands of the rulers, they were subservient to these. Ibn-Taymiyya, following in the tradition of Ibn-Hanbal, stood up for what he believed to be right, regardless of the suffering it might bring upon him personally.[74]

---

[70] Ibid., 158.
[71] Watt, *Philosophy*, 142.
[72] 'Abdul Azim Islahi, "Economic Concepts of Ibn Taimiyyah" in *Readings in Economic Thought*, ed. Abul Hasan M. Sadeq (Dhaka, Bangladesh: Islamic Foundation Press, 2006), 183.
[73] Baeck, 100.
[74] Watt, *Philosophy*, 142.

Ibn Taymiyya's scrutiny of Islam—in particular his separating the *Sunnah* from man's traditions—was timely since the Mongol invasions had roused the conscience of the people.[75] His criticisms also extended to Islamic theology *(kalam)* and philosophy since he advocated "the absolute dissimilarity of God and man . . . [thereby making it] impossible to attain knowledge of God by rational methods."[76]

The centrality of the Qur'an and the *Sunnah* to Ibn Taymiyya was reflected in his views on possessions and wealth. For example, he affirmed the rights of individuals to obtain property through "the means recognized by the *Sharī'ah*, such as securing possession of unowned uncultivated land and making it cultivable, [and subject to] inheritance, purchase, etc."[77] The right to have and use possessions and wealth, however, was limited. The owner cannot spend extravagantly, nor may he spend on the objects of vice and forbidden luxuries.[78] Ibn Taymiyya also rejected interest (*riba*) and did not differentiate between loans for production purposes and loans for consumption purposes, because *riba* in any form was clearly prohibited in the Qur'an.[79]

With respect to his writings on the subject of business in Islam, it has been observed that "Ibn Taymiyya's study of questions pertaining to the market is richer than that proposed in the *[hisbah]* manuals; in any case his approach is distinctly more analytical."[80] Although he was never a merchant or trader, "he had contacts with such people and hence understood their problems, as is evident from the *fatāwā* in which a large number of enquiries were addressed

---

[75] Goldziher, 240.
[76] Watt, *Philosophy*, 144.
[77] Abdul Azim Islahi, *Economic Concepts of Ibn Taimīyah* (Leicester, UK: Islamic Foundation, 1988), 113.
[78] Ibid.
[79] Ibid., 130.
[80] Essid, 171.

to him about trade, commerce, business enterprises and contracts."[81]

Ibn Taymiyya also wrote that, as a *muhtasib*, "he acquired much practical experience as to the manner in which surplus value originates—for example, in the processing of raw materials by artisans, or with merchants, money changers, renters of public baths, etc."[82] Consistent with most Islamic jurists, his views on trade and commerce were favorable, for he opposed only those economic activities that were explicitly prohibited by the *Sharī'ah*.[83] He was, however, supportive of strict control of the marketplace. One scholar notes that Ibn Taymiyya did not . . .

> conceive of the market as an open space in which anyone can engage in trade without previous approval. Market commerce should be practiced only by people with specific authorization to purchase goods for resale. Permitting individuals from outside a given profession to engage in trade in that profession is not only an injustice to other tradesmen, but disrupts prices.[84]

With respect to prices in the marketplace, Ibn Taymiyya understood that price fluctuations do not always stem from injustices in the marketplaces. Shifts in peoples' desire for products and "deficiency in production or decline in import of the goods in demand" can also affect prices.[85] In commenting on Muhammad's refusal to set prices in the marketplace, he stated that the context of the Prophet's statement and contemporary conditions at the time must be factored in when interpreting Muhammad's decision.[86] In the

---

[81]Islahi, 59.
[82]Baeck, 103.
[83]Islahi, 151.
[84]Essid, 168.
[85]Islahi, 88.
[86]Essid, 167.

final analysis, Ibn Taymiyya adopted what one scholar termed an intermediate position since . . .

> he is an advocate of an *ad hoc* market regulation on the basis of concrete situations. Occasional intervention by the central authorities may be helpful to ensure the fulfillment of the basic needs of the people. Thus, he is a proponent of control for the purpose of curbing speculative peaks that hurt the poor, but he rejects general price setting by market guilds or by the authorities as being inefficient.[87]

Ibn Taymiyya's analysis of fair prices also extended to the question of fair wages. He argued that the *muhtasib* must determine the "fair rate of remuneration" if craftsmen are compelled to "put their skills . . . at the disposal of the public which is in need of them."[88] With respect to the matter of profits, he again takes a mediating position. While recognizing the seller's right to a profit, it should only be the . . .

> "profit of the equivalent" [defined as] the normal profit which is generally earned in that particular type of trade, without harming others. He does not approve an abnormal rate of profit, exploitative *(ghaban fāhish)* of a situation where people are ignorant of market conditions *(mustarsil)*.[89]

Since the economic activities of Muslims in the waning years of Abbasid rule were spread over a wide geographic area, Islamic business partnerships were common. Ibn

---

[87]Baeck, 104.

[88]Ibn Taymīya, *Public Duties in Islam: The Institution of the Ḥisba*, trans. Muhtar Holland (Leicester, UK: The Islamic Foundation, 1982), 43.

[89]Islahi, 86.

Taymiyya stressed that justice be maintained in such partnerships and that . . .

> the partners should share in the fruits of their partnership whether positive or negative, profit or loss. No partner should be guaranteed any particular amount of profit: their contract should be on the basis of a percentage share in profit, mutually agreed beforehand, and not on a percentage to be earned on the capital supplied.[90]

Both Ibn Taymiyya and Ibn Khaldun spent time in Egypt—with only about 50 years separating them. It is highly likely that the latter was familiar with the former's writings.[91] While similarities exist between Ibn Khaldun's work and those of Ibn Taymiyya and other predecessors, Ibn Khaldun significantly advanced Islamic thinking in the area of business and economics—as will be presented in the following section.

Ibn Khaldun

Ibn Khaldun was born in 1332 in Tunis and died in 1406 in Cairo. His family was originally from southern Arabia, although they were "believed to have immigrated to Spain in the 8th century in the early years of the Muslim conquest."[92] He received a classical education, which included studies in "Islam, logic, philosophy, law, grammar and poetry."[93] His family had many jurists, and Ibn Khaldun was a chief justice. Despite this history, his writings transcend disciplines in that

---

[90]Ibid., 157.
[91]Ibid., 251.
[92]Zeitlin, 21.
[93]Charles Issawi, "Ibn Khaldun's Analysis of Economic Issues," in *Readings in Islamic Economic Thought*, ed. Abul Hasan M. Sadeq and Aidit Ghazali (Dhaka, Bangladesh: Islamic Foundation, 2006), 332.

... he did not completely adhere to juristic tenets which required reality to submit to the exigencies of economic rules drawn from principles of law. He was neither a philosopher nor a jurist nor a believer in political ethics because, for him, moralizing solutions suit only societies not limited to force and violence but where there is also room for speech. There should, he felt, be reliance on discourse as well.[94]

In comparing Ibn Khaldun with Ibn Taymiyya, one Islamic scholar writes, "Reflection on economic problems and economic analysis never ceased in the Islamic world ... But none of these surpasses Ibn Taimīyah or Ibn Khaldūn."[95] Ibn Khaldun wrote about 100 years after Ibn Taymiyya. Whereas Ibn Taymiyya's economic work "is best described as 'Islamic Political Economy' [which stresses] the desirable economic practice of the individual and just economic policy of the state," Ibn Khaldun's writings on the economy—particularly in his widely known work, *The Muqaddimah*—are "economic sociology," in that he "first proposes a theory then supports it with evidence. Thus, his economics is a positive economics or, let us say, based on empirical study."[96] For purposes of this book, Ibn Khaldun's views on business in Islam will be limited to *The Muqaddimah*.

Before presenting Ibn Khaldun's views on business, it would be helpful to understand how he "sets the stage" for his analysis. In *The Muqaddimah*, "two different kinds of social milieu have characterized human development, the *'umrān al-badaoui* (nomad civilization) and the *'umran al-ḥadhari* (urban civilization)."[97] Ibn Khaldun clearly sees more virtue in nomad (or rural) civilization. Concerning this preference, one scholar noted, "The virile and moral virtues

---

[94]Essid, 89.
[95]Islahi, 252.
[96]Ibid., 246.
[97]Essid, *Islamic Economic Thought*, 90.

of the nomad are replaced by the depravity and vice of the urbanite who, subverted by pleasure, luxury, and idleness, lacks the fortitude to defend himself."[98] Nevertheless, the rural and urban parts of society are interrelated. Many of Ibn Khaldun's economic observations stem from his analysis of the "productive activities which provide man's subsistence: farming, animal breeding, hunting and fishing, fabricating goods, and exchanging products" along with "the art of managing the production and distribution of wealth."[99]

According to Ibn Khaldun, work and effort form the basis of man's ability to obtain sustenance. While some, by means of power or taxing authority, may be able to take their sustenance from others, sustenance is most often gained from human labor. This fact accounts for the various crafts. Ibn Khaldun writes lengthy paragraphs describing and categorizing the types of crafts. For example, some "are necessary to society, or honourable by their very nature . . . The necessary crafts are agriculture, building, tailoring, carpentry and weaving. The honourable ones include midwifery, writing, papermaking, singing, and medicine."[100] Man's need for sustenance also accounts for commerce in that "Profit may come from merchandise and its use in barter; merchants can make such profit either by travelling around with (merchandise) or by hoarding it and observing the market fluctuations that affect it. This is called commerce."[101]

Ibn Khaldun's views of the market and price mechanisms are quite detailed. In analyzing the various crafts, he writes the following: "If a particular craft is in demand and there are buyers for it, that craft, then, corresponds to a type of goods that is in great demand and imported for sale. People in the

---

[98]Ibid., 92.
[99]Ibid., 91.
[100]Issawi, 342.
[101]Ibn Khaldûn, *The Muqaddimah: An Introduction to History*, abr. ed., trans. Franz Rosenthal, abr. and ed. N.J. Dawood (Princeton, NJ: Princeton University, 2005), 299.

towns, therefore, are eager to learn that craft, in order to make a living through it."[102]

Also, he recognized that production costs impact the prices of goods. Drawing upon his experience in Spain, he noted that . . .

> The cost of agricultural production also affects the value of foodstuffs and determines their price, as may be seen today in Andalusia. For when the Christians, taking for themselves the rich and fertile land, drove the Muslims into the coastal and hilly regions, whose soil is unfit for agriculture, the latter were forced to apply themselves to improving the conditions of those fields and plantations. This they did by applying valuable work and manure and other costly materials. All this raised the cost of agricultural production, which costs they took into account when fixing their price for selling. And ever since that time Andalusia has been noted for its high prices.[103]

Further, he understood the impact of falling prices. If, therefore, the price of any goods remains low, whether it be a foodstuff, article of dress or any other goods in general, and there is no offsetting increase in sales (or while the market shows no sign of improving), losses are incurred and the market for these goods is depressed. Traders will therefore not seek to work in that line and their capital is diminished.[104]

Fluctuating prices in the marketplace in response to changing supply and demand translated naturally into profit.

---

[102]Ibid., 316.
[103]Issawi, 334.
[104]Ibid., 336.

"Commerce means the attempt to make a profit by increasing capital, through buying goods at a low price and selling them at a high price, whether these goods consist of slaves, grain, animals, weapons, or clothing material. The accrued (amount) is called 'profit.'"[105]

After describing some strategies that could be used to make a profit (e.g., storing products for later sale when supplies are tighter and importing scarce products from another country), Ibn Khaldun summarized commerce as follows: "Buy cheap and sell dear."[106] He realized, however, that profitable trades, if they occur only infrequently, would not lead to success in commerce. He noted, "Prosperity is best insured by moderate prices and a quick turnover."[107]

Ibn Khaldun's assessment of merchants is decidedly negative—perhaps stemming from his view of urban civilization. He links success in commerce with bad character:

> In the preceding section, we stated that a merchant must concern himself with buying and selling, earning money and making a profit. This requires cunning, willingness to enter into disputes, cleverness, constant quarrelling, and great persistence. These are things that belong to commerce. They are qualities detrimental to and destructive of virtuousness and manliness, because it is unavoidable that actions influence the soul.[108]

In his view, the result is that honesty is not found in many traders.[109] It comes as no surprise, then, when he supports the role and functions of the *muhtasib*. "The office of market supervisor is a religious position. It falls under the religious

---

[105]Ibn Khaldûn, 309-10.
[106]Ibid., 310.
[107]Issawi, 337.
[108]Khaldûn, 313.
[109]Ibid., 312.

obligation 'to command to do good and forbid to do evil,' which rests with the person in charge of the affairs of the Muslims."[110] In the marketplace, the *muhtasib*...

> investigates abuses and applies the appropriate punishments and corrective measures . . . he has authority over everything relating to fraud and deception in connection with food and other things and in connection with weights and measures. Among his duties is that of making dilatory debtors pay what they owe.[111]

Ibn Khaldun's writings openly criticize certain actions of the state as they relate to economics. In his commentary on the various crafts, he notes "It is the goods demanded by the state which enjoy the highest sales. Other goods, not demanded by the state but only by private individuals, cannot compare with them, for the state is the greatest market, spending on things without too much of calculation."[112] Still speaking of state spending, he says that the money goes "to the courtiers whose expenditure finds its way to the large number of private citizens inhabiting the metropolis, who have dealings with the court and officials, whose fortune consequently grows."[113] "Crony capitalism," it appears, was also present in Islam.

Ibn Khaldun also warned of negative effects of government appropriation of private property. "Know then that the arbitrary appropriation by the government of men's property results in the loss of all incentive to gain, when men realize that what they have accumulated will be taken away from them. A loss of incentive will lead to a slackening in

---

[110]Ibid., 178.
[111]Ibid.
[112]Issawi, 334.
[113]Ibid., 347.

enterprise."[114] And in what is a 14th century precursor of the Laffer curve,[115] he cautions the state about raising taxes. "In the early stages of the state, taxes are light in their incidence but fetch in a large revenue; in the later stages, the incidence of taxation increases while the aggregate revenue falls off."[116] He warned the state that customs duties would increase prices in that "All middlemen and traders add to the price of their goods all that they have spent on them, including their own expenses."[117]

As if to top off his conservative bona fides, Ibn Khaldun emphasized the role of precious metals in the economy when he stated, "God created the two minerals, gold and silver, as the measure of value for all capital accumulations."[118] To maintain confidence in the currency, he emphasized the importance of the office of the mint to guard coins "against possible falsification or substandard quality (clipping) . . . and with all else relating to (monetary matters)."[119]

A Muslim scholar had previously made a tenuous comparison between Ibn Taymiyya and Adam Smith. In Ibn Khaldun, however, the parallels to Adam Smith are more striking, and there are even parallels to Milton Friedman and other Western conservative economists and political leaders.

Business in Islamic Law

As mentioned in the first section of this chapter ("Intellectual and Legal Landscape"), two comprehensive handbooks of Islamic law will be consulted to describe the

---

[114] Ibid., 343.
[115] The Laffer curve was popularized by economist Arthur Laffer in the 1970s. It demonstrated that, as tax rates increase, total tax revenues decline.
[116] Issawi, 345.
[117] Ibid., 335.
[118] Khaldûn, 298.
[119] Ibid., 179.

legal situation of various business topics in Islam. The two are al-Misri's *Reliance of the Traveller* and al-Marghinani's *The Hedaya*. The former was written from the perspective of the Shafi'i school of law, the latter from the perspective of the Hanifi school. While other Islamic Sunni schools of law aren't represented, according to one source, 75% of the legal conclusions of the four Sunni schools of Islamic law are identical; and in the remaining cases, "variances within a single family of explainers of the Holy Koran and prophetic *Sunnah* are traceable to methodological differences in understanding or authentication of the primary textual evidence."[120]

The methodology will be the same as in prior chapters—i.e., possessions and wealth will be addressed first, followed by trade and commerce. An area that developed significantly as Islam expanded geographically, which also had profound effect on Islamic business even to current times, was that of business partnerships. This area will be discussed in a separate section.

Possessions and Wealth in Islamic Law

Private Use and Possession of Property

Islamic law protected the Muslim's right to own and use private property. In the matter of moveable property, the law prescribed stiff penalties for stealing. Since the penalty for stealing was amputation of the thief's right hand, certain minimal conditions were specified in order for the penalty to be exacted. These conditions were that the thief: (a) had reached puberty, (b) was sane, (c) acted voluntarily, (d) stole goods worth at least a quarter of a dinar, which was approximately one gram of gold, (e) stole the goods from a

---

[120] Ahmad ibn Naqib al-Misri, *Reliance of the Traveller*, rvd. ed., ed. and trans. Nuh Ha Mim Keller (Beltsville, MD: Amana Publications, 1994), vii.

secured location, and (f) could give no other explanation but thievery.[121] Multiple instances of theft were punished ever more harshly—"If a person steals a second time, his left foot is amputated; if a third time, then his left hand; and if he steals again, then his right foot."[122] Individuals who found valuable property were required to attempt to find the owner who lost the property by "advertis[ing] its having been found for a ... year on the doors of mosques, in the marketplaces, and the vicinity where he found it, in the manner customary for advertising such things."[123]

Non-moveable property, including land and houses, was also protected under Islamic law. The most common way private land was owned was as *mulk* land "in which the owner held full rights of ownership."[124] The law also recognized a division of the rights connected with land. Such a division occurred primarily relative to the lease of land. According to one Islamic law specialist,

> Where such a leasehold was created, the owner of the land, the lessor, was said to retain the *raqabah* of the land, its title or fee. Accordingly, Islamic law conceived of full ownership (*mulk tamm*) as comprising two elements: the *raqabah*, or fee, and the *manfa'ah*, or usufruct.[125]

This distinction was also critical in the formation of *waqfs*, to be discussed in the following section.

Protection of private property rights in Islamic law was not unlimited. Specified parties were accorded preemptive rights to purchase land. These rights gave the preemptive

---

[121] Al-Misri, 613-4.
[122] Ibid., 614.
[123] Ibid., 447.
[124] Richard A. Debs, *Islamic Law and Civil Code: The Law of Property in Egypt* (New York, NY: Columbia University, 2010), 17.
[125] Ibid., 21.

party the ability to step into a contract of sale with the effect that the owner of a property "could not always sell his property to a person of his own choice."[126] The owner of a property was limited in the exercise of his legal rights if "such exercise would cause intentional or unwarranted damage to others, disproportionate to the benefit accruing to the individual vested with such rights."[127] This was particularly relevant in cities where different parties owned adjacent buildings, but also in rural areas where the equitable distribution of water was critical.[128]

Establishment of Waqfs

While Islamic law affirmed the private use and possession of property, there was a significant development with regard to the right use of possessions. Islam taught that . . .

> "Once wealth is accumulated . . . Muslims are ordained to redistribute this wealth voluntarily. It is believed that those who redistribute their wealth voluntarily shall be rewarded in the hereafter perpetually, while those who do not shall be punished."[129]

While the Qur'an and *hadith* make frequent reference to paying the *zakat* tax, which was used to assist the poor, among other purposes, legal interpretations of certain *ahadith* gave rise to an entirely new way to earn the favor of Allah with one's possessions. One such *hadith* quotes Muhammad as saying, "When a man dies, all his good deeds come to an end except three: ongoing charity, beneficial knowledge, or a righteous son who will pray for him" (Mu

---

[126]Ibid., 24.
[127]Ibid., 19.
[128]Ibid.
[129]Çizakça, 78.

25:3:4223). In order for charity to be ongoing, assets were allowed to be placed in what was tantamount to an unincorporated, non-profit Islamic charitable trust or foundation known as a *waqf*.[130] "Lexically, *waqf* means 'to be retained.' In Sacred Law, it refers to the retention of any property . . . with the financial proceeds of it going to some permissible [usually charitable] expenditure."[131]

In early Islam, *waqfs* were endowed with cash, land, and buildings. Moveable property was not allowed to be placed in a *waqf*, although exceptions were made for moveable assets connected with land and building and (in the opinion of Muhammad) "horses, camels, or arms, to carry on war against infidels."[132] All of an individual's eligible assets could be placed in a *waqf*, if such intentions were legalized during the person's lifetime. Bequeathing assets to a *waqf* on a person's deathbed was allowed, but only up to one-third of that person's property.[133]

Islamic law held that all property in a *waqf* belonged to Allah.[134] This gave rise to an entirely separate class of assets. In *waqfs*, "the *raqabah*, or title, was immobilized in perpetuity; as a result, the only property interests existing in *waqf* land were limited to and based on the usufruct."[135] Thus, regardless of its complexity, *waqfs* became very popular with the wealthy. One Islamic historian noted,

> Zakât, collected by public law, had been the original vehicle for financing Islam as a society; zakât continued as the main justification for a Muslim government's various urban taxes or as a ritualized form of personal charity, but no longer as the

---

[130] Ibid.
[131] Al-Misri, 453.
[132] Burhan al-Din al-Marghinani, *The Hedaya, or Guide: A Commentary on the Mussulman Laws*, vol. 2, trans. Charles Hamilton (London, UK: T. Bensley, 1791; reprint, Cambridge, UK: Cambridge University, 2013), 343.
[133] Ibid., 338.
[134] Al-Misri, 454-5.
[135] Debs, 25.

material foundation for most specifically Islamic concerns. Private *waqf* foundations largely took its place in this role. The properties set aside in *waqf* were guaranteed inalienable under the Sharî'ah and were very rarely touched by a Muslim ruler.[136]

Islamic *waqfs* are still prevalent in Muslim-majority nations today in the non-profit sector. It is important to note that *waqfs* were designed to benefit Muslims and are not strictly analogous to western (especially Christian) non-profits, which typically benefit all those with a need, regardless of their religious affiliation.

Trade and Commerce in Islamic Law

The Qur'an and *hadith* were favorable toward trade and commerce; and this continued as Islamic law developed, although the control of the markets also became more pervasive in Islamic law. Following are some examples of the law's positive view of business.

Based on the statement in the Qur'an that "God has allowed trade and forbidden usury" (2:276), Islamic law states, "that this verse is general in meaning, referring to all sales except those specifically excluded by other evidence."[137] A Muslim is allowed to miss some of the required daily prayer times if he "fears harm in earning his living" or if he finds "it is impossible to leave his work."[138] The penalty for robbery along trade routes is also doubled. Assuming the conditions for theft were met (the six points discussed in the previous section), the highwayman's "right hand and left foot are amputated . . . [since] the offense of the highwayman is far greater [than a thief] because he menaces the lifeline of

---

[136] Hodgson, vol. 2, 124.
[137] Al-Misri, 376.
[138] Ibid., 197.

the community, its trade routes."¹³⁹ The law also approved "Moorâbihat, or a sale of profit [sic], [which] means the sale of any thing for the price at which it was before purchased by the seller, with the superaddition of a particular sum by way of profit."¹⁴⁰

Islamic law addressed, in minute detail, the types of products that could be sold in the marketplace and the methods of sale. A "legal product" must meet the following requirements: (a) be pure, (b) be useful, (c) be deliverable, (d) be the property of the seller or an authorized person, and (e) have known characteristics.¹⁴¹ Certain products were banned outright. "The sale of a woman's milk is unlawful, although it be in a vessel ... The sale of the bristles of a hog is unlawful, because the animal is essentially filth."¹⁴² Selling animals that are the offspring of offspring was not valid, since such a product "is not owned, known, or deliverable."¹⁴³ Sellers must also not sell products to someone if they suspect that the product will be a means to disobedience (e.g., selling grapes to someone for the purpose of making wine).¹⁴⁴ Islamic law recognized valid sales only if "there is a spoken offer ... and spoken acceptance ... by equivocal expressions such as [I will] 'take it for so-and-so much' ... [although] a mute's gesture is as binding as a speaker's words."¹⁴⁵ While the Qur'an and *hadith* clearly intended to prohibit transactions that involved *gharar* (chance), Islamic law allowed pathways around such restrictions. For example,

> If a person wish[es] to purchase [unripened] fruit, artichokes or melons, and afterwards to have it in his power to let them remain until they become ripe, or

---

¹³⁹Ibid., 616.
¹⁴⁰Al-Marghinani, vol. 2, 469-70.
¹⁴¹Al-Misri, 381-2.
¹⁴²Al-Marghinani, vol. 2, 438.
¹⁴³Al-Misri, 387.
¹⁴⁴Ibid., 390.
¹⁴⁵Ibid., 377-379.

> until they shall yield a new crop, so as to have a lawful claim to the property, the expedient to be practiced, in order to render such conduct legal, is to purchase the tree or bed itself, and after clearing it of the fruit when ripe, to undo the contract of sale with regard to the tree or bed.[146]

It appears that the common Western tax stratagem of "form over substance" has an Islamic counterpart.

As Islamic trade expanded, accommodations were made in Islamic law for division of labor and for joining land and labor in economically viable forms. Islamic law required that, in the case of job wages, the amount of compensation must be specified along with a general description of the task to be performed, cautioning, "Whoever works when no wage has been stipulated does not deserve anything."[147] There were also distinctions made between types of laborers. "Hirelings [the term for laborer used in *The Hedaya*] are of two descriptions—common and particular. A common hireling is one with whom a contract of hire is concluded for work of such a nature as may be perceived by examining the subject."[148] A leatherworker hired to make shoes would thus be a "common" laborer. This is opposed to a "particular" laborer, which . . .

> signifies one who is entitled to his hire in virtue of a surrender of himself during the term of hire, although he do[es] no work; as, for instance, a person who is hired as a servant for a month, or to take care of flocks for a month, at a certain rate, under a

---

[146] Al-Marghinani, vol. 2, 376-7.
[147] Al-Misri, 445.
[148] Burhan al-Din al-Marghinani, *The Hedaya, or Guide: A Commentary on the Mussulman Laws*, vol. 3, trans. Charles Hamilton (London, UK: T. Bensley, 1791; reprint, Cambridge, UK: Cambridge University, 2013), 350.

condition that he shall not serve or tend the flocks of any other person during that term.[149]

Islamic law even allowed a Muslim to hire a Christian to act as an agent with respect to products that were forbidden for a Muslim to sell. According to the Hanifi school, "If a Mussulman desire a Christian either to purchase or sell wine or a hog on his account, and the Christian acts accordingly, in that case . . . such sale or purchase is valid."[150] Leasing buildings for the purpose of conducting business was also permissible, although the lessee was held responsible for any of his activities that would "be injurious to the building."[151]

Financing trade and commerce through debt was also permitted in Islamic law. These debts were often secured by pledges of land or other property, which required a refinement of the legal language to precisely describe the collateral. Where land was used as collateral, one Islamic legal scholar noted, "It required that the creditor take possession of the property . . . The creditor, however, did not have a right of usufruct in the land, but a right of possession only; the owner of the property retained his full rights of ownership, subject to the rights of the creditor."[152] An outside party could guarantee a debt[153] and debts could be cross-guaranteed in the event that a loan was given to two parties.[154] Islamic magistrates were also given the authority to declare a debtor bankrupt, thereby preventing him from disposing of any of his property to the detriment of creditors.[155] There is also an indication that judges took into consideration the views of creditors before rendering

---

[149] Ibid., 354.
[150] Al-Marghinani, vol. 2, 445.
[151] Ibid., vol. 3, 324.
[152] Debs, 22.
[153] Al-Misri, 414-5.
[154] Al-Marghinani, vol. 2, 598.
[155] Al-Misri, 407.

decisions with respect to the disposition of a debtor's assets.[156] Notwithstanding a judge's ruling, the payment of *zakat* took precedence over the repayment of any debt.[157] As in the West, death and taxes cannot be avoided.

The payment of *riba* in connection with any debt was not permissible, nor could the lender "impose as a condition that the loan be repaid on a certain date."[158] There were exceptions in the law when Muslims found themselves in enemy lands where Islamic law was not used. In such cases, they were allowed "to put their money in the banks of non-Muslims and take interest from them, and . . . loan the state money for interest."[159] As discussed previously, the use of *hiyal* methods were common, thereby resulting in a situation where, in one scholar's opinion, "The prohibition of *riba* had little practical effect . . . [in that] the doctors of the Law demonstrated great ingenuity in finding ways of getting round the theoretical prohibitions."[160]

Partnerships in Islamic Law

As noted in Chapter 3, early Meccan caravans required substantial sums of invested capital. As Islam expanded geographically, the scope of trade expanded as well. Merchants needed methods for "pooling resources, whether in the form of cash, goods, skills, or a combination of these."[161] The prohibition of *riba* in Islam, however, necessitated business arrangements where the owners of capital could be compensated other than through overt interest payments. Business partnerships of various types met this need. As one scholar notes, "Business partnerships

---

[156] Ibn Rushd, *The Distinguished Jurist's Primer*, vol. 2, trans. Imran Khan Nyazee (Reading, UK: Garnet Publishing, 1996), 341.
[157] Al-Misri, 248.
[158] Ibid., 403.
[159] Ibid., 943.
[160] Rodinson, 66.
[161] Udovitch, 3.

constitute one of the institutions, probably the most important one, by which the rate of interest is substituted in the Islamic economy."[162] Muslims, however, did not invent partnerships:

> At the dawn of Islam, partnerships among non-kin were common in the Mediterranean region. Hence, the Muslim jurists who developed an Islamic law of partnerships did not start from scratch. They built on established customs of Arabia, Mesopotamia, Persia, and Greece, and also Jewish and Christian traditions.[163]

The three most significant of the partnership types for business in Islam are identified and discussed here.

1. The basic form of partnership in Islam was a *mudaraba* (also known as *qirad* or *commenda*).[164] Muhammad was a party to such a partnership. Its basic characteristics are described as follows: The classical *mudaraba* was an arrangement in which a principal, *rab al-mal*, entrusted his capital to an agent, *mudarib*, who was to trade with it and then return to the investor the original capital plus a previously agreed-upon share of the profits. As a reward for his entrepreneurship the agent received the remaining share of the profits. Any loss resulting from unexpected dangers of travel or from an unsuccessful business venture was shouldered exclusively by the investor . . . The maximum loss of the principal, however, is limited to his [the investor's] invested

---

[162] Çizakça, 29.
[163] Kuran, *Divergence*, 49.
[164] Udovitch, 35.

> capital. In this sense, *mudaraba* was a limited-liability partnership.[165]

The percentage of profits paid to each partner can be varied to suit the circumstances.[166] Each party has the right to terminate the partnership so long as no work has yet been done.[167] However, there is one area that is forbidden—introducing *gharar* (chance) into the partnership. For example,

> If an additional profit is stipulated by one of the parties for himself, beyond that on which *qirāḍ* has been contracted, it is not permitted. This is so as it renders the ratio of profit over which *qirāḍ* has been concluded uncertain. This is a basic principle according to Mālik, which maintains that no sale, hire, loan, (additional) work, or facility be stipulated.[168]

The *mudaraba* or *qirad* partnerships filled "the need for a contract suitable for long distance trade . . . [and] a more flexible distribution of profits."[169]

> 2. If the agent or merchant (the *mudarib*) wished an opportunity to make more money, he would contribute some capital to the partnership in exchange for a greater percentage of the profits. This was referred to as an *inan* (or *musharaka*) partnership. "*Inan* partners usually contribute unequal amounts to the partnership capital, with

---

[165]Çizakça, 30.
[166]Ibid., 31.
[167]Ibn Rushd, 286.
[168]Ibid.
[169]Udovitch, 35.

the passive partner contributing the larger and the active partner the smaller part. But once committed, this combined capital becomes the joint capital of the partnership."[170]

One Islamic legal scholar noted that the *inan* partnership "is perhaps best rendered as a limited-investment partnership."[171] In both of the two types of partnerships discussed to this point, the liability of the passive investor (who is contributing the majority of the capital) was "limited to his own investment. Liability for damages to third parties fell entirely on the merchant who caused the harm."[172] A risk-averse investor could also "constrain a merchant's mandate. He could limit the merchant's mission, geographic range, duration, expenses, and contacts. He could also make profit shares contingent upon the merchant's commercial choices."[173]

3. The most comprehensive form of partnership was known as <u>mufawada</u>. In this type of partnership, the partners "contribute capital in exactly equal amounts to the venture and share profits, as well as losses, in exactly equal proportions . . . In *inan*, each partner's contribution is specified, in *mufawada* the communality comprehends all things."[174] *Mufawada* partnerships have been referred to as a "universal or unlimited investment partnership."[175] They are analogous to what, in the United States, is referred to as a general partnership.

---

[170]Çizakça, 31.
[171]Udovitch, 40.
[172]Kuran, *Divergence*, 51.
[173]Ibid.
[174]Çizakça, 33.
[175]Udovitch, 40.

It is significant to note that all of the major schools of Islamic jurisprudence adopted rules to strengthen mutual trust among unrelated individuals and "three of the four major Sunni schools, including the Hanafi school, allowed partnerships between Muslims and non-Muslims."[176] Furthermore, "The treatment of partnership and *commenda* in Islamic legal treatises remained essentially the same from the time of Shaybānī to that of the Ottoman *Majallah*"[177]—a period of about 1,000 years. Islamic law related to partnerships, therefore, had a substantial influence upon how business was conducted throughout Islamic history, which will be among the topics discussed in the following chapter.

---

[176]Kuran, *Divergence*, 49-50.
[177]Udovitch, 14.

CHAPTER 5

Business in Islamic History

This chapter will review how business was conducted in three Islamic societies during periods of time when Islam achieved hegemony. The three will be examined in chronological order. The first is known as the "Islamic Golden Age," which began with the Muslim expansion under the "rightly guided" caliphs and continued under the Umayyads, reaching its zenith under the Abbasids. While the geographic center of this "Golden Age" consisted primarily of Syria and Iraq, it included (until the early 10th century) all of the areas conquered by the Muslims from North Africa in the west through the Middle East and into Central Asia. As the Abbasid dynasty declined beginning in the 10th century, the trading centers of Islam slowly shifted westward. Cairo, in particular, became an important center under the Fatimids in the 10th and 11th centuries. Thus, "Fatimid Egypt" will be the second Islamic society of focus. The third societal period examined will be pre-modern Egypt during the Middle Ages through the end of the 19th century. Preceding the discussion of how wealth, possessions, trade, and commerce were practiced in each of these Islamic societies, a historical overview will be presented to provide the necessary context.

Business in the Golden Age of Islam

Historical Overview

After the death of Muhammad, leadership passed into the hands of four caliphs who had been, in varying degrees, his companions. This period of the "rightly guided" caliphs lasted from Muhammad's death in 632 until 661. It was during those years that Muslims began to raid and conquer adjacent territories and people groups. Scholars have cited numerous factors to explain the raids and subsequent conquests. One Orientalist, Leone Principe di Caetani, said that the Muslim conquests

> were brought about by climatic changes which had begun many centuries before. The aridity of Arabia had been growing during long ages.... The discrepancy between the worsening conditions and the increase of the population had resulted in periodical migratory movements.[1]

Another historian explained that the Muslim actions "started as raids to provide new outlets for the warring spirit of the tribes now forbidden to engage in fratricidal combats, the objective in most cases being booty and not the gaining of a permanent foothold."[2]

Economic considerations were likely a major factor in Islam's expansion, the lands surrounding Arabia being especially tempting targets. One historian described Syria and Mesopotamia as composed of a network of fertile oases as follows:

---

[1] E. Ashtor, *A Social and Economic History of the Near East in the Middle Ages* (London, UK: Collins, 1976), 10.
[2] Hitti, 145.

In Cilicia, irrigation made it possible to grow tropical crops such as sugar-cane and cotton. In the Biqa (the Crusaders knew it as "Bouquee") corn was grown. In Ghawr ("the hollow"), a rift-valley containing lakes, the Jordan, and the Dead Sea, tropical crops were also grown: sugar-cane, cotton, later on rice, which was introduced during the Muslim era. The Damascus oasis, watered by streams flowing down from the Anti-Lebanon and Mount Hermon, was one enormous garden, the Ghuta, a kind of orchard planted with walnut trees, olive trees, fig trees, and other fruit trees. In the Middle Ages preserves from Damascus were famous the world over; they were made from Damascus fruits and Syrian sugar. Similarly, along the coast, there was a series of garden oases.[3]

Upper Mesopotamia, Syria, and areas southward as far as the Negev and the port of Eilat produced an excess of wheat and "was in the days of the caliphs a granary for the surrounding countries."[4] Lower Mesopotamia, due to the improvements in irrigation under the Sassanids, "grew palm trees, corn, barley, and also rice . . . [and] it was the most important area for growing sugar-cane."[5] In addition, Egypt's "agricultural products of corn, flax, and papyrus were of world-wide importance."[6] The value of possessing such lands did not elude the caliphs and Muslim leaders, particularly those who came from a merchant background. "Expansion was clearly regarded not only as an opportunity to spread the faith, acquire booty, and enlarge the base for land taxes; it

---

[3] Maurice Lombard, *The Golden Age of Islam*, trans. Joan Spencer (Princeton, NJ: Markus Wiener, 2003), 26-7.
[4] Ashtor, 42.
[5] Lombard, 25.
[6] Ibid., 22.

was also seen as a way to gain control over commodities, trade routes, and customs revenues."[7]

The Muslim expansion began under the first caliph, Abu Bakr, and accelerated under Umar, who became the second caliph upon Abu Bakr's death in 634. Durant says, "In 635 Damascus was taken, in 636 Antioch, in 638 Jerusalem; by 640 all Syria was in Moslem hands; by 641 Persia and Egypt were conquered."[8] Conquest became so much the focus of Umar that he even articulated a vision of a Muslim empire that, according to Ashtor, consisted of a

> dominant Arab military class, and working classes, to which would belong the native non-Arabs and non-Moslems. The Arabs would live apart and be maintained by taxes paid by the subjects of the Moslem state. Every Arab would get from the Treasury a pension, the so-called *ata*.[9]

Creation of a military class of Muslims would have far-reaching implications since, in many respects, its interests would clash with those of the established merchant class (as discussed in Chapter 3). The fact that the third caliph, Uthman, was a member of the Umayyad merchant clan further exacerbated tensions between the "new segment" and the "traditional segment" of Muslim society.[10] A backlash occurred, resulting in the assassination of Uthman and the selection of Ali as the fourth caliph. One prominent historian describes Ali's accession to caliph as follows:

---

[7] Patricia Risso, *Merchants and Faith: Muslim Commerce and Culture in the Indian Ocean* (Boulder, CO: Westview, 1995), 14.
[8] Will Durant, *The Age of Faith: A History of Medieval Civilization—Christian, Islamic, and Judaic—from Constantine to Dante: A.D. 325-1300* (New York, NY: Simon and Schuster, 1950), 188.
[9] Ashtor, 22.
[10] Ibrahim, 126.

> Around the charismatic figure of 'Alî, companion of Muhammad and the fighting man's hero, the common soldier's sense of Islamic justice crystallized, even in the first generation, against what were felt to be the backslidings of a wealthy clique which had got control of the Muslims' conquests for its own benefit.[11]

The impact of these societal divisions, as well as Islamic policies regarding the disposition of conquered lands, will be examined in greater detail in the section below entitled "Wealth and Possessions."

When the Umayyads, under the leadership of Muawiya, wrested control away from Ali and moved the capital city to Damascus, it marked the beginning of a period of trade that exceeded anything prior. One scholar characterized the Umayyad rule as "a kind of military occupation by Arab tribal kings, who had superimposed themselves upon the Byzantine and Persian administration."[12] The Abbasids, who succeeded the Umayyads in 750, further Islamized trade and the marketplace; but as one Islamic scholar noted, "The Abbasids did it on a grand scale. It is no wonder, then, that capital accumulation increased to unprecedented levels, making the 1st century of the Abbasids the 'golden age of Islam.'"[13] The impact of the development of pan-Islamic markets will be addressed below in the section entitled "Trade and Commerce."

---

[11] Marshall G.S. Hodgson, *The Classical Age of Islam*, vol. 1, *The Venture of Islam: Conscience and History in a World Civilization* (Chicago, IL: University of Chicago, 1974), 83.
[12] Ashtor, 71.
[13] Ibrahim, 192.

Wealth and Possessions

Two factors significantly impacted the nature and distribution of wealth and possessions in the early Islamic expansion and during the rule of both the Umayyads and Abbasids. The first, was the acquisition and disposition of conquered land and property; and the second, the emergence of classes within Islamic society.

Acquisition of Conquered Land and Property

Muhammad and all of the early caliphs took ownership of conquered land directly and used grants of land to favored individuals both to establish Islam and, in the case of the caliphs, to solidify their reigns.[14] One scholar noted that

> the land in the subjugated territories consisted of two broad categories: (i) treaty land conquered without war, and (ii) land conquered by force. The first category was governed by the terms of treaty and regarded as the common property of the Muslims *(Fay')* and hence inalienable, while the second category was treated as state owned. It included land under cultivation, arable, waste or barren. Of these the latter was unoccupied and was generously allotted.[15]

The lands allotted in Mesopotamia, for example, were

> mostly crown lands of the Sassanids or estates whose proprietors had abandoned them, such as the high Persian aristocrats. These estates were given to the land-hungry Arabs . . . [and] were in fact considered

---

[14]Ibid., 185.
[15]Zaman, 123.

as private property: the proprietor usually did not live there."[16]

Development of idle conquered land for agricultural use was a major priority, particularly during the time of the Abbasids. According to one scholar,

> Deserted farms and ruined villages in different parts of the empire were gradually rehabilitated and restored. The lower region of the Tigris-Euphrates valley, the richest in the whole empire after Egypt and the traditional site of the garden of Eden, was the object of special attention on the part of the central government. Canals from the Euphrates, either old and now re-opened or else entirely new, formed a "veritable network."[17]

Another scholar noted, "Where Middle Easterners really showed their skill was in irrigation—in the organization and maintenance of an elaborate system of dykes (or dikes) and reservoirs and canals to preserve and distribute the floodwaters of the great rivers."[18]

In addition to the wealth derived from land conquest, the spoils of wars (e.g., gold, silver, other valuables, sheep, goats, camels, horses) added greatly to the wealth of Muslims, particularly those who fought in the campaigns. In one early campaign, "According to the Arabic sources, the booty taken at Ctesiphon was estimated at 900 [million] *dirhams*, the share of every Arab warrior amounting to 12,000 [*dirhams*]."[19] During the campaigns into Egypt, "The Arabs, when they became aware of the fact that the Pharaonic

---

[16] Ashtor, 37.
[17] Hitti, 349.
[18] Bernard Lewis, *The Middle East: A Brief History of the Last 2,000 Years* (New York, NY: Scribner, 1995), 165.
[19] Ashtor, 23.

tombs included hidden treasures, began systematic searches and apparently found considerable quantities of gold."[20] One historian noted that

> the weight of pure gold removed from the tomb of Tutankhamun amounted to several thousand kilogrammes. . . . But Tutankhamun was a minor monarch; it is difficult to conceive of the value of the gold stored in all the tombs of the Pharaohs, most of which were violated![21]

Emergence of Classes Within Islamic Society

The Ruling Aristocracy

The rapid accumulation of land and possessions as a result of conquest directly benefitted two groups in Muslim society—the ruling aristocracy plus the soldiers and warriors. Initially, what would become a ruling aristocracy consisted of the caliphs, extended family members, and associates. One scholar described the wealth of such individuals as follows:

> The third successor of Mohammed, the caliph Uthman (644-56) is said to have left estates worth 100,000 or even 200,000 dinars. . . . The riches of Abdarrahman b. Auf, a close friend of Mohammed, were proverbial. He left ingots of gold to the value of 400,000 dinars. He was a great merchant and also possessed large estates. Talha b. Ubaid-allah, one of the earliest converts to Islam and one of those to whom Mohammed promised a place in Paradise, was the proprietor of many estates in Irak (or Iraq) and in Transjordan. . . . The estates and the merchandise

---
[20]Ibid., 80.
[21]Lombard, 106.

which he left amounted to 30 [million] dirhams. The crops of his estates in Irak alone yielded him every year 100,000 dirhams—and all this without ever holding a post in the Moslem government. Abdallah, the son of the caliph Omar, was a very rich man too. He could well afford to be generous and was known to make a single gift of alms amounting to 20,000 or 30,000 dirhams.[22]

Under the Umayyads and Abbasids, large bureaucratic courts complete with wealthy courtiers came into being. These courtiers "derived substantial profit simply by receiving, directly or indirectly, a share of the tribute levied from the peoples and countries they had conquered... [and by occupying] profitable administrative positions."[23]

The Soldiers and Warriors

The second group that benefited directly from the early conquests were those soldiers and warriors who participated in the campaigns. Although rewards were routinely given to individuals engaged in *jihad* during the time of Muhammad, under the second caliph payments were institutionalized, thereby creating a separate class within Islamic society. "Umar institutionalized the new social structure based on an Islamic hierarchy by creating what came to be known as *Diwan* Umar."[24] The *diwan* was

> a register of all the Muslims of Medina and Mecca and of the conquering armies (and their descendants). The booty from the conquest was to be distributed in individual pensions to the men (and sometimes

---

[22] Ashtor, 24-5.
[23] Rodinson, 59.
[24] Ibrahim, 129.

women) listed in the dîwân, according to their rank therein.[25]

While the amount of the payments varied by how long the person had been a Muslim[26] plus factors related to the campaign he had participated in, one scholar stated that the "military pay amounted to double the average income of a highly qualified craftsman."[27]

The *diwan* system also created new markets, since the Muslim recipients of military pensions typically lived in "big camp-towns, the so-called *amsar* . . . [which] became permanent settlements and developed into large towns. . . . [where] many non-Arabs from the surrounding districts and even from distant regions flocked to these camp-towns."[28] Two such towns, Basra and Kufa,

> generated great commercial exchange between Iraq and the Hijaz, on the one hand, and with other points in Arabia, on the other. And with the creation of Fustat [another of the *amsar*] in Egypt, Medina linked the economy of Iraq and the eastern provinces with the economies of Syria, Egypt, and, later, North Africa.[29]

The Merchant Class

The merchant class in Arab society had always been an influential group (as discussed in Chapter 3); but in the era of Islamic conquest, they increased their wealth substantially. In the early Islamic campaigns of expansion, leading merchants often "had a visible and commanding role in the service of Islam, whether in administration or in leading the

---

[25] Hodgson, *The Classical Age of Islam*, vol. 1, 207-8.
[26] Ibrahim, 129.
[27] Ashtor, 23.
[28] Ibid., 18.
[29] Ibrahim, 120.

armies of the state."³⁰ Since the Umayyads were originally merchants, their rise to power provided the merchant class with many opportunities. Relocation of the Umayyad capital to Damascus served that class well, since

> Damascus was an ancient city with an already-developed infrastructure that could support a politically and economically advanced merchant class much more easily than the newly created Basra, Kufa, and Fustat could. Also, Mecca and Medina could not adequately serve the interests of the triumphant merchants after the expansion transformed their political and economic position.³¹

Writing of the Umayyad dynasty, one Islamic scholar noted, "The position of the merchants, therefore, changed significantly not only in that they came to control an empire, but . . . they also came to control its resources, such as land, trade routes, and productive forces."³²

As Islam proceeded into the "golden age" under the Abbasids, the merchant class continued to rise in wealth and prestige, with one scholar writing,

> These merchants formed the spearhead of the economic expansion. . . . [They] pooled capital resources and founded trading and banking companies. The merchant-cum-contractor founded industries, provided work, supplied the raw materials, advanced the money, and undertook to find an outlet for the products. He was adventurous, he struck out into foreign lands and reached the Sudan, where he traded gold for salt and trinkets,

---
³⁰Ibid., 127.
³¹Ibid., 183.
³²Ibid., 182.

loading his camels to capacity. He reached the Indian Ocean too, where, like Sindbad the Sailor, he bartered his wares over and over again.[33]

Also, merchants were often highly educated, with knowledge of numbering systems (including the Arabic system), ciphers, accounting, and scientific treatises, with some of them possessing "real culture . . . religious erudition and [the ability] to write poetry."[34] Much like modern businessmen turning into philanthropists in their later years, a great Islamic merchant

> played the part of patron and benefactor by giving alms and affording help to the poorer people in the community. He contributed towards the embellishment of places of worship . . . and [established] pious foundations. . . . The merchant offered food and shelter to students and teachers, and he entertained people on pilgrimages . . . [while living] on a grandiose scale in his stately townhouse, surrounded by a host of slaves and hangers-on, in the midst of his collections of books, travel souvenirs, and rare ornaments.[35]

The Underclasses

While the aforementioned three classes of Muslim society (predominantly Arab) amassed great amounts of wealth and possessions through the Islamic expansion, a large underclass also emerged, consisting of several groups.

---

[33] Lombard, 147-8.
[34] Ibid., 149.
[35] Ibid.

The first group was the *mawali*. These were

> non-Arabs who had embraced Islam. . . . They participated in military expeditions and fought valiantly against the heathen but were not entered on the payroll, the *diwan*, they either had a meagre share in the booty or none at all, and—worst of all—they had to pay the poll tax, considered a token of inferiority.[36]

The second group was the *dhimmis*. These were not converts to Islam but rather, predominantly Christians, Jews, and Zoroastrians, who were placed in an inferior position in the Muslim state and required to pay a poll tax (known as *jizya*). According the one scholar, during Islam's golden age, they "were granted security of life and property, protection against external enemies, freedom of worship, and a very large measure of internal autonomy in the conduct of their affairs."[37] Despite being *dhimmis*, Jews and Christians did business with Muslims, one scholar recording, "Muslim merchants used the following formula when writing business letters: 'May God prosper your affairs and those of the Muslims.'"[38] Also, the Jews lived in their quarter of the merchant part of Baghdad, and the leader of the Jewish community there "was an important figure at the caliph's court and enjoyed a specific rank in official ceremonies."[39] It should be noted that the relatively benign impact of *dhimmitude* (as described by Lewis and Lombard) is not representative of its heavily oppressive impact in later

---

[36] Ashtor, 29.
[37] Lewis, 210.
[38] Lombard, 213.
[39] Ibid., 207.

Islamic history, as evidenced by the research of such scholars as Bat Ye'or and Mark Durie.[40]

A third underclass group was composed of large numbers of slaves. "The large-scale, long-range commerce in human beings was, in the main, a development of the Islamic period.... Slaves came from three main areas: from Europe, from the Eurasian steppe, and from Africa."[41] In documenting the prevalence of slavery under the Abbasids, one historian wrote that

> the palace of al-Muqtadir (908-32), we are told, housed 11,000 Greek and Sudanese eunuchs. Al-Mutawakkil, according to a report, had 4000 concubines, all of whom shared his nuptial bed. On one occasion, this caliph received as a present two hundred slaves from one of his generals. It was customary for governors and generals to send presents, including girls received or exacted from among their subjects, to the caliph or vizir *[sic]*; failure to do so was interpreted as a sign of rebellion.[42]

The more valuable of these slaves were sent to Medina, where they were trained to sing, play music, and dance.[43] The large number of them (as will be discussed later in this chapter) played a key part in the overthrow of the Abbasids and the decline of Islamic trading hegemony.

The last group that comprised the underclass was rather amorphous. It included many who lived in cities and worked in or around the marketplaces as "craftsmen, labourers both free and slave, hawkers, and street-porters."[44] It also included

---

[40]See, for example, Bat Ye'or, *The Dhimmi: Jews and Christians under Islam*, and Mark Durie, *The Third Choice: Islam, Dhimmitude and Freedom*.
[41]Lewis, 174.
[42]Hitti, 342-3.
[43]Lombard,18.
[44]Ibid., 151.

those who lived in rural areas. "The agricultural class, who constituted the bulk of the population of the empire and its chief source of revenue, were the original inhabitants of the land, now reduced to the position of *dhimmis*."[45] Both of these groups suffered from a decline in their purchasing power due to the influx of gold and silver and the resulting rising prices.

Since the underclass had no power to pass along price increases, their increasing impoverishment triggered riots in the cities and flight from the land in rural areas "in an attempt to evade the taxes and their urban creditors, and gradually slipping into brigandage."[46] As will be discussed further in Chapter 6, many modern Muslim scholars and economists write of the superiority of the Islamic economic system, especially in the treatment of the poor through the Islamic concepts of *zakat* and *sadaqah*, yet during the Islamic Golden Age, it appears that the poor were ever present and in great numbers.

Trade and Commerce

The Islamic conquests impacted trade and commerce in numerous ways. A major impact was the unification, under Islam, of many regions that had been controlled by competing groups (e.g., the Byzantines, the Persians, the Egyptians, and various tribal groups). This unified area experienced growth in its internal economy as well as the benefits of international trade. Toward the end of Abbasid rule, however, a number of factors combined to bring about the decline of Islamic trade dominance. Each of these factors will be discussed in further detail below.

---

[45]Hitti, 352-3.
[46]Lombard, 151.

Development of Pan-Islamic Trade

The Islamic conquests created "a gigantic economic unit never before equaled in the history of the old world."[47] One scholar noted that Islam succeeded in wiping out the "unnatural frontier between Syria and Mesopotamia"[48]—something the Greeks after Alexander, the Romans, and the Byzantines each failed to do. In place of numerous borders,

> a network of routes ran through the world of Islam and beyond it. Along them moved not only caravans of camels or donkeys carrying silks, spices, glass and precious metals, but ideas, news, fashions, patterns of thought and behaviour. When merchants and leaders of caravans met in the marketplace, news was exchanged and its meaning assessed. Merchants from one city settled in others and kept a close and permanent link between them.[49]

Muslims extended their influence into central Asia. "Colonies of merchants settled in Balkh, Merv, Bukhara, Samarkand, and Kashgar. The exchange of personnel, merchandise, ideas, and techniques was intensified."[50] Islam also united

> [the] two arteries of long-distance trade known in antiquity between the Indian Ocean and the Mediterranean. The twin channels of the transcontinental trade of Asia—the seaborne traffic through the Red Sea and the combined sea, river, and overland journey across the Persian Gulf, Iraq, and

---

[47] Ashtor, 71.
[48] G. Hourani, 52.
[49] Albert Hourani, *A History of the Arab Peoples* (New York, NY: MJF Books, 1991), 128.
[50] Lombard, 42.

the Syrian desert—were brought under the political control of [a single authority].[51]

Since the conquests were relatively quick, much remained intact in the conquered territories, including "institutions, administrative machinery and personnel, legal processes, offices, taxes, and even currency."[52] Upon this base, however, were added some unifying elements. First, Islam provided a common language. Ashtor writes,

> According to the prevailing tradition it was the caliph Abdalmalik (685-705) who made Arabic the official language of the administration, replacing the Persian and Greek languages which had been used before.... In Egypt, Arabic was introduced in 706, whereas it had already become the official language in Irak in 699.[53]

Second, Islam required that all Muslims undertake a pilgrimage to Mecca (*hajj*) at least once in their lifetime, which contributed to Pan-Islamic trade. "The *ḥajj*, held every year, brought together great numbers of Muslims from every part of the Islamic world to share in the same rites and rituals at the same holy places, and certainly helped to create and maintain a sense of common identity."[54]

Third, a common currency was adapted early in the reign of the Umayyads. Abd-al-Malik minted the first Arabic coinage, gold *dinars* and silver *dirhams*, at Damascus in 695.[55] The pervasiveness of Arabic coinage increased over time, not only by reason of the plundered gold from Egypt, the Sassanid palaces, and the Syrian and Mesopotamian

---

[51] K. N. Chaudhuri, *Trade and Civilization in the Indian Ocean: An Economic History from the Rise of Islam to 1750* (Cambridge, UK: Cambridge University, 1985), 44-5.
[52] Lombard, 4.
[53] Ashtor, 21-2.
[54] Lewis, 173.
[55] Hitti, 217.

churches, but also from the collection of the poll tax and land tax, which were often paid in gold.⁵⁶ The mining and subsequent monetization of gold originating in western Sudan also raised Islam's economy to an unprecedented level.⁵⁷

Development of the Islamic Economy

In pre-Islamic Mesopotamia, a number of staple crops were grown, including barley, wheat, rice, and dates.⁵⁸ During the Islamic Golden Age, the variety and range of agricultural products increased considerably. One historian described the busy economy of Islam as follows: "Men raised cattle, horses, camels, goats, elephants, and dogs; stole the honey of bees and the milk of camels, goats, and cows; and grew a hundred varieties of grains vegetables, fruits, nuts, and flowers."⁵⁹ Agricultural products were also introduced westward "from Iran to the Fertile Crescent and North Africa and Europe. . . . [The products included] rice, sorghum, sugar cane, cotton, watermelons, aubergines, artichokes, oranges, and condiments, and other plants required for both medicinal and cosmetic purposes."⁶⁰ Certain areas also experienced a marked increase in productivity, one being the Iranian plateau when cotton came into widespread production.⁶¹

The most important industry in the Golden Age of Islam was likely textiles. One scholar who studied occupational epithets concluded that, "For individuals dying during the ninth/third and tenth/fourth centuries, textiles accounted for a remarkably consistent 20 to 24 percent of occupational

---

⁵⁶Lombard, 105.
⁵⁷Ashtor, 81.
⁵⁸Hitti, 350.
⁵⁹Durant, *Age of Faith*, 205.
⁶⁰Lewis, 164.
⁶¹Richard W. Bulliet, *Cotton, Climate, and Camels in Early Islamic Iran: A Moment in World History* (New York, NY: Columbia University, 2009), 1.

involvement."⁶² The wide array of textiles produced in the Middle East is evidenced by their names—for example, "muslin (from Mosul), damask (from Damascus), or technical terms, like gauze *(qazz)*, mohair *(mukhayyar)*, [and] taffeta (Persian *tāftah*)."⁶³ The demand for cotton clothing rose dramatically since Muhammad was reported to have worn a white cotton shirt and trousers, as did the caliphs Umar and Ali.⁶⁴

Although other industries developed in Islam, they typically involved an "artisan working in his own home, perhaps with his family or in a small workshop... primarily for community, family, and local needs."⁶⁵ The nature of the goods produced via such hand industry included "rugs, tapestry, silk, cotton and woolen fabrics, satin, brocade (*dībāj*), sofa (from Ar. *ṣuffah*) and cushion covers, as well as other articles of furniture and kitchen utensils."⁶⁶

Throughout the Golden Age and well into later Islamic history, the type of industry developed by Muslims was, in comparison to the West, relatively simple and small scale. Referring to the period of classical Islam, one scholar noted,

> Industrial techniques were and remained rudimentary. With few exceptions, the only source of energy was human and animal muscle.... One obvious reason for the lack of progress in the generation of energy is the absence of suitable raw materials—of anything comparable with the firewood and charcoal and coal of Western Europe, or the water power available from so many rivers and waterfalls.⁶⁷

---

⁶²Ibid., 3.
⁶³Lewis, 168.
⁶⁴Bulliet, 49.
⁶⁵Lewis, 171.
⁶⁶Hitti, 345.
⁶⁷Lewis, 169.

This is not to say that the territories under Muslim control were devoid of natural resources, since there is substantial evidence that gold, silver, and precious stones were mined and traded, along with other mineral resources and ores.[68]

To summarize the Islamic economy during the Golden Age as "booming" does not appear unreasonable. Although detailed records are not available, one scholar painted this vivid word picture that provides a sense of the depth and breadth of this trade:

> Grain was shipped from Northern Mesopotamia to Southern Irak, olive oil from Syria, Palestine and Tunisia to Egypt. Dates from Irak were exported to many provinces of the Moslem world. Khuzistan, Makran and Yemen produced sugar, Syria was famous for its fruit-culture, the products of which were highly appreciated in Irak and in Egypt. Barca supplied Egypt with cattle for slaughter. The textile industries of Khurasan, Bukhara, and Samarkand exported their cotton goods to all the provinces of the Near East. The cotton cloth of Herat, Merw and Nishapur was sold everywhere. The Caspian provinces produced silk and woolen stuffs renowned in all parts of the Abbasid empire. Khuzistan and Fars, the two provinces of South-western Persia bordering on the Persian Gulf, exported precious silk and cotton fabrics, Armenia its famous carpets. Egypt had from time immemorial a highly developed linen industry; and when it was united, under the scepter of the caliphs, with Irak and Persia, these latter countries became a big market for its products. The North African provinces, lastly, exported coarse

---

[68]Hitti, 348-9.

woolen fabrics, destined for the lower classes of Oriental society.[69]

Development of International Trade

During the Golden Age, the fact that Muslims controlled the land and water bridges between West and East greatly enhanced their ability to conduct international trade. One scholar has advanced the argument that, due to their inability to overcome the Byzantines and thereby to completely secure the Mediterranean, the Abbasids moved their capital to Baghdad in order to assure "access to the Persian Gulf and Indian Ocean, to South Asian and Tang Chinese trade."[70] The Muslim historian Tabari wrote that al-Mansur said, in describing the siting of Baghdad, "This is the Tigris... there is no obstacle between us and China; everything on the sea can come to us on it."[71] Furthermore, since Islam did not disdain trade as they did agriculture, over time, Muslims superseded the early Christian, Jewish, and Zoroastrian merchants and caused "such ports as Baghdād, al-Baṣrah, Sīrāf, Cairo, and Alexandria ... [to develop] into centres of active land and maritime commerce."[72]

The basis of international trade between Muslims and regions outside their control was complex since it involved, in addition to products produced within the Islamic economy, the transit trade of items imported into the Islamic economy and then exported to other regions. For example, Muslims acquired slaves from Africa and Central Europe, some of whom were then used in trade with the Chinese. The range of goods imported into the Islamic territories included numerous luxury items and skilled slaves. According to Lopez & Raymond,

---

[69] Ashtor, 78.
[70] Risso, 15.
[71] Chaudhuri, 47.
[72] Hitti, 343.

From India are imported tigers, panthers, elephants, panther skins, rubies, white sandal, ebony, and coconuts. From China are imported silk stuffs, silk, chinaware, paper, ink, peacocks, racing horses, saddles, felts, cinnamon, Greek unblended rhubarb. [Also] ... female slaves, knickknacks with human figures, fast locks ... hydraulic engineers, expert agronomists, marble workers, and eunuchs.[73]

In return, there was demand in India and China for such Middle Eastern products as "gemstones, pearls, incense, perfumes, sandalwood, and spices,"[74] along with carpets.[75] One scholar noted that international trade using ships would not have been limited to luxury items, since heavy lower-value cargo would also have been needed as ballast. "The range of goods brought to India or China would almost certainly have included heavy cargo such as dates, sugar, building material, and timber [from Africa], just as the export of porcelain from China provided the staple ballast for ships."[76]

Decline of Arab Islamic Trading Hegemony

The rule of the Abbasids represented the high point of Arab Islamic dominance in trade, with Abu-Lughod writing,

> Of the three routes between Europe and the Far East, Sindbad's "middle way" through the Persian Gulf was the easiest, cheapest, and, not unexpectedly then, the most ancient and enduring. When it functioned well,

---

[73]Robert S. Lopez and Irving W. Raymond, *Medieval Trade in the Mediterranean World: Illustrative Documents Translated with Introductions and Notes* (New York, NY: Columbia University, 2001), 28.
[74]Chaudhuri, 53.
[75]Lewis, 171.
[76]Chaudhuri, 53.

this middle route through the Levant and Baghdad took precedence over all alternatives.[77]

Beneath the surface, however, trouble was brewing for the Abbasids in that, "most roads were poor or nonexistent, ships were small, coinage was barely adequate, and the conspicuous consumption of a few rich people did not make up for the destitution of the masses."[78] As the Abbasid dynasty wore on, economic activity and trade began to shift away from Baghdad. There were a number of factors that accounted for this.

The first was a lack of unified leadership. For several centuries, leadership of Islam was restricted to Arabs. The Abbasids, however, "set no value on Arabian blood.... Among the Abbāsids only three caliphs were sons of free mothers.... Soon the Arabian aristocracy was superseded by a hierarchy of officials representing diverse nationalities, at first preponderantly Persian and later Turkish."[79] Another historian noted that,

> From about 950 to 1050, members of a Persian family called the Buyids were able to marshal a more effective army than that of the Abbasids, which gave them the necessary leverage to dominate the empire from behind the throne, setting a precedent for the Saljuq Turks who came after them.[80]

Even though the Abbasids retained the caliphate, power was decentralized among competing lords, not unlike the feudal society of Europe.

---

[77] Janet L. Abu-Lughod, *Before European Hegemony: The World System A.D. 1250-1350* (New York, NY: Oxford University, 1989), 185.

[78] Robert S. Lopez, *The Commercial Revolution of the Middle Ages 950-1350* (Cambridge, UK: Cambridge University, 1976), 24.

[79] Hitti, 332.

[80] Risso, 15.

A second factor was a sustained decline in agricultural productivity, the lack of a unified central government exacerbating this problem. According to one scholar, "irrigation and soil conservation vanished in the days of the Abbasids."[81] One soil conservationist concluded that between 3 to 6 feet of topsoil were eroded.[82] Another scholar noted, "The situation was surely worsened by the increasing tendency towards the state direction of the economy, and the control of agricultural land by military officers with no great knowledge of agriculture and no great interest in the long-term prosperity of their domains."[83] In addition to man-made factors, the climate of the Iranian plateau entered into a long-term cooling trend during the last half of the Abbasid rule, which negatively impacted agricultural output, particularly cotton.[84]

A third factor was oppressive taxation. Despite lowered land productivity, the Abbasid state's need for tax revenue to support its large army and bureaucracy was unabated. The rich bourgeois and merchants were squeezed through higher land taxes and through "the imposition of arbitrary 'contributions' (*musadara*)."[85] The heavy tax burdens also extended to rural peasants who often fled their land to escape these taxes, only to be hunted by authorities.[86]

A fourth factor included revolts and social upheavals, which were the culmination of the previous three. For example, the Zindj revolt, which involved thousands of slaves in the swamp area of lower Iraq, diverted substantial resources of the Abbasid military to quell it and caused much commercial loss, since the Zindj targeted the cargoes of merchant ships which negatively affected trade on the

---

[81] Ashtor, 48.
[82] Ibid., 52.
[83] Lewis, 166.
[84] Bulliet, 1.
[85] Ashtor, 114.
[86] Ibid., 67.

Persian Gulf.[87] Another upheaval was the 10th century Qarmat movement, which began among skilled laborers, who organized labor guilds that one scholar described as, "a close-knit association, a brotherhood in fact, with initiation rites, secret oaths, elected leaders known as 'masters,' councils composed of these leaders, and a doctrine with both mystical and social elements."[88] Qarmatism was Shi'ite in orientation and allied for a time with the Isma'ilis, who founded the Fatimid dynasty in Egypt.[89] Although these revolts and upheavals alone did not topple the Abbasids, the Mongol invasions from the East proved decisive when, in 1258, the Mongols captured Baghdad.[90] After the fall of Baghdad, the center of Islamic trade shifted definitively to Cairo. (However, this shift had been under way for several centuries prior to the Mongol invasions.)

Business in Fatimid Egypt

Historical Overview

During the reign of the Abbasids, "Egypt was nominally a province of the 'Abbāsid caliphate in Baghdad, but it had in effect been independent since 868 under various dynasties of governors, and it carried on its own commercial relations with both the *Dār al-Islām* and the *Dār al-Ḥarb*."[91] With the decline of Baghdad during the 10th century, many merchants migrated to other centers of trade including Aden, Oman, and Egypt.[92] One of the chief beneficiaries of this trend was

---

[87]Ibid., 121.
[88]Lombard, 155.
[89]Farhad Daftary, *The Ismāʿīlīs: Their History and Doctrines*, 2nd ed. (Cambridge, UK: Cambridge University, 2007), 116.
[90]Abu-Lughod, *Hegemony*, 146.
[91]Subhi Labib, "Egyptian Commercial Policy in the Middle Ages," in *Studies in the Economic History of the Middle East from the Rise of Islam to the Present Day*, ed. M. A. Cook (New York, NY: Oxford University, 1970), 65.
[92]Ibid.

the former Muslim military settlement of Fustat, which was built on a hill about a mile south of Cairo. Fustat was described as having "seven- and even fourteen-story structures . . . surrounded on all four sides by exceedingly prosperous markets."[93] Fustat and Cairo were prime targets for the various factions operating in the power vacuum left by the declining Abbasid dynasty. Foremost among these was a Shi'ite group (founded by Sa'id ibn Husayn) known as Isma'ilis. The Isma'ilis, which originated in Tunisia, made several abortive attempts to capture Cairo and Fustat in 914 and 921. They ultimately succeeded in 969 and established what became known as the Fatimid Caliphate.[94]

After consolidating their position in Egypt, the Fatimids developed complex financial systems and expanded their trade network by redeveloping the Red Sea trade route to China and India from which it received substantial import duties. These trade activities, when combined with a flourishing agricultural sector based on the Nile, along with other domestic industry, allowed the Fatimids to support "armies, and its vast fleet operating throughout the Mediterranean Sea. For much of the 5th through 11th centuries, Fāṭimid Egypt was a major sea power, competing with the Byzantine empire from Sicily to the shores of Syria."[95] One scholar noted that, after the Fatimid conquest, Cairo and Fustat were "awash in money and geographically more central to the Islamic world as a whole . . . [which made them] a magnet for immigrants from throughout the Islamic world at every social level."[96]

Among the residents of Fustat who immigrated there after Cairo became the Fatimid capital were Jewish

---

[93] Janet L. Abu-Lughod, *Cairo: 1001 Years of the City Victorious* (Princeton, NJ: Princeton University, 1971), 19.
[94] Abu-Lughod, *Cairo*, 16.
[95] Daftary, 138.
[96] Jessica L. Goldberg, *Trade and Institutions in the Medieval Mediterranean: The Geniza Merchants and Their Business World* (Cambridge, UK: Cambridge University, 2012), 43.

merchants from Tunisia and other parts of Egypt.[97] From the time of their arrival and throughout the 11th century, these merchants traded in regional agricultural products as well as a variety of transit goods and elite luxuries.[98] It has been determined that they engaged in 265 occupations related to trade and industry.[99] However, one scholar noted, "Despite the enormous diversity of goods handled by individual merchants, it is evident that each had his specialties in which he was prominent."[100]

Whereas much of the trade with Egypt was conducted overland via caravans, which were scheduled annually based on the destination and season,[101] the majority of the trade of the Jewish merchants of Fustat was conducted by sea. This was due, in part, to Jewish Sabbath law restrictions, which "allowed one to stay aboard a moving ship but prohibited overland travel. This restriction meant these Jewish merchants could not travel in the great caravans."[102]

While some of the Jewish merchants were stationary, most traveled throughout the Mediterranean on a seasonal basis. The value of such travel was captured in a popular business saying of the time: "A man present sees what a man absent can never see."[103] The wealth of these merchants was described as "middling," which according to one scholar meant that, while they had movable capital to invest, their livelihood depended upon keeping their limited capital constantly invested in trading activities (i.e., they were not able to live off passive sources of income).[104] Their guiding rule was, "Do not let idle with you one single dirhem . . . but

---

[97]Ibid.
[98]Ibid., 338.
[99]Udovitch, 213.
[100]S.D. Goitein, "Mediterranean Trade in the Eleventh Century: Some Facts and Problems," in *Studies in the Economic History of the Middle East from the Rise of Islam to the Present Day*, ed. M. A. Cook (New York, NY: Oxford University, 1970), 57.
[101]Ibid., 58.
[102]Goldberg, 54.
[103]Goitein, *Facts and Problems*, 58.
[104]Goldberg, 48.

buy whatever God puts into your mind and send it on with the very first ship sailing."[105]

The significance of this group of Jewish merchants from Fustat lies in the fact that over 10,000 mercantile letters and documents that they wrote have been retrieved from the ancient synagogue of Fustat, which provides a unique source of information on daily trade practices. These ancient manuscripts are referred to as the "Geniza Documents" since, in Hebrew, "*genīza*, or rather *bēth-genīza*, designates a repository of discarded writings."[106] One scholar has summarized the content of these mercantile letters as follows:

> [M]ore than 95 percent of the material is directly related to mercantile affairs, with the remainder allocated to news that is personal, familial, or concerned with the religious community. Five general topics make up the great bulk of letter text: discussing commodity transactions; talking (and often complaining) about the behavior of other merchants; sharing a few key types of business news; writing about correspondence itself; and narrating business trips.[107]

Some recent scholars have argued that the Geniza Documents do not reflect the broad spectrum of Mediterranean trade and commerce, since the Jewish merchants of Fustat were interacting primarily on the basis of Jewish law and culture.[108] However, this view is in direct opposition to the established Princeton School of

---

[105] S. D. Goitein, *Economic Foundations*, vol. 1, *A Mediterranean Society: The Jewish Communities of the Arab World as Portrayed in the Documents of the Cairo Geniza* (Berkeley CA: University of California, 1967), 200.
[106] Ibid., 1.
[107] Goldberg, 77.
[108] Phillip I. Ackerman-Lieberman, *The Business of Identity: Jews, Muslims, and Economic Life in Medieval Egypt* (Stanford, CA: Stanford University, 2014), 3.

Interpretation (growing out of the pioneering work of S.D. Goitoin), which argued the Jews were reflective of the greater Islamic society. Among the points made by the Princeton School to support its contention was the fact that

> no ghetto [occupational or otherwise] existed in Fusṭāt, Alexandria, or Qayrawān (then the capital of the country now known as Tunisia), or even in a holy city like Jerusalem, or a provincial capital and industrial centre like al-Maḥalla in Lower Egypt, [and that,] we find partnerships between Muslims and Jews in both industry and commerce, and there were many other ways of cooperation.[109]

Jews also served in the Fatimid Caliph's court. For example, Yaqub ibn-Killis was a Jew from Baghdad who, after converting to Islam, became a vizier, and through his "expert administration laid the basis of the economic prosperity of the Nile valley under the early Fāṭimids."[110] The Princeton view is also supported in that

> through much of the Islamic world in the eleventh century, Jewish and Islamic law recognized very similar forms of commercial contract.... Jewish legal scholars in the Islamic world often took care to ensure that their co-religionists were not at a commercial disadvantage, occasionally bending or even breaking Talmudic precepts to do so.[111]

For purposes of this book, the information contained in the Geniza Documents will be treated as representative of

---

[109] Goitein, *Facts and Problems*, 52.
[110] Hitti, 627.
[111] Goldberg, 150.

trade and commerce in the broader Mediterranean Islamic society.

Trade and Commerce in Fatimid Egypt

This section will examine the trade policies and commercial practices of the Islamic economy in Egypt during the late 10th and through 11th centuries when the Fatimids ruled Egypt. Prior to such an examination, however, it is necessary to understand the nature of the Mediterranean trade of which Fatimid Egypt was a part.

Nature of Mediterranean Trade

While the Abbasid dynasty in Iraq was declining, the western part of the Islamic empire increased in economic importance. Mediterranean trade integrated various port cities—east and west, Muslim and non-Muslim. Demand from the Mediterranean also diverted trade away from the Persian Gulf toward the Red Sea to Egypt. "From Egypt, goods were disseminated along the east-west trunk route to markets in Ifriqiya and al-Andalus, and from there along spur routes to Christian lands and other satellite markets."[112]

While the scope of products traded in the various cities and areas varied greatly (as will be discussed below), the largest share of Mediterranean trade related to textiles ranging from finished goods to raw materials. The second largest area consisted of spices which included "chemicals, medicines, perfumes, and dyes as well as culinary substances."[113] Since the Abbasids had instituted regional

---

[112]Olivia Remie Constable, *Trade and Traders in Muslim Spain: The Commercial Realignment of the Iberian Peninsula, 900-1500* (Cambridge, UK: Cambridge University, 1994), 5.
[113]Goldberg, 96.

mints to govern coin production,[114] another significant export item from the Muslim West to the Muslim East was gold *dinars* and silver *dirhams*.[115] This was particularly true of Fatimid Egypt, which controlled Sudan's gold production as well as gold from Syria and Sicily.[116]

Egyptian transit trade, where products were imported with the goal of exporting them at a profit, was an important dimension of the economy. In the 10th century, Al-Kindi wrote that Egypt was the center of all trade, describing it as

> endowed by God with all manner of commodities and advantages: it was the emporium for Mecca and Medina, for Ṣanʿāʾ, Aden, Oman, Shiḥr, India, Ceylon, China, and many other lands. Perfumes, spices, precious stones, and tools came by sea as far as Qulzum. Egypt also possessed important Mediterranean ports, emporia for Syria, Antioch, Byzantium, and Rome, as also for the lands of the Franks, Sicily, the Maghrib, Cyprus, and Rhodes. From these regions came slaves, silk, brocades, mastic, coral, amber, saffron, furs, gall-nuts, and various metals, [such] as iron, copper, silver, lead and tin, and finally timber.[117]

In addition to its established trading partners of Iraq, Syria, Arabia, and North Africa, Egypt's Mediterranean partners in the transit trade now included Spain, Sicily, Italian cities, and Greek cities, including Constantinople. Even though the Geniza merchants did not trade directly with Europe,[118] Egypt's Mediterranean trade with Spain and the Italian cities of Venice, Genoa, and Pisa also enabled it to

---

[114] Andrew S. Ehrenkreutz, "Monetary Aspects of Medieval Near Eastern Economic History," in *Studies in the Economic History of the Middle East from the Rise of Islam to the Present Day*, ed. M. A. Cook (New York, NY: Oxford University, 1970), 39.
[115] Goitein, *Facts and Problems*, 57.
[116] Lombard, 115.
[117] Labib, 65.
[118] Goldberg, 107.

benefit economically as Europe emerged from the Dark Ages. One scholar noted, "al-Andalus was a point of contact with the Islamic trading domain and one of the channels through which desirable luxuries—eastern spices, precious metals, textiles, paper, and other items—might be obtained."[119]

Italian merchants also transported goods over the Alps for sale in Germanic markets, which created demand for Eastern (Islamic and Oriental) exporters.[120] The Venetians in particular had strong commercial ties to Egypt during the Fatimid period, which continued through most of the Crusade period, due to the Venetians' neutral stance.[121] The Geniza Documents also describe trade with Greek merchants ("*Rūm*" in Arabic) who were European Christians.[122] One Geniza merchant advised another:

> "Keep your pepper, cinnamon and ginger . . . for the Rūm are keen solely on them and all of them are about to leave for Fusṭāṭ. They are only awaiting the arrival of two additional ships from Constantinople." In another letter from Alexandria, the business correspondent in Old Cairo is advised to hold his date-palm fibre until the Rūm arrive from Damietta. In a report from Fusṭāṭ itself we read that the Rūm did not leave there a single piece of odoriferous wood.[123]

Although the transit trade was clearly important to the Geniza merchants, other scholars have argued that the textile trade was the lynchpin of medieval Egyptian economic prosperity.[124] Another scholar linked the two

---

[119]Constable, 2.
[120]Heck, *Arab Roots of Capitalism*, 162.
[121]Ibid., 194.
[122]Goitein, *Facts and Problems*, 54.
[123]Ibid.
[124]Gladys Frantz-Murphy, "A New Interpretation of the Economic History of Medieval Egypt: The Role of the Textile Industry 254-567/868-1171," in *Manufacturing and Labor*, ed. Michael G. Morony (Hampshire, UK: Ashgate, 2003), 119.

factors together when he noted that the buoyant Mediterranean transit trade facilitated development of vertically integrated regional production networks.[125] Such networks were described in the Geniza Documents because numerous transactions were entered into in order to turn raw flax into finished textiles. Regardless of the relative significance of the transit trade versus domestic production, the Geniza Documents portray a highly diversified economy, with more than 210 industries and 18 major industrial centers functioning in Egypt.[126] Such centers included

> al-Fusṭāṭ, near Cairo, which was distinguished by sugar, glass, and soap manufacturing, boat-building, textiles weaving, and gold, silver, and copper craftsmanship; Tinnīs, the largest textile and weaving center; Alexandria, famous for its silks and engaged in shipbuilding and soap and candle production; and Damietta, also involved in shipbuilding and the export of silk textiles.[127]

Considering the vast array of products and services comprising the Fatimid Egyptian economy, it is not surprising that new commercial policies and trade practices emerged which, while still seeking to conform to Islamic law, were also a departure from the policies and practices of the Abbasids, the Umayyads, and the early caliphs. These new developments are the subject of this next section.

Commercial Policies and Trade Practices of Fatimid Egypt

While the Abbasid dynasty presided over a decline in trade and commerce in the Arab East, the Fatimids

---

[125] Goldberg, 339-40.
[126] Heck, *Arab Roots of Capitalism*, 129.
[127] Ibid.

established an economic framework that supported a rapid increase in Egyptian trade and commerce. There were a number of components in this. One scholar described the Fatimid economy as a "capitalistic state economy" that integrated three components of capitalism: "the possession of private property, the pursuit of private profit, and the quest for quality private capital."[128] The Fatimids' legal system protected an individuals' right to private ownership of property.[129] More than previous Islamic states, the Fatimids also adopted many free-market or *laissez faire* policies.[130] This was particularly true when it came to the transport of products between the various markets. "From references [in the Geniza Documents] to ship-owners and camel-drivers and discussions of freight rates, for instance, it is clear that commercial transport was largely in private hands—it was an open, competitive market."[131]

At the same time, the Fatimids monopolized strategic industries such as the manufacture of weapons including the production of natron and alum.[132] The rulers of Egypt were also frequently involved in trade. Biographies chronicle how one Fatimid ruler had expanded the textile trade and how a certain Fatimid *wazir* at his death owned cloth valued at 500,000 *dinars*, which he invested in large quantities in the textile trade.[133] The production and sale of sugar and paper were also linked to the Fatimid rulers.[134] However, the transit trade was not exempt from ruling class incursions. "Rulers bought, sold, and filled their storehouses with native and foreign goods . . . possessed several *funduqs* [warehouses] and shops, and were at the same time the largest merchants, producers, and consumers in the realm."[135] Thus, in their

---

[128] Heck, *Arab Roots of Capitalism*, 127.
[129] Ibid., 130.
[130] Ibid., 78.
[131] Goldberg, 97.
[132] Heck, *Arab Roots of Capitalism*, 128.
[133] Frantz-Murphy, 134.
[134] Goitein, *Economic Foundations*, 81.
[135] Labib, 76.

mixing of government and business, the Fatimids were no different than the Abbasids and the Umayyads.

Aside from the overall economic environment, the Geniza Documents shed light on a variety of trade practices during the rule of the Fatimids. Some of these practices were extensions of developed Islamic law adapted to the expanded Mediterranean trade environment, while others were new.

The Marketplace and Prices

The marketplace under the Fatimids continued to be at the center of trade and commerce. Commensurate with the importance of the marketplace, the position of the *muhtasib* also grew in stature. Abu-Lughod says,

> In Fatimid times the *muḥtasib* was the third highest ranking official among the "men of the pen" (i.e., religious rather than military), inferior only to the chief *qāḍi* and the supervisor of religious knowledge (*Dār al-'Ilm*). So important was he that his appointment was announced from the pulpits of the Friday mosques in both al-Qāhirah and Miṣr (Fusṭāṭ), where he also sat in judgment on alternating days. His authority in moral matters was absolute.[136]

The *muhtasib,* together with an assistant (known as the *arif*), supervised the different kinds of craftsmen and traders in the marketplace.[137]

There were daily, weekly, and annual markets. The weekly markets were largely farmers' markets, while the annual markets,

---

[136] Abu-Lughod, *Cairo*, 24, note 31.
[137] Gabriel Baer, "Guilds in Middle Eastern History," in *Studies in the Economic History of the Middle East from the Rise of Islam to the Present Day,* ed. M. A. Cook (New York, NY: Oxford University, 1970), 13.

provided for exchange over longer distances, raised agricultural production, and strengthened commercial exchanges over the whole area of the country [and] were timed to occur in conjunction with much-frequented religious festivals, and located at the intersections of great maritime or terrestrial trade routes.[138]

The marketplaces also became more specialized. The Geniza Documents refer to "streets and markets named for the types of merchants located there, such as the clothiers, wool merchants, dealers in second-hand garments, vendors of wax or of seeds [or] of spices."[139]

Buying and selling was conducted "either by man-to-man dealings, 'in sitting' namely in a store, a bazaar street, a bourse, or in a toll house, or by public auction through participation 'in a circle,' *fī 'l-ḥalqa*."[140] Unless monopolized by the government, prices of most products were not fixed and reflected changing conditions. As such, a high value was placed upon market intelligence. The Geniza Documents describe merchants inquiring "first about prices [and then about] the volume of business, the availability of capital, the movements of ships and caravans, the arrival and departure of merchants, the general situation in a country, and the safety of communications."[141] Once a price was agreed to, transactions were closed with the clasping of hands.[142] The major participants in the marketplace were *mawali*, since Arabs preferred not to engage in commerce directly or sitting in the markets to buy and sell.[143]

---

[138] Labib, 72.
[139] Goitein, *Economic Foundations*, 193.
[140] Ibid., 192.
[141] Ibid., 201.
[142] Ibid., 195-6.
[143] Jamal Judah, "The Economic Conditions of the Mawālī in Early Islamic Times," in *Manufacturing and Labor*, ed. Michael G. Morony (Hampshire, UK: Ashgate, 2003), 172-3.

Marketplaces also adapted to the increased importance and complexity of the transit trade. When products arrived at a port city, they were typically wrapped in large canvas bundles with the name of the recipient written on the outside or perhaps just the name of the owner/shipper. Inside the bundles were often many separate packages owned by other merchants and destined for different merchants in the city.[144]

The person in charge of the entire bundle was the *wakil*, who acted as a representative of the merchants. In the Geniza Documents, *wakils* were often also *qadis* (judges).[145] Under supervision of the *wakil*, the contents of the bundles were often sent to a *wakala*, which was typically a two-story building (also known as caravanserais or *funduks* [in Greek]). The ground floor of the *wakala* provided places where merchants could rent space to store and sell their merchandise, while the second story provided rooms for lodging, which the merchants could rent until their business was concluded.[146] These *wakalas* "dominated the townscape of the great cities. Cairo, for example, possessed at the time of the Crusades four *funduqs* for commercial exchange between Egypt and Syria."[147]

New Uses for Partnerships

The primary motivation of Egypt's merchants was to make a profit in their trading activities. The Geniza Documents provide evidence of the merchants' "ongoing efforts to acquire new capital and then productively engage it in lucrative mercantile ventures and other worthwhile

---

[144]Goldberg, 111.

[145]Goitein, *Economic Foundations*, 187.

[146]G. Wiet, V. Elisséeff and Ph. Wolff, "The Development of Techniques in the Medieval Muslim World," in *Manufacturing and Labor*, ed. Michael G. Morony (Hampshire, UK: Ashgate, 2003), 8-9.

[147]Labib, 72.

private investments."¹⁴⁸ As discussed in previous chapters, Islam established partnerships as the accepted means of forming joint trading relationships. In Fatimid Egypt, the majority of partnerships were short-term partnerships that related to a specific venture and period of time.¹⁴⁹ Most of the partnerships recorded in the Geniza Documents were of short duration and limited to specific undertakings.¹⁵⁰ Islam's ban on forming partnerships with goods and merchandise became particularly onerous when a merchant's capital was invested in goods at a location where a profitable sale could not be made. The Geniza Documents illustrate how "legal fictions" of the type mentioned in Chapter 4 were used to create the appearance of a sale, with the proceeds used to form a new partnership—when no actual sale occurred.¹⁵¹

In addition to short-term venture partnerships, ongoing family partnerships were also formed, typically between a father and his sons or between a group of brothers. These were of the *mufawada* type, where each of the partners had general liability.¹⁵² While families often worked together, they "preferred to keep their accounts separate. *Taḥābabū wa-taḥāsabū*, 'love each other, but make accounts with each other' is a principle recommended in a saying used all over the Arab world."¹⁵³

Partnerships were also extended to certain special situations. For example, while most included two, or at most a handful of partners, the Geniza Documents make reference to a

> joint venture involving a sugar factory, [where] two brothers who agreed to serve as "operating

---

¹⁴⁸Heck, *Arab Roots of Capitalism*, 131.
¹⁴⁹Goldberg, 124.
¹⁵⁰Udovitch, 125.
¹⁵¹Ibid., 63.
¹⁵²Goldberg, 126.
¹⁵³Goitein, *Economic Foundations*, 183.

managers," contrived to take in new outside investors to raise 600 *dīnārs* needed for facilities expansion–with the implementing agreement stipulating that the brothers and the financiers were to share equally in the profits.[154]

There was also evidence of partnerships that were formed between Muslims and non-Muslims. Although Muslim religious authorities accepted the legality of such agreements, they viewed such partnerships with disdain and reprehension if the Muslim partner was not the dominant party in the agreement.[155]

The variety of partnerships in Islam gave rise to "a frequent point of contention between collaborating merchants... concern[ing] the nature of their relationship; e.g., one party might claim it to be a *commenda* or partnership, while the other might contend that it was a loan or deposit or *ibḍā*!"[156] The lack of clarity in regard to how partners shared profits and losses certainly inhibited the flow of capital into commerce, since such ambiguity was in addition to the normal risks associated with commerce (e.g., theft, shipwreck, adverse price fluctuations).

The continued proliferation of partnerships was due not only to Islam's prohibition of interest, but also the need for merchants to enlist employees in the operation of their businesses. The Geniza Documents indicate that many partnerships were essentially employment agreements.[157] Why such was the case is examined in the following section.

---

[154] Heck, *Arab Roots of Capitalism*, 150.
[155] Udovitch, 227-8.
[156] Ibid., 188.
[157] Goitein, *Economic Foundations*, 170.

Labor and Agency Arrangements

The craftsmen of Fatimid Egypt appeared to be highly specialized. For example, among woodworkers were carpenters, sawyers (who cut timbers to required dimensions), chest-makers, turners and "makers of wooden door locks, who were of particular importance, since 'the safety of property and the guarding of women' depended upon them."[158] Dyers specialized by type of material and type and color of dye. Among metal workers, "There were specialists for knives, ladles and spoons, tongs, hooks (such as those used in butchers' shops), razors, needles, and the like."[159] These craftsmen appeared to work independently of one another, since there is no evidence in the Geniza Documents of labor guilds.[160]

The trades, however, were divided into two categories—those that were "base" and those that were "raised." The base trades included tanners, cuppers (those engaged in blood-letting), blacksmiths, and weavers. Weavers were especially looked down upon because of their supposed low intelligence. ("Of the ten tenths of stupidity found in the world, you will find nine tenths among the weavers.")[161] The raised trades included many types of merchants (including cloth and spice merchants), goldsmiths, and moneychangers.[162] Since marriages could only be arranged within categories, social mobility was restricted.

Regardless of one's trade or business, the Geniza Documents reveal that being employed by someone was looked down on, since depending on others for income was

---

[158]S.D. Goitein, "The Working People of the Mediterranean Area During the High Middle Ages," in *Manufacturing and Labor*, ed. Michael G. Morony (Hampshire, UK: Ashgate, 2003), 213.

[159]Ibid.

[160]Baer, 12.

[161]Ignaz Goldziher, "The Crafts Among the Arabs," in *Manufacturing and Labor*, ed. Michael G. Morony (Hampshire, UK: Ashgate, 2003), 149.

[162]Robert Brunschvig, "Base Trades in Islam," in *Manufacturing and Labor*, ed. Michael G. Morony (Hampshire, UK: Ashgate, 2003), 164.

viewed as humiliating.[163] A Tunisian merchant who through difficult circumstances was forced to be an employee complained, "I eat bread in the service of others; every minute of the day I gulp the cup of death because of my degradation and that of my children."[164] The only type of wage labor referred to in the Geniza Documents is that of manual labor.[165] Yet an individual merchant could not manage all the details involved in shipping and receiving products to and from different locations simultaneously, especially as his business grew. Thus, he needed clerks and others he could rely on to perform certain tasks at distant ports—without making them employees.[166] This situation gave rise to new types of labor and agency relationships.

One type of "agency agreement" was known as a *subha*, which typically involved two merchants located in distant cities or areas. It gave "the ability to unilaterally designate one's associate as an agent for particular goods, and to request specified tasks on specified goods through written instructions in a letter."[167] This was typically a reciprocal relationship with each merchant performing similar services for the other—all without monetary compensation.[168] One Geniza merchant referred to such a relationship as follows: "You are in my place there, for you know well that I am your support here."[169]

Another type of arrangement was referred to as *ashabuna*, which literally means "our colleagues" or "our associates."[170] One scholar referred to *ashabunas* as networks of mentors and apprentices, where the apprentices traveled for their mentors' business, learned how to trade,

---

[163] Udovitch, 184-5.
[164] Ibid., 185, note 50.
[165] Goldberg, 124.
[166] Goitein, *Economic Foundations*, 162.
[167] Goldberg, 128.
[168] Goitein, *Economic Foundations*, 169.
[169] Udovitch, 103.
[170] Goldberg, 38.

and were supervised by a group of mentors in different locations. Over time, the apprentices would be allowed to trade for their own accounts and might even become full-fledged merchants and members of the *ashabuna*.[171] The Geniza Documents refer to several of these supra-regional *ashabunas*, indicating that membership in them was essential to a merchant's success.[172]

The informality of *subha* arrangements, as well as the shifting roles of apprentices in mentor-apprentice relationships, gave rise to much misunderstanding. "It is not surprising that the Geniza records teem with cases in which the parties were not sure on what conditions they had collaborated, or who made contradictory statements about the subject."[173] Such inefficiencies certainly played a role in the relative decline of Islamic trading hegemony during the High Middle Ages.

Credit Facilities

Contrary to the perception created by Louis Massignon (a French Arabist) that "banking during the Middle Ages consisted mainly of money-lending and that the Jews were the Rothschilds of the Islamic world,"[174] the Geniza Documents contain very few references to commercial loans in the 10th and 11th centuries. Only in the latter half of the 12th century is it noted that "commercial credit becomes more prominent and seems partly to replace the previously paramount practices of partnerships and commendas."[175] Although there was not a conventional banking sector in the modern sense, Fatimid Egypt did have *jahābidhah* or merchant bankers. One scholar describes them as "trade vendors who were concurrently in the business of financing

---

[171]Ibid., 136.
[172]Ibid., 353.
[173]Goitein, *Economic Foundations*, 186.
[174]Ibid., 229.
[175]Ibid., 253.

and facilitating the commercial transactions of others. At certain times, to augment their capital stocks, these functionaries would likewise accept deposits and take in outside investors."[176] Such bankers issued paper monetary instruments that functioned like checks or letters of credit to free the merchant from having to carry large amounts of currency if traveling long distances.[177]

Trade credit between merchants and their customers was commonplace, particularly at the wholesale level. Under the Fatimids, "forward-sales-on-credit" contracts became standard practice.[178] The normal waiting period for payment after a sale was two months, although with certain commodities there could be a delay of up to four months.[179] In light of the Qur'an's prohibition of *riba,* it is interesting to note that "When Maimonides was asked whether this procedure was not religiously objectionable since it involved some sort of veiled interest, he replied that without it most livelihoods would come to a standstill."[180] He also found that a transaction involving interest was permissible if the profit accrued to a Muslim.[181]

The repayment of trade credits and loans, however, was a problem in Fatimid Egypt. Evidence of this was the sizable discount given to purchasers who had ready cash. "In one letter, Ya'qūb b. Yūsuf al-Iṭrābulusī reports that he has sold part of Nahray b. Nissīm's flax in Ascalon on credit and part for cash. The cash price was 15 percent lower than the credit price."[182] The Geniza Documents also frequently mention "the pernicious habits of procrastination and delay of payment. The more important a person was the more

---

[176] Heck, *Arab Roots of Capitalism*, 152.
[177] Ibid., 154.
[178] Ibid., 144.
[179] Goitein, *Economic Foundations*, 197.
[180] Ibid., 197.
[181] Ibid., 199.
[182] Goldberg, 114.

difficult it was to enforce payment."¹⁸³ As a result, creditors tried to protect themselves by taking collateral. The Documents refer to a wide range of collateral as follows:

> Everything could serve as collateral: gold and silver, vessels, jewelry, clothing of all description, for poorer people even bedding and household goods, books, very common, but, above all, houses, that is, the property titles and transfer deeds were mortgaged. In extreme cases, children were pledged.¹⁸⁴

Written Contracts and Ethics

As their trade expanded across the Mediterranean, the Geniza merchants found it necessary to document their business transactions with extensive written records. "The elaborate care taken of written contracts is exemplified by the fact that, in several instances, copies of the same contract were dispatched by two or three different routes in order to ensure the safe arrival of at least one at the desired destination."¹⁸⁵ In addition, detailed records were kept of income and expenses, including "expenses involved in the shipment, handling and ultimate sale of merchandise from one city to another. The number of individual expense items recorded in such accounts reaches as high as eighty."¹⁸⁶ The Geniza Documents also contained rudimentary bookkeeping ledgers in two-column format where "the 'credit column' entry is labeled: *lahu* ('for him'); and the 'debit column' entry is marked: *alayhi* or '*indahu* ('against/with him')."¹⁸⁷

Notwithstanding such records, a merchant's reputation and standing "*jāh*" within both the business and broader

---

[183] Goitein, *Economic Foundations*, 258.
[184] Ibid., 259.
[185] Udovitch, 87-8.
[186] Ibid., 237-8.
[187] Heck, *Arab Roots of Capitalism*, 156.

community was vital.[188] An individual merchant's *jah* "did not give him any defined rights or privileges. It opened instead myriad possibilities of favors, advantages, and preferential treatment: [e.g.] access to flax from government estates."[189] To maintain their *jah,* merchants found themselves enmeshed in a complex web of patron-client relationships. For example, a merchant

> might be a patron to a number of customs officers in Fustat and Alexandria, through whose modest authority he would ship an endless series of bales and packages throughout many trading seasons, providing the officer with a significant and steady source of revenue while ensuring that his own goods received preferential and undisturbed treatment.[190]

Merchants also made payments to shipowners and sailors in exchange for their bundles' safe passage.[191] Although to modern Western sensibilities such payments constitute corruption, in the cultural milieu of Fatimid Egypt they were clearly acceptable. There is no indication from the Geniza Documents as to how, or whether, such practices were reconciled with the Qur'an or the *Sunnah*.

Business in Pre-Modern Egypt

The final section of this chapter will focus on pre-modern Egypt from the Middle Ages until the end of the British occupation after World War I. For the sake of analysis, this lengthy time period can be divided into the following four periods: (1) the rule of the Mamluks in the Middle Ages, (2) the Ottoman rule from 1517 to just before Napoleon's

---

[188]Goldberg, 147.
[189]Ibid., 352.
[190]Ibid.
[191]Ibid., 108.

invasion in 1798, (3) the impact of the French invasion and the rule of Muhammad Ali, and (4) the modernizing efforts of Ali's successors and actions of the British during their occupation and administration. An examination of these periods will provide a foundation to understand the historical and cultural currents that gave rise to (among other factors) the Islamist movement, which has greatly impacted business in modern Islam and is the subject of Chapter 6.

While key historical events of each period will be presented to provide appropriate context, the emphasis will be on how the conduct of business changed over these periods—i.e., on the shifts in ownership and use of wealth and possessions, plus changes in the patterns of trade and commerce. Due to the many rulers and changed circumstances in Egypt in the pre-modern period, the analysis of wealth, possessions, trade, and commerce will be addressed as each period is discussed, as opposed to being in separate sections.

Business in Egypt During the Middle Ages

The decline of the Fatimids in Egypt can be attributed to a number of factors. According to one historian, it was clearly linked to the policy of importing Turkish and black African mercenary soldiers, which resulted in much infighting between these groups and the Fatimids' Berber bodyguards. "It was Circassian and Turkish soldiers and slaves who later usurped the supreme authority and established independent dynasties."[192] There was also a famine "caused by the low level of the Nile for seven consecutive years, from 457/1065 to 464/1072, [which resulted in] the constant plundering and ravaging of the land by Turkish troops . . . [and] the total disruption of the country's agriculture."[193]

---

[192]Hitti, 620.
[193]Daftary, 194.

During this period of famine, the Fatimid palaces and Fustat were looted and burned by the Turkish guards.[194] Historians also noted that Egypt was smitten by "the Great Plague of 1063" and an earthquake in 1138.[195] In the 12th century, it was further negatively impacted by the Crusades. For example, in 1168 an Egyptian *wazir* "feared that the crusader forces ... would use indefensible Fustat as a base from which to launch a fatal thrust to fortified Cairo, and he therefore ordered the city burned to the ground. Burn it did—for 54 days and nights."[196]

The Crusades, however, brought to Egypt the legendary figure of Saladin, who displaced the Fatimids and founded the Ayyubid dynasty, which lasted from 1171 to 1250. One Egyptian scholar noted that, "According to most Arab historians, Ayyubid rule had been relatively good for Egypt. The country was opened to European trade, especially to Venetians and Pisans, and the sultans were friendly to Christians."[197] The Ayyubids also instituted a new system of land-tax administration known as the *iqta*. Under this system, revenues from specific parcels of land were assigned to various recipients (including the sultanate and various commanders of military units) in exchange for military service. The Ayyubid form of the *iqta* system did not, however, transfer ownership of land to the recipients of the revenues, since the Ayyubid rulers did not want to create a landed aristocracy.[198] As power shifted from the Ayyubids to various Mamluk families and clans, land ownership also shifted. "By the fifteenth century, most of the land in Egypt was the property of the sultan and his military commanders. Peasant cultivators were soon converted into mere

---

[194] Ibid.
[195] Abu-Lughod, *Cairo*, 19.
[196] Ibid., 20.
[197] P.J. Vatikiotis, *The History of Modern Egypt: From Muhammad Ali to Mubarak*, 4th ed. (Baltimore, MD: Johns Hopkins University, 1991), 18.
[198] Kenneth M. Cuno, *The Pasha's Peasants: Land, Society, and Economy in Lower Egypt, 1740-1858* (Cambridge, UK: Cambridge University, 1992), 20.

agricultural workers, tied to the soil as vassals of the fief holders."[199]

Under both the Ayyubids and the Mamluks, the use of *waqfs* expanded greatly. Whereas in classical Islam *waqfs* consisted primarily of urban land and buildings, the Ayyubids and Mamluks allowed arable land to be placed into *waqfs*. In addition, the use of family *waqfs* became widespread. "The income of a 'family' *waqf* was assigned to the heirs of its maker and was transferred to a designated charitable or pious activity only upon the extinction of the family line."[200] Clearly, the implementation of tax avoidance strategies transcends cultures.

There were some areas of the Egyptian economy that prospered. Foremost was the spice trade with Europe that, in the early 15th century, produced fortunes for the Karimi merchants engaged in the trade.[201] The wages of urban artisans and craftsmen also multiplied many times over due to shortages in the labor force caused by the plagues.[202] The rise in wages, along with a persistent urban inflation, negatively impacted the ruling Mamluks, who were based in urban centers and whose revenues from their agricultural holdings were diminishing. They responded by means of "increasingly blatant intervention in the urban economy in the form of taxes, confiscations and finally, in the 1420s and 1430s, to the late medieval equivalent of nationalization of the spice, sugar and other trades."[203] This continued Egypt's long history of creating state monopolies and fixing prices, which was certainly far from the reluctance to fix prices found in the Qur'an and the *hadith*. Interestingly, it was the Mamluk monopolies and "[t]he resulting disruption of the

---

[199] Vatikiotis, 18.
[200] Cuno, 21.
[201] Robert Lopez, Harry Miskimin, and Abraham Udovitch, "England to Egypt, 1350-1500: Long-Term Trends and Long-Distance Trade," in *Studies in the Economic History of the Middle East from the Rise of Islam to the Present Day*, ed. M. A. Cook (New York, NY: Oxford University, 1970), 123.
[202] Ibid., 122.
[203] Ibid., 123.

transit trade [that] was one of the main motives which led the Portuguese to set out on their journey around Africa."[204]

Although the Qur'an and the *hadith* supported the concept that those who worked the land should reap its benefits (if not also its ownership), Egypt in the Middle Ages moved away from this concept. During the roughly 250-year rule by the Mamluks, the amount of land-tax revenue collected declined by about 90 percent and the number of rural villages decreased by 80 percent.[205] The decline in agricultural output decimated Egypt's textile industry.[206] Along with agriculture and domestic industry, the level of commerce also declined. For example, annual revenues from a toll station on the main road from Egypt to Syria fell from 350,000 *dinars* in 1326 to 96,000 *dinars* by the end of the century, and to 8,000 *dinars* by the end of the 15th century.[207] However, in fairness, it should be noted that Egypt also experienced repeated plagues during the Middle Ages which, according to the Egyptian historian Maqrizi, reduced the its population by one-third.[208] In addition, "the ambitions of ruthless Mamluk factions plunged the empire into a quarter century of unrelieved civil wars."[209]

Business in Egypt Under Ottoman Rule

The Mamluks, who ruled Egypt prior to the Ottoman conquest, were from ethnic groups outside of Egypt: Turkish, south Russian, east European and north African. According to one scholar, the plagues affected the Mamluks disproportionately because they had no genetic resistance to

---

[204] Lewis, 172.
[205] Lopez, *England to Egypt*, 115.
[206] Ibid., 116.
[207] Ibid.
[208] Ibid., 120.
[209] Ira M. Lapidus, *Muslim Cities in the Later Middle Ages*, student ed. (Cambridge, UK: Cambridge University, 1984), 9.

the diseases.²¹⁰ They were further weakened by the slowing influx of slaves and mercenaries from Turkish areas due to the receding Mongol threat in the early 15th century.²¹¹ All these factors contributed to the Mamluk defeat by the Ottomans in 1517.

When the Ottomans assumed control of Egypt, they treated it as a province of their empire, with the Ottoman sultan appointing a governor (or viceroy) to administer it. The Ottoman garrison in Egypt consisted of seven corps including one elite infantry corp Janissaries who guarded Cairo and the Citadel.²¹² The Ottoman garrison, however, was still only about 10,000 men strong.²¹³ The Ottoman Mamluks, who were mostly Georgians that had intermarried with the earlier Mamluks, continued to exert influence (verging, at times, on outright control) throughout the centuries of Ottoman rule.²¹⁴ These Mamluks even formed one of the seven military corps that comprised the Ottoman garrison.²¹⁵

From a financial perspective, the Ottoman goal in Egypt was to maximize tax revenues. One scholar of Ottoman finances noted that, "For a healthy 'budget,' Ottoman statesmen expected a surplus after expenditures so that those receiving a salary from the sultan's treasury would not have any concerns about their income."²¹⁶ In setting tax rates, "It was believed that one-third of a peasant's income was the maximum amount which could be collected as tax for the public treasury, one-third was for the maintenance of the

---

²¹⁰Lopez, *England to Egypt*, 119.
²¹¹Vatikiotis, 19.
²¹²Michael Winter, "Ottoman Egypt, 1525-1609" in *Modern Egypt, from 1517 to the End of the Twentieth Century*, vol. 2, ed. M. W. Daly, The Cambridge History of Egypt (Cambridge, UK: Cambridge University, 1998), 9.
²¹³Ibid., 4.
²¹⁴Bruce McGowan, "The Age of the *Ayans*, 1699-1812," in *An Economic and Social History of the Ottoman Empire, 1300-1914*, ed. Halil İnalcik and Donald Quataert (Cambridge, UK: Cambridge University, 1994), 675.
²¹⁵Winter, 9.
²¹⁶Halil İnalcik, "The Ottoman State: Economy and Society, 1300-1600," in *An Economic and Social History of the Ottoman Empire, 1300-1914*, ed. Halil İnalcik and Donald Quataert (Cambridge, UK: Cambridge University, 1994), 77.

tillage, and one-third was for the nourishment of his family and himself."[217] Initially, the Ottomans used salaried *emins* (tax collectors).[218] The Ottomans also used periodic surveys and inspections of land titles to centralize land control.[219] By the 17th century, the system of salaried tax collectors gave way to

> tax-farming, or *iltizam*, whereby officials and local notables bid at auction (*muzayada*) for the right to collect the taxes of a given subprovince, district, village, or urban property or enterprise. In this fashion, virtually every significant office, from customs director to the governor of Egypt, came to consist of a tax-farm.[220]

Once again, it can be observed that Muslim rulers imposed a heavy tax burden upon their subjects—a burden not prescribed in the Qur'an or the *hadith*.

Egyptian merchants, who engaged in the transit trade in spices (a key component of the Egyptian economy) were also negatively impacted in the early 16th century by the Portuguese discovery of the Cape of Good Hope trade route to India. This new route cost Egypt's European trading partner, Venice, most of its northern markets. One scholar calculated that Venetian purchases of spices at Alexandria decreased by 75 percent.[221] Egypt's merchants were able to replace some of the lost transit trade with other products

---

[217] Ibid.

[218] Roger Owen, *The Middle East in the World Economy: 1800-1914* (London, UK: I. B. Tauris, 2002), 12.

[219] Cuno, 21.

[220] Jane Hathaway, "Egypt in the Seventeenth Century," in *Modern Egypt, from 1517 to the End of the Twentieth Century*, vol. 2, ed. M. W. Daly, The Cambridge History of Egypt (Cambridge, UK: Cambridge University, 1998), 38.

[221] İnalcık, 341.

(notably coffee from Yemen) and by supplying Muslims on pilgrimage along with towns in the Hejaz.[222]

The societal differences in status accorded in the *hadith* to various trades and crafts continued under Ottoman rule. For example, from a religious point of view, the buying and selling of textiles were regarded as "honorable," whereas tanning and oil-pressing were not (activities like gold smithery were in between).[223] Craftsmen and shopkeepers were segregated in the cities and organized into guilds that included both Muslims and non-Muslims.[224] These guilds, which were led by elected sheikhs, participated in public ceremonies and paid taxes as a group, with the total tax amount being apportioned to the members of the guild by the *sheikh*.[225]

Individual traders and craftsmen were often in partnership with the various paramilitary corps (such as the Janissaries) located in Cairo and other cities. While some of these partnerships may have involved a business investment, others were simply a means of fleecing the business for protection.[226] One scholar also noted that, when the military ruling class penetrated the artisan class, it was detrimental to the artisans because it limited their flexibility and their practice of "capitalism from below."[227]

Several factors in the 18th century had a profound effect upon Egyptian trade and commerce. The first was Europe's Industrial Revolution and the resulting increased activity of European nations in Egypt, particularly France and Britain. One scholar noted that, during the last half of the 18th century

---

[222]Suraiya Faroqhi, "Crisis and Change, 1590-1699," in *An Economic and Social History of the Ottoman Empire, 1300-1914*, ed. Halil İnalcik and Donald Quataert (Cambridge, UK: Cambridge University, 1994), 507.
[223]Ibid., 591.
[224]Ibid., 590.
[225]Ibid., 592.
[226]McGowan, 705-6.
[227]Nelly Hanna, *Artisan Entrepreneurs in Cairo and Early Modern Capitalism: 1600-1800* (Syracuse, NY: Syracuse University, 2011), 26.

techniques of production were improving, especially in the field of textile production. The French, for example, were importing vast amounts of cotton from Egypt . . . [and producing] medium-priced French cloth [which] was cheaper than the equivalent Egyptian product, so that French production was not only destroying the Egyptian textile export market but was also undermining the local internal trade in textiles.[228]

France also looked to Egypt as a nearby source of food supply for her growing population (especially in southern France) since, after losing the Seven Years' War to Britain, she also lost control of the seas.[229] Meanwhile, Britain's interest in Egypt was more strategic, since Egypt was strategically located on the Eastern trade route to India.[230] The trade between Europe and Egypt was not without restriction, in that European governments erected trade barriers against Egyptian products, which negatively impacted its trade balance. For example, "Barriers to imports erected at Marseilles caused France's intake of Egyptian textiles to fall. By 1783, the French-Egyptian trade balance began to tilt against Egypt, in contrast to other Ottoman provinces."[231]

Another factor was the exemption of Europeans and their agents in Egypt from the civil laws of Egypt and the Ottoman state. This exemption stemmed from the "Capitulations," originally agreed to by Suleiman the Magnificent in 1535, which

---

[228] Afaf Lutfi al-Sayyid Marsot, *Egypt in the Reign of Muhammad Ali* (Cambridge, UK: Cambridge University, 1984), 16.

[229] Peter Gran, *Islamic Roots of Capitalism: Egypt, 1760-1840* (Syracuse, NY: Syracuse University, 1998), 7.

[230] Robert L. Tignor, *Modernization and British Colonial Rule in Egypt, 1882-1914* (Princeton, NJ: Princeton University, 1966), 12.

[231] McGowan, 732.

confirmed and codified the prevailing practice that European nationals in the Empire should be ruled by their own law. The system originated in the concept of law as something personal rather than territorial; there was also the feeling that Christians could not be expected to live and trade with each other in accordance with the alien usages of Moslem society. With the passage of time, however, the privileges freely accorded by successive sultans were converted into prescriptive rights.[232]

Local merchants found it difficult to compete with the Europeans' *beratli* representatives, who were typically from Christian minority groups, such as Syrian Christians. This greatly reduced the role of indigenous Egyptians in handling Egyptian trade.[233]

A third factor was the continued infighting between Mamluk factions that was tantamount to a civil war. One scholar noted, "Conflict was thus the norm for all but seven of the thirty-five years from 1777 to 1812. There can be little doubt that the prolonged warfare, in conjuncture with natural disasters, contributed to a decline in population and production."[234] These three factors primarily set the stage for Napoleon's invasion of Egypt in 1798 and the subsequent rise of Muhammad Ali, whose influence upon Egypt's economy and business climate was far-reaching.

Business in Egypt Under Muhammad Ali

The long rule of Muhammad Ali (from 1805 to 1848) was preceded by the French invasion of Egypt in 1798. While a detailed explanation of the French occupation from 1798 to

---

[232]David S. Landes, *Bankers and Pashas: International Finance and Economic Imperialism in Egypt* (Cambridge, MA: Harvard University, 1958), 90.
[233]Marsot, 14.
[234]Cuno, 28.

1801 is beyond the scope of this book, that occupation did result in profound changes to the economy and manner in which business was conducted in Egypt during the 19th century. One scholar noted that

> when Napoleon came to Egypt in 1798, there were probably less than one hundred Europeans resident in the entire country, most of them traders in centres like Alexandria and Damietta. They lived in closed quarters, for like the Jew of medieval Europe, the Christian of Mameluke Egypt was an inferior being, a pariah whose presence was tolerated only on condition of physical isolation.[235]

Napoleon brought with him experts in a number of areas who conducted field research and analysis to determine Egypt's potential. For instance, they recommended that irrigation projects to support agriculturally-based industries should be the highest priority. In addition, the French built "factories in Cairo for gunpowder, beer, hats, arsenals for field guns, tanneries and windmills to make flour—all intended for the supply of the occupation troops."[236] Napoleon also sought to win over the *ulama* and especially the *shaykhs* and notables at al-Azhar (the leading institution of Muslim learning and culture).[237] Although French plans for Egypt were left largely uncompleted due to Napoleon's return to Europe in 1801, his courting of the Muslim religious authorities reinvigorated them to a degree. As the decades of the 19th century passed, their deference to various ruling factions decreased, even though they lacked the power to control the country.[238]

---

[235]Landes, 86.
[236]Vatikiotis, 59.
[237]Ibid., 43.
[238]Arthur Goldschmidt Jr. *Modern Egypt: The Formation of a Nation-State*. 2nd ed. (Boulder, CO: Westview, 2004), 19.

In the power vacuum created by Napoleon's withdrawal from Egypt, the person who emerged victorious was Muhammad Ali, an Ottoman army officer of Albanian descent who founded modern Egypt.[239] For the first ten years after Napoleon's departure, Ali removed any "contenders for authority. . . . He was not a nationalist or a pan-Islamist; rather, he treated Egypt as a tax farm or exploitable personal property, much as the Mamluks had done before him. His goal was personal aggrandizement."[240] In the words of one scholar, Egypt under Ali was to become "one great farm, held at a nominal rental of the Sultan. From this Muhammad Ali derived his usufruct; his bureaucracy were the overseers, and the population of Egypt the servants."[241]

Prior to becoming an army officer, Muhammad Ali was engaged in the tobacco trade in his Macedonian hometown of Kavala.[242] Although his involvement in trade and commerce was limited, when he came to power, he "understood well [that] Egypt had the potential for trade and sat astride a network of commercial routes that functioned in spite of all opposition to the orderly pursuit of commerce and all disruptions."[243] To maximize Egypt's economic value, he rejected free trade ideas and began to implement policies in accord with the prevailing theory of economy known as "mercantilism." Matsot says,

> Mercantilists believed the state must control and direct the flow of commerce, that agriculture and industry must be encouraged, and import trade controlled and limited to those commodities

---

[239] Ibid.
[240] Tignor, 32.
[241] Vatikiotis, 52.
[242] Henry Dodwell, *The Founder of Modern Egypt: A Study of Muhammad 'Ali* (1931; repr., Cambridge, UK: Cambridge University, 1967), 9.
[243] Marsot, 60.

necessary for creating an infrastructure, as long as the imports allowed a favourable balance of trade.[244]

Mercantilism well-suited "the philosophy of an adventurer who had seized power, and who, in order to stay in power, had to dominate the country, which otherwise would revert back to the control of the Ottoman empire."[245] To achieve the goals of mercantilism, Muhammad Ali took effective personal control of the government (although still nominally a viceroy under the Ottoman sultan) and instituted a number of radical changes in how wealth and possessions were owned and trade and commerce practiced. In line with the mercantilist emphasis on imperialism and expansion, Ali engaged in frequent military campaigns of conquest (but these are largely beyond the scope of this book).

Throughout his rule, Muhammad Ali sought to increase Egypt's agricultural output. In 1800, "The cultivation of the soil was almost exclusively the working of peasant families, farming small plots of land and using only the most simple tools."[246] In the first ten years of his rule, "Muhammad Ali succeeded in virtually nationalizing land in Egypt by destroying the agrarian position of the privileged classes he found in the country."[247] The government told the peasants what to sow; supplied the seed, tools, and fertilizer; irrigated the fields; and set the prices for the crops.[248]

Muhammad Ali also introduced a new strain of cotton, known as *Jumel* (named after the Frenchman who developed it). *Jumel* cotton was of very high quality, second only to American cotton.[249] Cotton accounted for over half of Egypt's

---

[244] Ibid., 164.
[245] Ibid., 177.
[246] Owen, 38.
[247] Vatikiotis, 54.
[248] Goldschmidt, 21.
[249] Landes, 74.

total exports in years where cotton prices were high. To raise more cotton, Ali also constructed new canals and installed pumps to provide fields with water during the summer months.[250] His rule also "saw the growth of a network of barge canals, river ports, and cart roads, together with grain weighing and storage facilities, cotton gins, sugar refineries, and other capital improvements."[251]

In order to increase revenues from the land, Muhammad Ali abolished the old Ottoman tax-farm system. According to Gran,

> During 1806-1808, he removed the tax collectors; during 1807-1809 he gained control of monies from *waqf* land and Uṣīya land. In 1810 he launched an attack on the Coptic clique in the financial administration... [and abolished] the *iltizām* system, replacing it with a system of government officials.[252]

These officials included descendants of Turko-Circassians as well as ethnic Egyptians from notable rural families. As the latter group became more numerous, Turkish was replaced by Arabic as the government language.[253]

Muhammad Ali's desire for military conquest required that he modernize Egypt's armed forces, which led to the development of industry.[254] In the view of one scholar, Egypt became "the first non-Western state to attempt an industrial revolution, introducing modern factories for the manufacture of soap, paper, cotton textiles, warships, and armaments."[255] To set up the industries, Ali invited groups of

---

[250]Tignor, 36.
[251]Goldschmidt, 22.
[252]Gran, 31.
[253]Eric Davis, *Challenging Colonialism: Bank Miṣr and Egyptian Industrialization, 1920-1941* (Princeton, NJ: Princeton University, 1983), 29.
[254]Vatikiotis, 56-7.
[255]Goldschmidt, 22.

foreigners with knowledge of each industry into Egypt.[256] Egypt's new industries, however, were organized as state monopolies, whereby

> the state was chief employer and paid cash wages: high wages to factory workers and students . . . and low wages to workers in the agricultural sector. Wage labor predominated throughout the economy, which was buffered by state policy from the direct impact of the world market.[257]

These industries fared well as Egypt's army grew to over 100,000 men and their demand for products grew accordingly. However, this came to an end when Muhammad Ali's occupation of Syria was repulsed by the Ottomans in 1840 (with help from the British) and the Egyptian army was limited to only 18,000 men.[258] In describing the failure of Ali's industrialization program, one scholar also noted, "The climate, and particularly the dust, caused breakdowns in the machinery, usually with no one to repair it. . . . The industries disappeared almost immediately after government supports were withdrawn."[259]

Muhammad Ali also opened Egypt to foreign trade. From the outset of his rule, he sold grain to both Britain and France, increasing Egypt's national income from four million francs in 1798 to over thirty million by 1812.[260] In addition, he opened Egypt to foreign businessmen. "He admired Greek, Armenian, and French businessmen, with whom he may have had working relationships in the course of his tobacco-trading career. During his rule, he invited a number of Greek businessmen to settle in Egypt and gave them his

---

[256]Marsot, 167.
[257]Gran, 111.
[258]Marsot, 249.
[259]Tignor, 37.
[260]Gran, 32.

patronage."[261] Egypt's trade with Britain was further expanded as a result of a commercial trade pact entered into by the Ottomans in 1838. While the treaty resulted in Britain becoming the Ottoman's most important trading partner for the remainder of the 19th century, it also weakened industries and craft guilds in the provinces (including Egypt), since the treaty limited "protective duties on manufactured goods imported into Ottoman territories . . . [which] enabled cheap British manufactures to undercut the local handicrafts."[262]

Egypt's exposure to worldwide changes in commodity prices exposed its population to recurring crises. When prices dropped, the peasants were forced to accept the lower prices; when prices rose, the government would largely retain the profits. Muslim religious leaders, judges, and doctors of religious law—all of whom had links to the peasants and noted these hardships—were powerless to resist the state.[263]

Although Muhammad Ali's rule ended with military and economic reversals, he was able to extract from the Ottoman sultan the right to pass along to his family the governorship of Egypt. The impact of these rulers on business, along with the resulting British occupation, will be the subject of the next section.

Business in Egypt Prior to and During the British Occupation

At the time of his death, "Muhammad Ali was not only the sole industrialist and agricultural master of Egypt, but also its only entrepreneur."[264] Ali's successors were faced with a largely depleted national treasury due to his military

---

[261] Marsot, 30.
[262] Goldschmidt, 25.
[263] Vatikiotis, 63.
[264] Ibid., 61.

expeditions and his unsustainable industrial monopolies.[265] Egypt was also highly dependent upon the sale of Jumel cotton. Aside from shifting agricultural production away from food grains, which negatively impacted Egypt's ability to feed its population,[266] cotton production and export required a large investment in infrastructure, including port facilities and ongoing irrigation, transportation and communications projects.[267] The Egyptian bureaucracy and intellectual class, many of whom were educated in the West or in Egypt's westernized schools, also favored modernization as the only means for the nation to survive in the world economy.[268]

Such infrastructure and modernization required increased levels of foreign technology plus a concomitant dependency upon foreign nationals. For example, in 1851, Abbas Hilmi I (successor to Muhammad Ali's son Ibrahim, who died after only six months in power) awarded the British a contract to build Egypt's first railroad, linking Alexandria with Cairo.[269] Certain actions by the Ottoman state that were applicable to Egypt further attracted foreigners. One such action was a new land law (enacted in 1858), which "permitted individuals, whether subjects or foreigners, to buy and own land or other property within the Empire. Ethnic Egyptians, as well as descendants of Turkish and Circassian Mamluks, bought land and created new estates."[270] Foreigners were also protected by the Capitulations (discussed earlier in this chapter). By the late 19th century, the Capitulations had resulted in a situation where Westerners were exempted from the jurisdiction of local laws or the obligation to pay any taxes unless their governments had agreed to them.[271] Understandably, the

---

[265] Davis, 21.
[266] Ibid., 24.
[267] Ibid., 21.
[268] Tignor, 25.
[269] Goldschmidt, 30.
[270] Ibid., 33.
[271] Ibid.

privileged position of foreign minorities and the advantages they provided (especially when such advantages were used illegitimately) occasioned much hatred.[272]

Egypt's infrastructure investments and modernization also required a large infusion of foreign capital, primarily in the form of loans. Initially, such loans were channeled through local commercial banks owned by Greek, Jewish, Syrian, and European merchants.[273] In an attempt to reduce the interest rates charged on these loans, Sa'id (another successor of Muhammad Ali) established the Bank of Egypt in 1854.[274] During the 1860s, however, British- and French-owned banks became the major lenders. By 1865, there were 47 different types of English credit companies and banks operating in Egypt, mostly to facilitate the development of foreign enterprises.[275] Aside from larger commercial ventures, even individual farmers were among the recipients of loans. One English prospectus from the Egyptian Commercial and Trading Company targeting "natives" boasted, "It is well ascertained that in Upper Egypt and the Sudan, cultivators and traders can afford to borrow money at 4 and 5 percent per month and still amass wealth, the field of operation is almost illimitable."[276]

However, many loans served no economic purpose and were used only to finance the spending of the ruling class. The Bank of Egypt, for example, had by 1861 "most of its capital tied up in loans to the more profligate princes of the Egyptian royal house."[277] Even Ismael (ruler of Egypt from 1861 to 1879), who was praised for his investment in schools and infrastructure projects, also borrowed heavily to bribe Turkish politicians, to "build palaces and yachts, to support his cronies, to buy Paris gowns for his wives, and to bribe

---

[272] Landes, 92.
[273] Ibid., 61.
[274] Davis, 23.
[275] Landes, 60.
[276] Ibid., 58.
[277] Ibid., 67-8.

influential journalists."[278] One scholar noted that, toward the end of his rule, Ismail was borrowing at 30 percent interest.[279] Due to his heavy indebtedness, he was forced to sell his shares in the Suez Canal to the British government in 1876.[280] The heavy indebtedness of Egypt's rulers also contributed to a high level of corruption in the government. Landes says,

> Government was personal, centring [sic] almost entirely in the Viceroy and his family, and capriciously authoritarian, with little if any concept of a continuing, sovereign body of law. Public offices were not the impersonal embodiment of public functions, but private properties exploited by their holders for whatever they would yield.[281]

Foreign governments were often willing participants in such arrangements, since their consulates in Egypt were typically headed and staffed by businessmen, who were often concurrently advancing their private interests.[282]

Fearing default on their loans, Egypt and France established the *Caisse de la Dette* (the Debt Commission) in 1876 to channel Egyptian finances toward debt repayment.[283] In an effort to gain control over Egyptian finances, the European powers removed Ismail in 1879, and the Commission diverted "more than half the government revenues in 1880 to start reducing the nation's huge debt to foreign creditors... [and instituted] government cutbacks for the army, schools, public works, and even essential maintenance."[284] This sparked widespread resentment

---

[278]Goldschmidt, 35.
[279]Landes, 317.
[280]Ibid.
[281]Ibid., 97.
[282]Ibid., 94.
[283]Tignor, 23.
[284]Goldschmidt, 42.

among the Egyptian population and a revolt in 1882 led by an Egyptian army officer. The British, to protect their use of the Suez Canal, and at the behest of its bondholders and cotton manufacturers,[285] put down the rebellion and began an occupation of Egypt, which lasted through the end of World War I. That rebels in a Muslim state were "suppressed by the force of arms of a Christian imperial power with the acquiescence, if not blessing, of the Sultan-Caliph and the Khedive" is indicative of the weakness of the Ottoman government at that time.[286]

The British occupation of Egypt was unusual in that Egypt remained "an autonomous state within the Ottoman Empire. The Khedive continued as the formal ruler of the country.... The Egyptian governmental apparatus was retained. Egyptian officials held the administrative positions, at least in name."[287] Behind the scenes, however, the British acted decisively to avoid an Egyptian bankruptcy, primarily by maximizing Egypt's agricultural output through enhanced irrigation of lands near the Nile.[288] In the words of one Egyptian political thinker, the British "transformed the entire Nile Valley into a gigantic cotton plantation."[289] The new land that was brought under cultivation was sold to the highest bidders (i.e., the wealthy classes) to bolster government revenues.[290] The British largely left small-scale agricultural lending to such private institutions as the National Bank of Egypt, which was created in 1898.[291]

It is argued by some scholars that, aside from the agricultural efficiencies they implemented, the British

---

[285]Davis, 42.
[286]Vatikiotis, 170.
[287]Tignor, 50.
[288]Ibid., 53.
[289]Davis, 45.
[290]Tignor, 79-80.
[291]E.R.J. Owen, "The Attitudes of British Officials to the Development of the Egyptian Economy, 1882-1922," in *Studies in the Economic History of the Middle East from the Rise of Islam to the Present Day*, ed. M. A. Cook (New York, NY: Oxford University, 1970), 489.

occupation left Egypt in a better position as it moved into the 20th century. For example, the British oversaw implementation of the "National Tribunals," which was a new court system for Egyptian subjects based on European concepts (primarily upon the Napoleonic Law Code).[292] The British also lowered taxes on the peasants and abolished forced labor, "except for the requirement to watch over the Nile and canal earthworks during the flood season."[293] Goldschmidt also notes that, during the British occupation

> government corruption had almost vanished. Once the financial crisis was over, Europeans resumed investing in Egypt. European entrepreneurship furnished Cairo and Alexandria with most of the amenities of Western cities: gas, electricity, street lights, piped drinking water, tram lines, and telephones. Many Westerners came to Egypt as tourists, and some as permanent residents, protected under the Capitulations from local laws and taxes, but their expenditures enriched the country. Egypt in the first decade of the twentieth century was more prosperous than it had been since early Mamluk times.[294]

The British occupation also gave rise to many opposition groups in Egypt. One such group was the "Nationalists," made up largely of Western-educated Egyptian intellectuals. "The nationalist objection was that the Egyptian people were not advancing toward self-rule but, rather, were being treated as tools serving British imperial interests."[295] Another group was comprised of Islamic religious leaders and other pious Muslims who were troubled by the discrepancies

---
[292]Goldschmidt, 49.
[293]Ibid., 48.
[294]Ibid., 58-9.
[295]Ibid., 59.

between what the Qur'an, *hadith*, and *sharia* taught versus what was occurring. For example, the acceptance of loans and payment of interest had become commonplace in Egypt by the late 19th century. In addition, Egyptian society was highly stratified along economic lines, with the Egyptian *fellah* (or peasant) long having been oppressed. Opposition Muslim religious leaders challenged this oppression, since Islam had provided for the care of the poor through the *zakat*. Furthermore, Egyptian society was dependent upon the West, e.g., in technology (for peaceful purposes such as irrigation and for war-making), in business organization (Islam's partnerships were no equivalent of the joint stock company), and in finance (banks were owned by Westerners).

While these discrepancies were being raised, those in authority were not responding to them. The rulers of pre-modern Egypt largely suppressed the influence of the Islamic religious authorities. The role of the Qur'an and the *hadith* in determining economic policy was subordinated to the needs of the rulers and (in the 19th century) to the desire of these rulers to "modernize Egypt." In the 20th century, certain Islamic teachers and groups attempted to make Muslim economies and business "more Islamic." This effort has raised issues for those who would do business in the modern Muslim-majority world. Several of these teachers and groups will be examined in the next chapter.

CHAPTER 6

Business in Modern Islam

Business in Muslim-majority nations has been shaped by the writings of Muslims, ranging from political and economic reformers who sought gradual change, to Islamists who favored radical reform. After a brief historical introduction, this chapter will focus first on the modernist movement in Egypt, as exemplified by Muhammad Abduh (1849-1905). Reformers like Abduh, who lived under the British occupation, sought to establish Egypt as an independent Islamic nation. While these early Egyptian reformers seem far removed from present-day events, they constituted one side of the debate with a younger generation of Muslims, known as Islamists, who favored more radical change and whose works are widely read throughout Muslim-majority nations to this day. This chapter will then examine the writings of selected Islamists, with particular attention paid to Sayyid Qutb (1906-1966). The analysis of each individual's writings, whether modernist or Islamist, will be limited primarily to their views on business and economics.

From the roots of both modernism and Islamism sprang the field of contemporary Islamic economics. Thus, this chapter's final section will look at three prominent themes in current Islamic economic literature. The first theme concerns Muslim arguments for the supremacy of an Islamic economic system versus other economic systems, particularly capitalism. The second theme relates to the need for an interest-free Islamic banking system; and the third revolves around how Islamic economic development should be carried out in Muslim-majority nations.

Historical Overview

Events over the course of the 19th century profoundly changed many Muslim societies, especially as England, France, Germany, and Russia made political, economic, and religious inroads into the Ottoman Empire. One scholar noted,

> Western penetration took on various forms: apart from extra-territorial rights, loans to the Istanbul Government, concessions for the building and exploitation of railways, municipal investments and the operation of foreign banks, of tremendous importance were the Christian missions, schools, hospitals and the "protection" by the Great Powers of various sectors of the local populations. Thus, France was the protector of the Lebanese Maronites, Russia was the patron of the Greek-orthodox faith, and Great Britain of the Druses and Jews. In the Arab countries situated on the eastern shore of the Mediterranean, France dominated the spheres of municipal investment and railways, as well as of education and culture. But other powers, too, held strong positions, among which one cannot ignore the American missions and university at Beirut, founded in 1886 by the American Presbyterian mission.[1]

Up to the middle of the 19th century, the reaction of many Muslims to the increased European presence was not particularly one of alarm. Rifaa Bey al-Tahtawi (1801-1873), a teacher at Al-Azhar, an advisor to Muhammad Ali, and the

---

[1] Lukasz Hirszowicz, *The Third Reich and the Arab East* (London, UK: Routledge & Kegan Paul, 1966), 2.

individual regarded as the initiator and symbol of the Egyptian Awakening,[2] wrote that "The *ulema* must come to terms with the new learning.... Doctors, engineers, all who had mastered sciences which were useful to the State should be honoured and consulted by the ruler."[3] Nevertheless, based on his studies in France and interaction with European culture, Tahtawi was "conscious of a certain moral danger" between Christianity and Islam; but he minimized the risk, at least where the French were concerned, since he argued that their real religion was human reason.[4]

Another early reformer, Khayr al-Din (d. 1890), who became prime minister of Tunisia in 1873, argued that Europe's strength was based on its political institutions and material success, which was due to free economic association.[5] Al-Din maintained that Christianity had nothing to do with Europe's progress since "Christianity is a religion which aims at happiness in the next world and not in this."[6]

The early reformers regarded Islamic law as being flexible. For example, al-Zurqani (1645-1710), a highly regarded Egyptian Islamic theologian, wrote "that laws should be adapted to circumstances."[7] In the opinion of such reformers, "As for the Islamic thinkers of the later Middle Ages, law was a negative restraining factor. It set the limits within which the ruler must act, not the principles in accordance with which he should act."[8]

The Muslim response to foreign influence was also shaped by Jamal al-Din al-Afghani (1838-1897). Al-Afghani travelled extensively across the Muslim world, taught at al-Azhar in 1870s and inspired numerous Azharites and

---

[2]*The Encyclopaedia of Islam*, CD-ROM ed., s.v. "Rifaa Bey al-Tahtawi."
[3]Albert Hourani, *Arabic Thought in the Liberal Age: 1798-1939* (Cambridge, UK: Cambridge University, 1983), 76.
[4]Ibid., 82.
[5]Ibid., 90.
[6]Ibid., 91.
[7]Goldziher, *Islamic Theology and Law*, 234.
[8]Hourani, *Arabic Thought*, 83.

Egyptian Muslims.⁹ His message was for Muslims to resist imperialism, seek political liberation, and undertake an intellectual reawakening rooted in a return to Islam.¹⁰ His premise was that "All is well with pure Islam: the basic evil is impure Muslims. There is perfection in the faith itself, rightly understood, if only it were rightly practiced."¹¹ In advocating a return to pure Islam, Al-Afghani saw himself in the same role as Martin Luther at the time of the Christian Reformation.¹²

Several events in 1881-82 radically changed the attitude of Muslims toward Europe. In 1881, France occupied Tunis. Also in 1881, an uprising by a group of officers in the Egyptian army led by Colonel Urabi led to the occupation of Egypt by Britain in 1882. After occupying Egypt, the British placed the nation under the supervision of its Foreign Office. The fiscal and administrative affairs of the nation were directed by the British Consul-General, although the bureaucracy, staffed by Egyptians, was largely kept in place.

The Modernist Movement in Egypt

The relative ease with which the British quelled the Urabi rebellion "caused many Muslim leaders to question the strength of Islamic institutions and to seek to reform them in such a way as to render them viable in the modern world."¹³ As one scholar noted, "For a Muslim . . . whether he was Turkish or Arab, the seizure of power by Europe meant that his community was in danger."¹⁴ Islam views history as the fulfillment of the divine will. Thus, when the historic events in the 19th century no longer seemed to affirm Islam, it

---

⁹Vatikiotis, 190.
¹⁰John L. Esposito, ed., *Voices of Resurgent Islam* (New York, NY: Oxford University, 1983), 6.
¹¹Kenneth Cragg, *Counsels in Contemporary Islam* (Edinburgh, UK: Edinburgh University, 1965), 35.
¹²Hourani, *Arabic Thought*, 122.
¹³Vatikiotis, 189.
¹⁴Hourani, *Arabic Thought*, 103.

created "an awareness that something is awry between the religion which God has appointed and the historical development of the world which He controls."[15]

The decades of British occupation were a further source of irritation among Muslims and resulted in organized forms of opposition. The earliest resistance movements were often comprised of Egyptian intelligentsia, many of whom had been educated in Europe or had exposure to Western training (e.g., in Egypt's schools for the military and teachers). Some viewed these individuals as part of the "Arab *nahḍah* (rebirth or renaissance) of the 19th century . . . [which] postulated that a regeneration of Islam and an acceptance of the 'positive' features of the West were not at all incompatible."[16] Others referred to such groups as secularist, nationalist, or modernist.

In this book, the term "modernist" will be used, since individuals in the various movements did not separate Islam from their views (as connoted by the term "secularist"), nor did the importance of the State overshadow their identity as Muslims (as the term "nationalist" implies). In general, modernists saw no need to bring all of society's activities under *sharia* law. Rather, they held that "Some areas of life are not subject to religion and in these areas changes may be relatively easily made and foreign ways introduced," although they valued Islam "as a heritage to be respected and drawn upon and . . . [were] prepared to have Islam as the official religion of state."[17]

The key figure among Egyptian modernists was Muhammad Abduh. As one scholar noted, "No one will dispute that the story of Egyptian 'modernism' is the story of

---

[15] Wilfred Cantwell Smith, *Islam in Modern History* (Princeton, NJ: Princeton University, 1957), 41.

[16] Ibrahim M. Abu-Rabi', *Intellectual Origins of Islamic Resurgence in the Modern Arab World* (Albany, NY: State University of New York, 1996), 6.

[17] William E. Shepard, *Sayyid Qutb and Islamic Activism: A Translation and Critical Analysis of* Social Justice in Islam (Leiden, Netherlands: E. J. Brill, 1996), xii.

'Abduh and his legacy."[18] He had been a fellow student with al-Afghani at al-Azhar in the 1870s. After graduating as an *alim* (Islamic scholar), Abduh became involved in politics, which resulted in his banishment to Paris in the aftermath of the Urabi uprising. While in Paris, he collaborated with al-Afghani in forming a society, and publishing a paper, that promoted nationalism. After being permitted to return to Egypt in 1889, he was appointed to the judiciary and became state *mufti* in 1899, the highest clerical post in Egypt. He also was part of the governing body of al-Azhar.[19]

When Abduh returned to Egypt, despite his associations with al-Afghani, his aims were not "the realization of the political unity of the Muslim countries and, still less, 'Holy War' against non-Muslims. He expressly refrained from holding pan-Islamic ideas."[20] Rather, "the fundamental conviction of his career was that Islamic response to the inroads and pressures of Europe, both political and intellectual, must be by educative action rather than revolt."[21] The goal of all Abduh's work was to reform Muslim society.[22] He and many other modernists intended no radical reformation of Islam.[23] According to one scholar, Abduh's "essential thesis was that a true Islam, freed from un-Islamic accretions, was perfectly reconcilable with modern thought and conditions."[24] Another scholar noted, "He was in effect demanding that *ijtihad*, the right of the Muslim to interpret and reinterpret the rules of the Sacred Law in the light of changed conditions, be permitted."[25]

---

[18]Kenneth Cragg, "The Modernist Movement in Egypt," in *Islam and the West: Proceedings of the Harvard Summer School Conference on the Middle East, July 25-27, 1955*, ed. Richard N. Frye (The Hague, Netherlands: Mouton, 1956), 149.
[19]*The Encyclopaedia of Islam*, CD-ROM ed., s.v. "Muhammad Abduh."
[20]Osman Amin, "The Modernist Movement in Egypt," in *Islam and the West: Proceedings of the Harvard Summer School Conference on the Middle East, July 25-27, 1955*, ed. Richard N. Frye (The Hague, Netherlands: Mouton, 1956), 177.
[21]Cragg, *Counsels*, 33.
[22]Amin, 177.
[23]Cragg, *Modernist Movement*, 155.
[24]Cragg, *Counsels*, 36.
[25]Vatikiotis, 195-6.

The modernism of Muhammad Abduh was opposed by the majority of the *ulema*, which complained, "What sort of *shaykh* is this, who speaks French, travels about in Europe, translates western books, quotes from Western philosophers, holds discussions with their scholars, and issues *fatwa*s on things that not one of the ancients would have known about?"[26] In some respects, Abduh and the modernists set the stage for Islamism:

> Without intending it, 'Abduh was perhaps opening the door to the flooding of Islamic doctrine and law by all the innovations of the modern world. He had intended to build a wall against secularism; he had in fact provided an easy bridge by which it could capture one position after another. It was not an accident that, as we shall see, one group of his disciples were later to carry his doctrines in the direction of complete secularism.[27]

In response, many Muslims felt the need to counter this by holding tighter to their Islamic religion. Since the door to *ijtihad* had been opened by Abduh, it gave Islamists the opportunity to "reapply *sharia*" (as opposed to the modernist's "rethinking of *sharia*") in ways that transcended the historical norms established by the various Islamic law schools and by the *ulema*.[28] One scholar noted that the Islamist response to modernism was "more insistent and purist."[29]

---

[26] Amin, 166.

[27] Hourani, *Arabic Thought*, 144-5.

[28] Shepard, xiii.

[29] William Shepard, "The Diversity of Islamic Thought: Towards a Typology," in *Islamic Thought in the Twentieth Century*, ed. Suha Taji-Farouki and Basheer M. Nafi (London, UK: I. B. Tauris, 2004), 74.

The Emergence of Islamism

For Egypt, the span of years from the British occupation in 1882 until after World War I were difficult economically. As still one of Egypt's principal export commodities, cotton production was experiencing a significant decline due to lower soil fertility, pest attacks, and that no higher-yielding varieties were being introduced. At the same time, prices on the international market were dropping. This resulted in many peasants becoming impoverished and forced to sell livestock and other possessions in order to survive. Although the British instituted a moratorium on bank debts in 1914, many banks still demanded repayment; and moneylenders made new loans, worsening the situation of the peasants further.[30] At the end of World War I, many Egyptians assumed that the British Protectorate and occupation would end.[31] When this did not occur, the people revolted in 1919, which led to Egypt being granted the status of a sovereign state in 1922—but Britain still exercised a great deal of control over governmental affairs (and would continue to do so until after World War II).

In the 1920s and 1930s, British capitalists were dominant in Egyptian economic life, although French capitalists were also active.[32] The Red Line Agreement, concluded in 1928, divided all oil concessions in Turkey, and in Arab lands, between British, French, Dutch, and American interests.[33] It seemed to many Egyptians that their economy was being controlled from abroad. "Such manufacturing as did exist was owned by Europeans ... [and] the preponderant foreign elements tended to perpetuate their dominance by employing local foreigners, and rarely employing

---

[30]Davis, 114.
[31]Ibid., 113.
[32]Hirszowicz, 9.
[33]Ibid., 11.

Egyptians."[34] At the same time, many farms were being divided into ever smaller (and uneconomical) parcels due to Egypt's rising population and Islam's inheritance laws, which divided the majority of all estates among family members based on established formulas.[35] The decline in agricultural income (discussed earlier) continued in the decades between World Wars I and II and was exacerbated by the worldwide depression of the 1930s.

During these times, the *ulama* did not seem to be able to represent Muslims effectively. One scholar noted that the *ulama*'s economic strength had eroded since many *waqfs* had been taken over by the State; and its traditional monopoly on education was broken due to the State's need for modern disciplines and skills, which were provided for in newly established schools.[36] The abolition of the Caliphate in 1924 created a further feeling of loss. As one scholar noted,

> The institution [the Caliphate] had endured, after all, from the immediate hours of the Prophet's death and through all its fortunes had been taken as a *sine qua non* of Islamic life and order. When the Turks terminated, first the Imamate, and then the Caliphate, bewilderment, indeed a sense of outrage, took hold of Muslims everywhere.[37]

It was out of this milieu that the Muslim Brotherhood was founded and began to grow.

---

[34] John Calvert, *Sayyid Qutb and the Origins of Radical Islamism* (New York, NY: Columbia University, 2010), 76.
[35] Davis, 110-1.
[36] Suha Taji-Farouki and Basheer M. Nafi, eds., *Islamic Thought in the Twentieth Century* (London, UK: I.B. Tauris, 2004), 6-7.
[37] Cragg, *Counsels*, 68.

Hasan Al-Banna and the Muslim Brotherhood

The Muslim Brotherhood's founder, Hasan al-Banna (1906-1949), was born in a small town some 90 miles from Cairo. His father, the local *imam*, was educated at al-Azhar when it was under the direction of Muhammad Abduh. In addition to his religious duties, al-Banna's father repaired watches.[38] Early in his life, al-Banna engaged in pious activities, one scholar noting,

> At the age of twelve, Banna was enrolled in a primary school, where he quickly joined the first of the many religious societies ... the Society for Moral Behaviour, the purpose of which was to sensitize its members to moral offences. A system of increasingly burdensome fines was levied on all members who cursed their fellows and their families or cursed in the name of religion. Within a short time, Banna became the leader of the society.[39]

He was also the secretary (at age 13) of the Hasafiyya Society for Charity, which promoted Islamic morality and resisted the efforts of local Christian missionaries.[40]

Al-Banna was trained as a teacher, and his first assignment was in a town near the Suez Canal. He noted, first, the opulence of the homes of the European employees of the Suez Canal compared to Egyptian workers and, second, the British military bases which were a constant reminder of Egypt's subordination.[41] Al-Banna considered materialism to be the driver of modern Western civilization[42] and the cause

---

[38] Richard P. Mitchell, *The Society of the Muslim Brothers* (New York, NY: Oxford University, 1993), 1.
[39] Ibid., 2.
[40] Ibid.
[41] Calvert, 81.
[42] Abu-Rabi, 81.

of Muslims departing from the tenets of their faith.[43] As a pious Muslim, he also "decried the presence of Christian and Bahai missionaries who, in his view, conspired to separate Egyptians from the Islamic source of their moral strength."[44]

Al-Banna's motivation in founding the Muslim Brotherhood in 1928 was to "go beyond reformist theory to political action."[45] Such action, however, could only occur "after the stages of propaganda, education, preaching, selection, formation, and mobilization."[46] Ideologically, al-Banna was situated between such early reformers as al-Afghani and Abduh, and the later Islamists who favored more revolutionary methods. One scholar stated that it is incorrect to view al-Banna as sanctioning Islamic terrorism since he opposed terrorism when he asked for the death sentence for the Muslim Brothers who committed two political murders in Cairo in 1948.[47]

The Muslim Brotherhood advocated a series of reform programs in order to guide the government.[48] Al-Banna stated that "any good economic system is welcomed by Islam" and noted that "Islamic jurisprudence is filled with rules for financial transactions, and it has given them in such minute detail as to obviate further elaboration."[49] Of the six foundational premises advanced by the Brotherhood, two related to economics. There must be "economic equality of resources and opportunity," a higher standard of living, and

---

[43] Mitchell, 6.

[44] Calvert, 82.

[45] Olivier Carré, *Mysticism and Politics: A Critical Reading of* Fī Ẓilāl al-Qur'an *by Sayyid Qutb (1906-1966)*, trans. Carol Artigues, rvd. W. Shepard (Leiden, Netherlands: E. J. Brill, 2003), 14.

[46] Roxanne L. Euben and Muhammad Qasim Zaman, eds., *Princeton Readings in Islamist Thought: Texts and Contexts from al-Banna to Bin Laden* (Princeton, NJ: Princeton University, 2009), 54.

[47] Carré, 14.

[48] Mitchell, 260.

[49] Hasan al-Banna, "Toward the Light," in *Princeton Readings in Islamist Thought: Texts and Contexts from al-Banna to Bin Laden,* eds. Roxanne L. Euben and Muhammad Qasim Zaman (Princeton, NJ: Princeton University, 2009), 67.

a struggle against poverty.⁵⁰ Among the Brotherhood's specific demands were the following:

> Usury in all its forms should be abolished.... The natural resources of the country should be nationalized.... The nation should be industrialized "immediately," with emphasis on industries dependent on "local raw materials" and on "war industries."... The National Bank of Egypt (*al-bank al-ahli*) should be nationalized.... Taxes should be reformed so that a levy of *zakat* was applied "progressively" on capital as well as profit.... Land reform should be pursued vigorously.... Labour legislation should be reviewed with an eye to reforms which (a) guarantee to all workers (including "farm labourers") security against unemployment, injury, illness, old age, and death; (b) compel labour organization; and (c) assure the wage-earner of a fair share of increased productivity.... Finally, every worker must be guaranteed "social security."⁵¹

The Muslim Brotherhood also founded small businesses. Such businesses included:

> The Muslim Brothers' Company for Spinning and Weaving.... In Alexandria, the Society founded the Company for Commercial and Engineering Works... which concerned itself with the construction of buildings, the production of construction materials, and the training of workers in such trades as plumbing, electricity, and carpentry.⁵²

---

⁵⁰Cragg, *Counsels*, 117-8.
⁵¹Mitchell, 272-4.
⁵²Ibid., 276-7.

These businesses were established in an effort to develop the national economy and destroy foreign control over the economy, which included the work of missionaries who, in the Brotherhood's perception, were gaining converts for economic reasons.[53]

One of the legacies of Hasan al-Banna was that "Political Islam emerged from within the intellectual crucible of the reformist project . . . [which] prepared the ground for the laymen, the modern Muslim intellectual, and the Muslim professional to speak on behalf of Islam."[54] Among the foremost of these spokesmen was Sayyid Qutb.

Sayyid Qutb—Beacon of Modern Islamism

Sayyid Qutb is regarded by many scholars as "the most significant thinker of Islamic resurgence in the modern Arab world."[55] He was born in 1906 in a town in southern Egypt near Asyut.[56] His father was a local landowner, regarded as pious and educated, and a member of the Nationalist Party.[57] In the years prior to World War I, the family was forced to sell portions of their estate, including their home, to pay debts. Qutb later wrote that the family "lived in fear of financial ruin and the possibility that it might have to join the growing throngs of destitute peasants."[58] Qutb was sent to Cairo in 1920 for his secondary education, after which he studied to be a teacher. During the 1920s, "he was a partisan of the *Wafd*, the party particularly associated with

---

[53] Ibid., 274.
[54] Basheer M. Nafi, "The Rise of Islamic Reformist Thought and its Challenge to Traditional Islam," in *Islamic Thought in the Twentieth Century*, eds. Suha Taji-Farouki and Basheer M. Nafi (London, UK: I.B. Tauris, 2004), 53.
[55] Abu-Rabi, 93.
[56] *The Encyclopaedia of Islam*, CD-ROM ed., s.v. "Sayyid Kutb."
[57] Shepard, *Sayyid Qutb*, xiv.
[58] Calvert, 43.

independence, parliamentary government, and the nationalist cause.[59]

By the 1940s, Qutb had turned against western influence and ideas as a result of British policies during World War II and the creation of the state of Israel.[60] As a result of political corruption, economic and social inequality, and ongoing European imperialism, Qutb wrote the first edition of *Social Justice in Islam* in 1948.[61] Ideologically, during the post-war period, he was moving closer to the Muslim Brotherhood, although "he still maintained his independence as an intellectual and was still prepared to cooperate with people of a more secularist orientation for common social and political goals."[62]

Although the Ministry of Education had employed him for many years, his criticism of the Egyptian government ultimately led to his being sent to the United States from 1948 to 1950 on a study tour. This trip left him with strong impressions. For example, "*In the Shade of the Qur'an*, he tells how his attention was drawn to a Christian missionary who proselytized among the ship's passengers and dared even to direct his attention at Qutb and five other Muslim passengers aboard."[63] Qutb chaffed at the West's "frantic pace [which] confirmed his preconception of the West's hard-nosed, materialistic ways."[64] He was also unnerved about "the 'dizzying speed' and 'abruptness' by which Egyptians adopted Western mores and practices of consumption. . . . [He maintained] the fast pace of Western style modernity . . . caught Egyptians off guard."[65] As opposed to the individualism and materialism of the West, Qutb saw the ethical world of Islam as the antidote. When he returned

---

[59] Shepard, xv.
[60] Yvonne Y. Haddad, "Sayyid Qutb: Idealogue of Islamic Revival," in *Voices of Resurgent Islam*, ed. John L. Esposito (New York, NY: Oxford University, 1983), 69.
[61] Shepard, xvi.
[62] Ibid.
[63] Calvert, 141.
[64] Ibid., 143.
[65] Ibid., 89.

from the U.S., his ties to the Muslim Brotherhood increased, and he became one of its leaders.

Beginning in 1955, Qutb was imprisoned for nine years by the Nasser regime, along with many other Muslim Brotherhood members. It was during his prison years that he completed his massive commentary on the Qur'an, titled *In the Shade of the Qur'an*, which has, in the words of one scholar, become

> [an] icon-text . . . for the militant Islamic movements not only in the Arab world but also in Turkey, eastern Europe and central Asia, in Iran and Afghanistan, in Pakistan and in India, also in Indonesia, in sub-Saharan Africa and, finally, in the Muslim Diaspora of Europe and America.[66]

Like al-Banna, Qutb viewed Islam as a *nizam* (an integrated system) with social, economic, and political dimensions.[67] For the purposes of this book, however, only Qutb's views regarding the economy—specifically his views on wealth and possessions, trade and commerce, and usury and capitalism—will be discussed. Special attention will be focused on *Social Justice in Islam* and *In the Shade of the Qur'an*. Qutb revised the former six times between 1948 and 1964, with each subsequent edition adopting a more radical Islamist position.[68] This book will focus on the final edition.

Sayyid Qutb on Wealth and Possessions

Qutb contended that Muslims have the right to individually own property, which included the right to preserve and defend it "against any kind of theft, robbery,

---

[66]Carré, 13.
[67]Calvert, 130.
[68]Shepherd, xviii.

looting or fraud, or confiscation unless for a public need with adequate and genuine compensation. It [Islam] also sets deterrent punishments to assure all this."[69] By allowing private ownership, Islam is in accord with human nature since private ownership balances effort and reward. Moreover, Qutb wrote that private ownership

> leads to self-respect, honor, independence and the development of individual personalities so that they are suited to be trustworthy agents for this religion, standing against wrong doing, calling the ruler to account and admonishing him without the fear of having their livelihood cut off if it is in his hands.[70]

He acknowledged that possessions would be unequal since they would be acquired "according to the diversity of individual capacities, circumstances, types of social relationships, etc."[71]

Private property, however, carries with it problems. In his commentary on Qur'an 83:1-6, Qutb noted that, while the Meccans were very rich, they were completely unscrupulous and monopolistic in their business affairs.[72] The proper management of wealth was, for Qutb, the essence of social justice.[73] Islam's restrictions on the use of wealth were at odds with the view of private property espoused by capitalism.[74] Accordingly, true Muslims must maintain a radical detachment to possessions, knowing that "the reward here on earth does not consist of property, wealth or luxury, but of serene inner joy already here on earth."[75] He preached that extremes in wealth were to be discouraged, but rather

---

[69]Ibid., 125.
[70]Ibid., 127.
[71]Carré, 207.
[72]Sayyid Qutb, *In the Shade of the Qur'ān*, vol. 18, trans. Adil Salahi (Leicestershire, UK: The Islamic Foundation, 2004), 109-10.
[73]Shepard, *Sayyid Qutb*, 123.
[74]Ibid., 130.
[75]Carré, 206.

"Islam aims for a golden mean. Opulence and destitution are equally proscribed."[76]

Qutb insisted that Islam was a comprehensive social system that guaranteed each person a livelihood.[77] Furthermore, he maintained that "Capital in Islam should not be restricted to the rich . . . thus if it appears to be in the public interest and in order to establish justice, the government may appropriate from the rich not only their profits but part of their capital."[78] The institutional mechanisms for redistributing income were *zakat, sadaqa*, and inheritance.[79] While the amount of *zakat* was determined in the Qur'an and *hadith*, the amount of *sadaqa* was freely determined, although it was obligatory as part of one's "spending for God (*infāq*)."[80] The Qur'an's formulas for distributing the wealth of a Muslim upon death between a broad group of family members was, for Qutb, a key Qur'anic element in Islam's economic system.[81] He vested the right of collecting these amounts, with the *imam*.[82]

Sayyid Qutb on Trade and Commerce

Qutb placed work at the foundation of the economy, regarding it as the only legitimate basis for wages and recompense. The wealth of those who do not work was unlawful. According to one scholar, Qutb maintained,

> Islam is the enemy of idleness that proceeds from laziness. . . . Those who beg and are capable [of work] . . . on the Day of Judgment they will have no flesh on

---

[76] James Toth, *Sayyid Qutb: The Life and Legacy of a Radical Islamic Intellectual* (New York, NY: Oxford University, 2013), 182.
[77] Haddad, 92.
[78] Ibid.
[79] Toth, 184.
[80] Carré, 211.
[81] Ibid., 210.
[82] Ibid., 215.

their faces! Islam is the enemy of idleness in the name of worship and religion. Worship is not an occupation of life. It has but its appointed time. The Quran says: When the Salat [daily ritual prayer] is done, disperse in the earth and seek the benefit of God.[83]

Qutb affirmed the varieties of work mentioned in the Qur'an and the *hadith*, including wage labor. Islam demands that every worker "do his work well and thoroughly . . . for dishonesty and negligence in work are signs of a corrupt conscience and a slack spirit."[84] He acknowledged that "People's livelihood and provisions in this present life are influenced by their individual talents, life circumstances and social relations," with the result that "some people will inevitably be made to serve others."[85] For him there was no place for religious asceticism; rather, such ascetics "need to attend to their work and earn their living. This is essential."[86] Employers should respect workers since they are part of the Muslim community. These employers demonstrate sound leadership when they consult their workers.[87]

Qutb also includes commerce as an approved type of work, which he defines as the "numerous stages that may be undertaken as a whole by one individual or by a number of individuals . . . [where] the final goal is to transfer raw or manufactured goods from one hand to another, thus increasing its utilization as raw material or as commodity."[88] In particular, the work of a merchant is useful and merits remuneration since buying and selling is "subjected to the risks of profits and losses, according to climatic conditions

---

[83]Haddad, 92-3.
[84]Shepard, *Sayyid Qutb*, 139.
[85]Sayyid Qutb, *In the Shade of the Qur'ān*, vol. 15, trans. Adil Salahi (Leicestershire, UK: The Islamic Foundation, 2008), 237.
[86]Sayyid Qutb, *In the Shade of the Qur'ān*, vol. 17, trans. Adil Salahi (Leicestershire, UK: The Islamic Foundation, 2009), 347.
[87]Sayyid Qutb, *In the Shade of the Qur'ān*, vol. 15, 193-4.
[88]Shepard, *Sayyid Qutb*, 137.

and prices, and according to the skill and effort of the seller and buyer."[89]

Qutb accepted that traders could make profits since trade "is a service to both producer and consumer, which results in a profit gained by the trader. Skill and effort are essential for the gain to be made."[90] Commerce could be carried out through a variety of partnership forms where risks are shared, and through "companies financed with shares (*saham*), which also involves the sharing of risks; [and] through bank deposits without fixed interest and with the certainty that banks will finance developing industrial and commercial enterprises."[91]

Sayyid Qutb on Usury and Capitalism

Qutb condemned usury in the strongest possible terms, saying that someone who engages in usury "greedily laps and avidly sucks up the sweat and blood of others while he sits and does nothing."[92] And there is no distinction between a moderate rate of interest and usury since the later "applies to all that exceeds the principal amount, without qualification."[93] Money can be lent to the poor; but "loans should be interest-free and repayment should be just for the full principal."[94] In the context of business, he "recommended that where loans are for productive purposes, then repayment should be based on the profit or loss of the enterprise. Such arrangements maintain harmony between the creditor and the borrower."[95]

---

[89] Carré, 218.
[90] Sayyid Qutb, *In the Shade of the Qur'ān*, vol. 3, trans. Adil Salahi and Ashur Shamis (Leicestershire, UK: The Islamic Foundation, 2001), 115.
[91] Carré, 219.
[92] Shepard, *Sayyid Qutb*, 146.
[93] Sayyid Qutb, *In the Shade of the Qur'ān*, vol. 2, trans. Adil Salahi and Ashur Shamis (Leicestershire, UK: The Islamic Foundation, 2000), 211.
[94] Toth, 188.
[95] Ibid.

Qutb also rejected the argument that money used to finance the ongoing purchase and sale of merchandise was not usurious because it facilitated commerce. He countered that "There can be no casuistic compromises. It is simply necessary to prevent the growth of industry and commerce from being solely determined by the profits of financiers, and not by people's needs."[96] Further, he linked usury with mankind's various woes when he wrote,

> Only today, in the light of widespread human suffering, can we appreciate the reasons behind the Qur'ān's determined onslaught on this evil practice [usury].... We can see what havoc and what misery a usury-based financial system has brought upon the world, as well as the insidious destruction it has caused to the morals, religion, health and economic strength of modern society.[97]

In *The Shade of the Qur'an*, one scholar noted that Qutb attempted to persuade Muslim entrepreneurs and financiers that capitalism, speculative profits and Western-type banking (with interest) were not pre-conditions to a modern economy and were the opposite of an Islamic system.[98]

Qutb was critical of the "invisible hand" that governed marketplace transactions, as articulated by Adam Smith in *The Wealth of Nations*. He claimed that the free market's invisible hand "in Egypt and elsewhere resulted in a class of capitalist freebooters that had no regard for the human cost of its economic activity."[99] One scholar noted that, "In essence, Qutb took the Hidden Hand of Adam Smith's *Wealth of Nations* and claimed that, instead, it is the hand of God that

---

[96]Carré, 217-8.
[97]Sayyid Qutb, *In the Shade of the Qur'ān*, vol. 1, rvd. ed., trans. Adil Salahi and Ashur Shamis (Leicestershire, UK: The Islamic Foundation, 2003), 451.
[98]Carré, 225.
[99]Calvert, 134.

regulates the economy . . . [through] moral principles stated in the Qur'an and . . . the *shari'a*."[100]

The Rise of Islamic Economics

Most of the Islamic reformers, whether they were modernist or Islamist, were primarily concerned about political issues rather than economics.[101] Islamist thought on the topic of economics, however, began to receive focused attention in the writings of Sayyid Abul-Ala Mawdudi (1903-1979). He was a Muslim journalist and writer who lived in India and wrote extensively at the time the state of Pakistan was formed. According to one scholar, he was, among Islamic authors, very popular and highly respected.[102] Muslims in India were in the minority, and being such, Mawdudi and other Indian Muslim economists of the 1940s were driven to defend Islamic society against encroachment of foreign influences.[103] Like Qutb, Mawdudi saw Islam as a complete way of life and popularized the phrase "Islamic economics."[104]

Mawdudi's views on economics can be summarized as follows. As to the private ownership of property, he affirmed that from time immemorial people have owned land and that "the Qurān did not forbid this ownership, issue a decree to check this practice, promulgate a law to replace the existing situation, or even make a critical reference to this

---

[100]Toth, 179.

[101]Rodney Wilson, "The Development of Islamic Economics: Theory and Practice," in *Islamic Thought in the Twentieth Century*, eds. Suha Taji-Farouki and Basheer M. Nafi (London, UK: I.B. Tauris, 2004), 195.

[102]Charles J. Adams, "Mawdudi and the Islamic State," in *Voices of Resurgent Islam*, ed. John L. Esposito (New York, NY: Oxford University, 1983), 99.

[103]Timur Kuran, *Islam and Mammon: The Economic Predicaments of Islamism* (Princeton, NJ: Princeton University, 2004), 39.

[104]Wilson, *Islamic Economics*, 196.

common practice."[105] Furthermore, *sharia* law gave Muslims the right to use their property for subsistence and to pursue lawful vocations.[106] He acknowledged that "under the Divine Dispensation, there is equity [in opportunity] but not necessarily equality in the distribution of His bounties."[107]

Mawdudi held that one's right to property and income was not unlimited, in that Islam based mankind's economic life "on the twin concepts of justice and fairplay."[108] He noted that other economic systems, like capitalism, do not have such limits, which allows for the rise of "exploitative people that includes bankers, brokers, and the heads of industrial and commercial cartels and monopolies."[109] He also noted that communism was no better since it allowed for "the emergence of one Super Capitalist out of the ashes of many large and small ones . . . who is simultaneously the Czar as well as the capital baron."[110]

In contrast, Islam provided for a redistribution of wealth through the 2.5 percent annual *zakat* tax, which provided basic necessities to every person in a Muslim society.[111] In addition, Islam's inheritance laws prevented wealth from being hoarded, in that, a decedent's heirs receive predetermined shares of the decedent's assets.[112] To finally break the backbone of the capitalist system and the human penchant toward materialism, Mawdudi argued interest should be prohibited.[113]

Building on Mawdudi's economic concepts, numerous Muslim economists who had been educated in Western neoclassical economics, published works on Islamic

---

[105] Sayyid Abul Aʻlā Mawdūdī, *First Principles of Islamic Economics*, ed. Khurshid Ahmad, trans. Ahmad Imam Shafaq Hashemi (Leicestershire, UK: The Islamic Foundation, 2011), 120.
[106] Ibid., xxxix.
[107] Ibid., xli.
[108] Ibid., xxxix.
[109] Ibid., 13.
[110] Ibid., 15.
[111] Ibid., xlii.
[112] Ibid., 21.
[113] Ibid., 19.

economics beginning in the mid-1960s.[114] "This new generation, all of whom were born in the 1930s, included amongst its most notable contributors Muhammad Abdul Mannan, Muhammad Nejatullah Siddiqi, M. Umer Chapra, and Syed Nawab Naqvi."[115] Their writings interacted not only with the forms of capitalism with which they were familiar, but also with socialist thought. This was caused "by the worldwide economic crisis during the thirties and forties and the increasing exposure of the Muslim mind to the Socialist doctrines, and the impact of the Russian Revolution."[116] While Islamic economics sought to distinguish itself from capitalism, communism, and socialism, it was not driven "to correct economic imbalances, injustices, or inequalities."[117] Islamic economists desired to make Islamic religious beliefs the foundation of an Islamic economic system.

M. A. Mannan (b. 1938) was the first of the Islamic economists to write an economics textbook from a Muslim perspective. He argued, "Islam has recognized all legitimate economic activities of man—activities which are consistent with the spirit of Islam. Trade, commercial partnership, co-operatives, joint-stock companies are all legitimate activities and operations."[118] He described economics as a behavioral science, "with the behavior of Muslims shaped by their religious beliefs."[119] Not dissimilar from Islamic modernists of the time, Mannan stressed that Islamic economics, although based on Islamic law, had the responsibility of applying that law through human reason.[120] In a candid statement, he described his version of Islamic economy as

---

[114] Kuran, *Islam and Mammon*, 103.
[115] Wilson, *Islamic Economics*, 197.
[116] Muhammad Nejatullah Siddiqi, *Muslim Economic Thinking: A Survey of Contemporary Literature* (Leicester, UK: The Islamic Foundation, 1981), 1.
[117] Kuran, *Islam and Mammon*, 39.
[118] M. A. Mannan, *Islamic Economics: Theory and Practice (A Comparative Study)* (Lahore, Pakistan: Sh. Muhammad Ashraf, 1983), 191.
[119] Wilson, *Islamic Economics*, 198.
[120] Mannan, 13.

"capitalistic in broad outline restricted very largely by socialistic institutions and ideas."[121]

During the mid-1970s, writings on Islamic economics began to proliferate, due largely to the rise in oil prices that produced substantial wealth in numerous Middle Eastern Muslim nations. The newly oil-rich nations of the Gulf formed the Organization of the Islamic Conference and agreed to sponsor the Islamic Development Bank. These states were sympathetic to the Islamic agenda, which enabled it to "triumph over Arab socialist philosophy and nationalist secularism."[122] One scholar chronicled the rise of Islamic economics as follows:

> In 1976, the First Islamic Conference on Islamic Economics was held in Mecca. For the first time in Islamic history, a high-level conference dealt exclusively with economic matters. Concrete steps were taken to survey the field and promote Islamic economics as an academic discipline. In 1979 King Abdul Aziz University established the International Center for Research in Islamic Economics (ICRIE) to conduct and support theoretical and applied research in various sub-fields. The number of research institutes increased throughout the 1980s and 1990s.[123]

Themes in Islamic Economics

Although Islamic economists sounded a variety of themes, I will focus on three of the most significant. The first was the claim that, if Islamic principles were applied, they would produce an economic system superior to capitalism,

---

[121] Ibid., 58.
[122] Wilson, *Islamic Economics*, 200.
[123] Ibrahim Warde, *Islamic Finance in the Global Economy*, 2nd ed. (Edinburgh, UK: Edinburgh Univ., 2010), 38.

socialism, communism, and any other "-ism." The second was that Islam's prohibition of *riba* meant all interest should be prohibited and all banking transactions should be interest-free. The third (building on the first two) posited that economic development should be distinctively Islamic. Each of these themes will be summarized and assessed in separate sections below.

The Superiority of Islamic Economics

Islamic economists sought to differentiate the Islamic economy from all others by establishing that its core ideas were different. The writing of Muhammad Nejatullah Siddiqi (b. 1931) illustrates this approach. In the opinion of one scholar, Siddiqi was "perhaps the most influential writer of the first generation of modern Islamic economists."[124] He argued that foundational to the economic philosophy of Islam was *tawhid*, which he defined as "a total commitment to the will of Allah, involving both submission and a mission to pattern human life in accordance with His will."[125] Siddiqi argued that, in Islam, "No inhibitions attach to economic enterprise" so long as the motivation for, and ends of the activity, were consistent with the will of Allah.[126] Islam's economic system rested "on three main planks: clearly specified goals, well defined moral attitudes and behaviour patterns on the part of economic agents, and specific laws, rules, and regulations enforceable by the state."[127]

Siddiqi defined the goals of the Islamic economy as including the fulfillment of both spiritual and material needs.[128] While it was appropriate for individuals to seek to fulfill such needs (indeed, this being part of "striving in the

---

[124] Wilson, *Islamic Economics*, 199.
[125] Siddiqi, *Muslim Economic Thinking*, 5.
[126] Ibid., 5-6.
[127] Ibid., 12.
[128] Ibid.

cause of Allah"), it also included meeting social ends, such as the "eradication of hunger and poverty, disease and illiteracy and mobilization of resources for strengthening the Islamic state and spreading the message of Allah."[129] On the negative side, Islam prohibited economic striving that involved

> dishonesty, fraud and deception, coercive practices, and [gambling] or usurious dealings . . . [as well as] hoarding, speculation and collusion among producers and traders against the interests of the consumers. Monopoly is also regarded as injurious to the interests of society.[130]

Syed N. H. Naqvi (b. 1935), a Muslim economist from Pakistan, wrote about Islam and economics in a similar vein as Siddiqi. He stated, "The central idea that defines Islamic economics, and which sets it apart from positive (neoclassical) economics, is its insistence on the *explicit* inclusion of an ethics *based on religion* in a unified analytical framework."[131] He maintained that Muslims' economic behavior is impacted by their belief that the Divine Presence sees their conduct.[132] He described four "ethical axioms" that represent the "Islamic vision of man in relation to himself and his social environment."[133] Like Siddiqi, Naqvi included unity (*tawhid*) but also "equilibrium, free will, and responsibility—which together form an irreducible, non-trivial set."[134] Over the course of several chapters, Naqvi translated these axioms into a set of economic hypotheses and ultimately a list of economic objectives, which included individual freedom, distributive justice, universal education,

---

[129]Ibid., 6.
[130]Ibid., 17.
[131]Syed Nawab Haider Naqvi, *Islam, Economics, and Society* (London, UK: Routledge, 2013), 14.
[132]Ibid., 15.
[133]Ibid., 26.
[134]Ibid.

economic growth, and maximization of employment generation.[135]

Some recent works of Islamic economists have argued that, "rather than some heavenly ideal, it is *falah* (best translated as 'well-being') that lies at the core of Islamic economics."[136] For example, M. Umer Chapra (b. 1933) argued that

> The goals of Islam . . . unlike those of the predominantly secularist systems of the present-day world, are not primarily materialist. They are rather based on its own concepts of human well-being (*falāh*) and good life . . . which give utmost importance to brotherhood and socio-economic justice and require a balanced satisfaction of both the material and the spiritual needs of *all* human beings.[137]

He also claimed that Islam provided "a moral filter for allocation and distribution of resources . . . that gives biting power to the goals of need-fulfillment and equitable distribution of income and wealth."[138] Islam's moral filter and accountability before God was needed to counterbalance "the urge to maximize profits [which] may lead to unfair business practices and disregard of market externalities and social costs."[139]

Although varying in their descriptions of the core of Islamic economics and its ethics, Muslim economists uniformly criticized other economic systems, particularly capitalism. Their attacks on capitalism were directed at its perceived materialism and unrestricted private ownership of

---

[135] Ibid., 88-94 passim.
[136] Warde, 43.
[137] M. Umer Chapra, *Islam and the Economic Challenge* (Leicester, UK: The Islamic Foundation, 1992), 6.
[138] Ibid., 7.
[139] Ibid., 42.

wealth, and at its injustice. One of the earliest economists characterized capitalism as signifying "a religion of money or Dollar Dictatorship."[140] Another one noted that materialism drives capitalism's commercial culture far beyond available resources.[141] Mannan criticized capitalism for its "unrestricted private ownership of the means of production, the motive force of which is private profit. The capitalist's motto is 'Everything for himself and devil take the hindmost.'"[142]

Muslim economists also rejected the argument that free markets in capitalism were efficient and equitable since they created "*Pareto optimums*" (i.e., results where no one can be made better off without someone else being made less well off). The outcomes of efficiency and equity were insufficient in that they "do not have a direct relationship with the objectives of removing poverty, fulfilling needs, and reducing inequalities of income and wealth."[143] While the economists did concede that the market system resulted in the prosperity of Western economies, they argued that

> inequalities of income and wealth have in fact increased. There has also been a substantial degree of economic instability and unemployment which have added further to the miseries of the poor. This indicates that both efficiency and equity have remained elusive in spite of the rapid development and the enormous growth in wealth.[144]

As described in Chapters 2 and 3, the Qur'an and the *hadith* gave high status to the honest merchant buying and selling in the marketplace. Thus, for a Muslim, the solution to market-driven inequalities was not in eliminating free

---
[140] Mannan, 32.
[141] Chapra, 22.
[142] Mannan, 57.
[143] Chapra, 19.
[144] Ibid., 32.

markets but in redistributing income and assets. A primary vehicle for accomplishing such redistribution in the Islamic economic system was the *zakat* tax. As Mannan noted, "Zakāt is the strong blow at the root of Capitalism."[145]

At the surface, Muslims found attractive elements in socialism since "It explicitly addresses the problems of an equitable distribution of income and wealth, deals directly with the phenomena of poverty and hunger, and shows a deep sense of responsibility to the least privileged in the society."[146] Under the surface, however, socialism severely limits individual freedom and private property—both of which run opposite to the tenets of Islam.[147] Mawdudi argued that the powerful role of the State and its "master-planners" would ultimately lead to a "slaughter of the self" and a "ruthless regimentation . . . [that would] put an end to the natural growth of civilization . . . eventually leading to the freezing of human potential and a severe mental and moral degeneration."[148]

In the final analysis, Islamic economists saw the Islamic economic system, versus capitalism and socialism, as the "Middle Way assimilating the good points in both the systems . . . [yet] free from the imbalances from which they suffer."[149] One Muslim scholar summarized the system as follows:

- under capitalism, human beings are selfish; under the Islamic economic system, human beings are selfish as well as altruistic;
- under capitalism, materialism is the supreme value; under the Islamic economic system, materialism should be controlled;

---

[145] Mannan, 220.
[146] Naqvi, *Islam, Economics, and Society*, 72.
[147] Ibid., 73.
[148] Mawdudi, 16-7.
[149] Siddiqi, *Muslim Economic Thinking*, 46.

- capitalism favors absolute private ownership; the Islamic economic system favors private ownership within a moral framework.[150]

Assessment of the Superiority of Islamic Economics

As has been already noted, the early Muslim economists sought to develop Islamic economics as a "distinct social science" since the basic principles of Islam, "altruism, cooperation, sacrifice, justice, fraternity, brotherhood" were not recognized in mainstream economics.[151] According to Muhammad Akram Khan,[152] this forced them "to develop a social science about a model economy that did not exist in the real world. They could not test and establish the veracity of their postulates,"[153] the result being that "most of the literature on Islamic economics is conceptual and theoretical. It is not related to real-life conditions of any Muslim country."[154] He goes so far as to say that "most of Islamic economics consists of theology on economic matters."[155] Even Naqvi, an advocate for Islamic economics, conceded,

> I tended to treat the subject in most of my writings as an Islamic economic philosophy. In doing so, I followed the practice of numerous notable thinkers and economists writing on the subject, who disregard the modern Muslim societies as real-world counterparts of Islamic economics.[156]

---

[150] Warde, 43.
[151] Muhammad Akram Khan, *What Is Wrong with Islamic Economics? Analysing the Present State and Future Agenda* (Cheltenham, UK: Edward Elgar, 2013), xiii.
[152] M.A. Khan was the Deputy Auditor General of Pakistan until 2003. Since Pakistan began to implement the principles of Islamic economics and finance in the late 1970s, his views of the actual results of Islamic economics and finance are both insightful and unique.
[153] Khan, *What Is Wrong*, 4.
[154] Ibid., 15.
[155] Ibid., 7.
[156] Naqvi, *Islam, Economics, and Society*, 21, note 2.

A related criticism focuses on Islamic economics' failure to properly consider the importance of cultural differences. Writing of Mawdudi, one Muslim scholar noted that Mawdudi's economic arguments were directed toward the universal Islamic *umma*, which was differentiated only by gender and was "supposed to transcend tribal, national, regional, and local ties. Having its own laws, values, and convictions, it is to be the individual Muslim's principal source of identity and the focus of his loyalty."[157] Kuran noted that this was an "imagined community" and that "the concept was sharply at variance with prevailing social realities. Economic relations among Muslim nations were minimal."[158]

The differing views of Islamic economics between Asian and Arab Muslims are illustrative of this point. "The Islam that spread into Southeast Asia appeared much more as a 'trader' religion and thus has a more modern character [socially progressive] . . . than it did as a reform movement within a pre-existent Arab tradition in the Middle East."[159] It was noted that Indonesia derived its five principles of civil religion (the *Panchasila*) from Islam. Yet, these five principles, identified as "belief in God, humanitarianism, national unity, democracy based on consensus, and social justice" would likely be acceptable by many Western capitalist nations.[160]

Islamic economics also doesn't appear to recognize the impact of large centralized governments. According to Khan,

> It seems that Muslim economists who delve into the romantic view of Islamic government do not have any

---

[157] Kuran, *Islam and Mammon*, 94.
[158] Ibid.
[159] William H. Swatos, "Islam and Capitalism: A Weberian Perspective on Resurgence," in *Religion and the Transformations of Capitalism: Comparative Approaches*, ed. Richard Roberts (London, UK: Routledge, 1995), 57.
[160] Ibid.

perception of the capacity and will of government functionaries in present-day Muslim societies. They have not realized properly that Muslim economies are steeped in corruption and fraud and have moved away from the pristine values of Islam.[161]

Although Islamic economics upholds the private ownership of property, empowering the State to enforce Islamic values is fraught with danger. Says Khan, "Intervention of the state machinery in private property rights will open the floodgates of coercion, abuse of authority, and bad governance."[162]

Another criticism of Islamic economists revolves around their portrayal of capitalism, which they often described as diametrically opposed to certain Islamic core values (e.g., self-interest, as described by Adam Smith in *Wealth of Nations*, being equated with selfishness). Yet within capitalist economies, there is much evidence that altruism is prized, whereas selfishness is not, and that Islamic "concepts of cooperation, brotherhood, and fraternity are not alien to conventional [capitalist] economics."[163] Ironically, several scholars have noted the similarities that exist historically between the Islamic economic system and capitalism. For example, some of the key commercial instruments used between the 11th and 13th centuries in trade between Muslims and Europeans mirrored each other.[164]

Perhaps the strongest critique of Islamic economics relates to the efficacy not only of one of the key elements of Islamic economics, but also of one of Islam's five pillars—the *zakat*. The actual impact of the *zakat* collection and redistribution has been disappointing. For instance, in Malaysia, its impact on the economy has been "negligible";

---

[161]Khan, *What Is Wrong*, 22.
[162]Ibid., 104.
[163]Ibid., 31.
[164]Heck, *Arab Roots of Capitalism*, 235-254 passim.

and "Even those sympathetic to the project have been obliged to acknowledge that it has had adverse outcomes as far as the peasantry is concerned, channeling resources away from the under-funded countryside towards the heavily subsidized cities."[165] In Pakistan, *zakat* revenues were a negligible percent of GDP many years after that nation made it legally enforceable; and in Iran it had "no measurable impact."[166]

If *zakat* greatly benefits Muslim societies and reduces economic inequities, why is it not more prevalent in Muslim-majority nations? A partial answer may lie in the fact that, if the *zakat* tax of 2.5 percent were assessed annually against all non-productive assets (including cash in savings accounts, precious metals, or other stores of value), it would amount to confiscation of these assets over a Muslim's lifetime. This is particularly true if Muslims are forced to use Islamic banks that pay no interest.

Interest-Free Banking

What began in the mid-20th century as a call for Islamic economics in reality shifted in the direction of Islamic finance. One Muslim economist recently noted, "Islamic finance was originally a subset of Islamic economics but now sits in the driver's seat. It has practically taken over the whole enterprise of Islamic economics."[167] Islamic finance, in turn, is centered on the elimination of *riba* from the economy. The debate over what constitutes *riba* has been the cause of much controversy since the early 1900s. In the first section below, the traditional interpretation of *riba* will be contrasted with the differing views of the modernists and the

---

[165] Charles Tripp, *Islam and the Moral Economy: The Challenge of Capitalism* (Cambridge, UK: Cambridge University, 2006), 125.
[166] Ibid.
[167] Khan, *What Is Wrong*, 12.

Islamists. Afterwards, the impact of these disparate interpretations of *riba* on Islamic banking will be addressed.

Islamic Interpretations of Riba

As was discussed in Chapter 2—"Business in the Qur'an," *riba* (meaning "increase"[168]) was strictly forbidden. Some scholars have noted that the origin of this prohibition has its roots in the pre-Islamic Meccan period when traders with unused capital (e.g., between caravan journeys) would enter into loan agreements with other traders.[169] The practice of "doubling" was often associated with these loans, whereby the creditors would demand that the debtors either pay their debt or extend it, in which case the debt would be doubled.[170] One scholar characterized such a practices as "loan-sharking."[171]

In addition to Qur'anic prohibitions of *riba,* "Muhammad also forbade *riba*, which includes both usury and interest. He 'cursed the accepter of interest and its payer, and one who records it, and the two witnesses;' and he said: 'They are all equal.'"[172] There are also numerous passages in the *hadith* that link the prohibition of *riba* to sales of various items, including "gold, silver, wheat, barley, dates, and salt."[173] Such passages have fueled ongoing debates among modern Islamic scholars as to whether *riba* is really meant to address commercial transactions and, if so, to what extent.

---

[168] *The Encyclopaedia of Islam*, CD-ROM ed., s.v. *"Riba."*

[169] Emad H. Khalil, "An Overview of the Sharia'a Prohibition of *Riba,*" in *Interest in Islamic Economics: Understanding Riba*, ed. Abdulkader Thomas (London, UK: Routledge, 2006), 57.

[170] Frank E. Vogel and Samuel L. Hayes, *Islamic Law and Finance: Religion, Risk, and Return* (The Hague: Kluwer Law International, 1998), 72-3.

[171] Saqib Rashid, "Islamic Finance and Venture Capital: A Practical Approach," in *Islamic Perspectives on Wealth Creation*, eds. Munawar Iqbal and Rodney Wilson (Edinburgh, UK: Edinburgh University, 2005), 231.

[172] Ram Swarup, *Understanding the Hadith: The Sacred Traditions of Islam* (Amherst, NY: Prometheus Books, 2002), 90.

[173] Khalil, 56.

There was also in Islam a prohibition against "idle gain." "Islam does not allow gain from economic activity unless it is also subject to a loss; the legal guarantee of at least nominal interest would be viewed as a sure gain.... In Islam wealth should be accumulated through personal activity and hard work."[174] An example of this comes from Muhammad when he

> gave Abyad ibn Hammal permission to mine salt at Maarib in the Hijaz, which looked at first sight the best way of exploiting this resource. When Muhammad was later advised how easy it was to extract the salt, he withdrew the franchise given to Hammal. The income Hammal was receiving was simply of a rentier nature, rather than because of any work which he had put into the mine.[175]

The traditional interpretation of *riba*, which included interest as part of *riba*, also relied on "the impermissibility of making money from money... because it involved no effort, and it was unjust because it did not share the risk (of profit or lack of profit) equally between the creditor and the debtor."[176] From the traditional viewpoint, this unequal division of risk was tantamount to gambling, which was prohibited as *"bay' al-gharar* (the sale of *gharar*)... [or the] unbundled and unnecessary sale of risk."[177] Another scholar noted, "Riba affords an extreme case of gharar."[178]

---

[174] John Thomas Cummings, Hossein Askari, and Ahmad Mustafa, "Islam and Modern Economic Change," in *Islam and Development: Religion and Sociopolitical Change*, ed. John L. Esposito (Syracuse, NY: Syracuse University, 1980), 32.
[175] R. Wilson, "Islam and Economic Development," in *Islam in the Modern World*, eds. Denis MacEoin and Ahmed Al-Shahi (New York, NY: St. Martin's Press, 1983), 121.
[176] Tripp, 132.
[177] Mahmoud A. El-Gamal, *Islamic Finance: Law, Economics, and Practice* (Cambridge, UK: Cambridge University, 2006), 60.
[178] Vogel, 84.

The Egyptian modernist, Muhammad Abduh, took a highly controversial position when he redefined the Islamic prohibition against *riba*. In his capacity as the *mufti* of Egypt, he issued a *fatwa* that "found ways to show that under the religious law savings banks and the drawing of dividends were admissible in Islamic society."[179] Further, Abduh distinguished between *riba* (which was prohibited) and interest. His *fatwa* advanced the notion "that the benefits of interest were permissible under Islam . . . at least among large segments of the upper class." This resulted in the Egyptian government opening the Post Office Savings Bank in 1901, "which sought to attract the savings of white collar workers and small cultivators . . . [and] to protect small landowners from usurers."[180]

Abduh's *fatwa* allowing interest also made possible the founding of Bank Misr (discussed in more detail later in this chapter). His disciple, Rashid Rida, sought to dispel the unease over Abduh's *fatwa* by claiming that funds raised by the Post Office Savings Bank would be used for small investments in risk-sharing partnerships that would benefit both the depositor and the Islamic community. Rida also reminded the people that Abduh fiercely condemned interest charged by banks in Egypt.[181]

Some 89 years after Abduh, the payment of interest by the Egyptian government on national and post office savings accounts was defended by the Deputy Prime Minister for Economic Affairs using arguments similar to Abduh's.[182] In 1989, the Grand Mufti of Egypt, Shaikh Tantawi, issued a *fatwa* that "declared legal the interest-bearing bonds issued by the Egyptian government and underwritten by Egyptian banks.[183] In the 1990s, Tantawi extended his position on the legality of interest to certain types of deposits at commercial

---

[179]Goldziher, *Introduction to Islamic Theology and Law*, 235.
[180]Davis, 72.
[181]Tripp, 127.
[182]Ibid., 128-9.
[183]Ibid., 129.

banks.[184] He considered that nothing in the Qur'an or the *hadith* "prohibits the pre-fixing of the rate of return, as long as it occurs with mutual consent of the parties."[185] Muslim intellectuals, such as Fazlur Rahman (1919-1988), argued that *riba* only applied to exorbitant increases as he made his case for to permit interest on commercial loans.[186] Others argued that interest was permissible if derived from non-Muslim countries (*Dar al-Harb*) since this would strengthen Muslims (*Dar al-Islam*).[187] And a further argument for interest was that "income from interest could be accepted, but that it should be 'purified,' that is, earmarked for charitable purposes."[188]

However, several groups have opposed the modernist interpretation of *riba*. As noted earlier in this chapter, Islamists like the Muslim Brotherhood and Sayyid Qutb have opposed interest, as have Islamic scholars at Al-Azhar. One such scholar wrote that interest "is the disruptive daughter of the mother capitalism."[189] And many Islamic jurists likewise remain opposed to interest. The Fiqh Academy of the Organization of Islamic Conference in 1986 stated, "There is complete unanimity among all schools of thought in Islam that the term *riba* stands for interest in all its types and forms."[190] Beginning in the late 1940s, Islamic economists have also argued that interest was prohibited in Islam and that banking should only be done on the basis of profit-sharing.[191] One such economist, while recognizing the concept of a return on capital, noted that capital had been divided into physical capital (buildings, equipment, etc.) and finance capital. He refused to recognize the legitimacy of a

---

[184] Ibid., 130.
[185] Khan, *What Is Wrong*, 175.
[186] Ibid., 176.
[187] Warde, 46-7.
[188] Ibid., 47.
[189] Tripp, 133.
[190] Ibid., 131.
[191] Siddiqi, *Muslim Economic Thinking*, 29-30.

return on finance capital since it wasn't a real factor of production.¹⁹² He further implied that the bifurcation of capital was part of a Jewish plan to thrive on money-lending.¹⁹³

The debate over whether interest is included in *ribā* remains unsettled among scholars. It has been observed, "Muslim scholars have never seriously and dispassionately discussed the three basic and inter-related questions. What is *ribā*? What is interest? Are *ribā* and interest co-equal or synonymous?"¹⁹⁴ Challengers of the position that *ribā* includes all forms of interest have also noted that "many learned scholars—notably M.A.S. Abdel Haleem and Arthur J. Arberry—in translating the Qur'ān from Arabic to English have translated *ribā* to mean usury, not normal interest."¹⁹⁵ In addition, "Muhammad himself sent Abu Bakr to the Qainuqa tribe of Medina with a message bidding them 'to lend to God at good interest,' using the very words of the Qur'ān, 'to lend to God a goodly loan' 5:12."¹⁹⁶ The camp that distinguishes *ribā* from interest also highlights the difference between the moneylenders of the 7th century and the banking institutions of today, which are merely intermediaries acting as custodians for depositors.¹⁹⁷

Islamic Banking and Finance

For much of Islam's history, the financing of trade and commerce was conducted by moneychangers, who were

---

¹⁹²Mohammad Uzair, *Interest-Free Banking* (New Delhi, India: Kitab Bhavan, 2000), 4.
¹⁹³Ibid., 9.
¹⁹⁴Aqdas Ali Kazmi, "A Window to the Unexplained: The Mythology of Islamic Banking is Being Propagated as a New Science While the Real Questions About *Riba* Remain Largely Unaddressed," *Hamdard Islamicus* 29, no. 3 (July-September 2006): 108-109.
¹⁹⁵Muhammad Saleem, *Islamic Banking—A $300 Billion Deception: Observations and Arguments on Ribā (Interest or Usury), Islamic Banking Practices, Venture Capital and Enlightenment* (np: Xlibris, 2005), 12.
¹⁹⁶Swarup, 90.
¹⁹⁷Saleem, 47.

located in "the majority of cities and towns in the Middle East with major souks or bazaars."[198] They were often related to their clients by ethnicity or religion. "In Bahrain, for example, Shia Muslims always dealt with Shia moneychangers and Sunni with their co-religionists, and the same religious loyalty was found amongst the Coptic Christians and Muslims of Cairo and the Marionite Christians and Muslims of Beirut."[199] Much of their financing activity was related to the purchase of specific goods or services, often from businesses owned by them or by family members.[200] Moneychangers were capable of providing relatively sophisticated banking services. For example, as early as the 11th century, they pioneered the use of checks for commercial purposes.[201]

In the arena of foreign-currency exchange, networks of moneychangers established direct dealings with the financial centers of Europe,[202] which allowed them to handle currencies from non-Muslim lands. While interest in foreign-exchange transactions could be hidden in the exchange rate, moneychangers did not refrain from lending money at interest. One scholar noted that they had lower costs and were often unregulated, which allowed them to extend credit on more favorable terms.[203] The "fairness" of such credit terms was clearly relative since, in Egypt, the moneylenders (frequently Greek) were widely regarded as charging usurious interest in connection with their loans to landowners.[204] Even today, moneychangers "continue to

---

[198]Rodney Wilson, *Banking and Finance in the Arab Middle East* (New York, NY: St. Martin's, 1983), 7.
[199]Ibid., 8.
[200]Ibid., 16.
[201]Sami Hassan Homoud, *Islamic Banking: The Adaptation of Banking Practice to Conform with Islamic Law* (London, UK: Arabian Information, 1985), 22.
[202]Wilson, *Banking and Finance*, 18.
[203]Ibid., 15.
[204]Ibid., 21.

serve a wider section of [Arab] society than the banks, which tend to cater for the middle and upper classes only."[205]

Some of the first commercial banks in Muslim nations were established in Egypt in the 19th century. They were foreign owned and lent money to members of the royal family for modernization projects and to large landowners. During the time of British rule, commercial banking was centered in Alexandria and Port Said:

> [The residents of Alexandria] regarded themselves as belonging to the Mediterranean rather than the Arab world. . . . Much of the population of the city was Christian [Greek and Italian] rather than Muslim, and even many of the Arabs were either Christian immigrants from the Levant or members of the Egyptian Coptic Church. Similarly, Port Said was an international town, and most of its wealthy residents likely to use modern banking services were foreigners, normally involved with the Canal either directly or indirectly.[206]

Although some banks with local ownership emerged at the turn of the century (e.g., the National Bank of Egypt, which was founded in 1898 with 50 percent of its capital in Egyptian hands[207]), commercial banks were clearly regarded as a foreign institution.

Egypt's economy prior to World War I was marked by times of "boom and bust." Under British direction, Egypt had a thriving stock market and was viewed as "a favorite among early 20th century 'emerging markets.'"[208] The flow of capital from Europe both before and during the war ballooned the balance sheets of Egyptian banks, which, in turn, created

---

[205]Ibid., 3.
[206]Ibid., 22.
[207]Warde, 46.
[208]Ibid.

speculative price bubbles in commodities and land. In response to a crash in farmland prices in 1907, the government enacted a law preventing foreclosure on land parcels of less than five *feddans* (approximately five acres). This legislation "effectively halted the granting of secured loans to small farmers,"[209] which caused hardship for many small landowners (including Sayyid Qutb's parents), as described earlier in this chapter. In 1920, Egypt was negatively impacted by "a repatriation of [bank] deposits back to Europe . . . [and by] a dramatic fall in cotton prices, which severely cut Egypt's export earnings, and caused a sharp decline in economic activity in general."[210] All of the factors mentioned above contributed to later attacks by Egyptian-born Islamists on the Western economic system that, in their experience, caused these hardships.

Abdul Hameed Shoman (1890-1974) founded the first Arab-owned commercial bank—the Arab Bank in Jerusalem—in 1929. It emphasized loans to "small businessmen such as traders, or to those who owned small manufacturing establishments."[211] While Middle Eastern governments were uneasy "about the spread of western banking practices... most governments, until the 1950s at least, were prepared to drop any reservations they had for the sake of modernization."[212] The exception was Saudi Arabia. During the early part of the 20th century, it largely resisted the establishment of foreign-owned commercial banks and even denied an Egyptian-owned bank permission to open a branch in 1936. However, two years later it allowed two money-changing families from Jeddah to open what became the National Commercial Bank.[213] A second commercial bank—the Riyadh Bank—opened in 1957, but

---

[209] Wilson, *Banking and Finance*, 26.
[210] Ibid., 28.
[211] Ibid., 44.
[212] Ibid., 74.
[213] Ibid., 87.

through poor lending practices nearly went bankrupt until it was effectively nationalized in 1964.[214] While the Saudi government resisted commercial banks on its soil, the royal family and wealthy elites routinely exported their capital (derived from oil revenues) to Bahrain, London, or New York where they could access international rates.[215]

Sharia-Compliant Finance

One Muslim economist, citing a long list of Islamic grievances pertaining to the capitalist system, stated that "the most criticized institution is interest."[216] Another scholar noted that the Islamist attack on *riba* had become "a feature of immense symbolic resonance," particularly since the "experience of *zakat* had not justified the hopes invested in it."[217] In the quest to eliminate interest, proponents of Islamic finance sought to replace interest with a form of profit-and-loss sharing known in Islamic law as *mudarabah*. (This form of partnership was discussed in Chapter 4.) To assure Muslims that *riba* was not present, proponents advocated that *sharia* boards be established, composed of experts in Islamic law "whose opinion is sought on the acceptability of new [financial] instruments, and who conduct a religious audit of the bank's activities—as well as other features reflecting their religious status."[218] By taking these steps, Islamic finance would become *sharia*-compliant.

The call for the elimination of interest and for the establishment of an Islamic system of banking and commerce first took root in Pakistan in the 1950s.[219] An early experiment with interest-free banking was launched in the late 1950s, whereby poor Pakistani farmers could access

---

[214]Ibid., 88.
[215]Ibid., 90.
[216]Siddiqi, *Muslim Economic Thinking*, 47.
[217]Tripp, 126.
[218]Warde, 7.
[219]Wilson, *Banking and Finance*, 75.

interest-free loans financed by interest-free deposits made by wealthier landowners. However, this government-sponsored institution "failed to grow and closed after a few years."[220] The movement toward interest-free banking reached a crescendo in Pakistan in the 1980s when official publications made sweeping attacks against interest, such as this one:

> The Council has all along expressed the view that the term *riba* encompasses interest in all its manifestations, irrespective of whether it relates to loans for consumption purposes or for productive purposes, whether the loans are of personal nature or of commercial type, whether the borrower is a government, a private individual or a concern, and whether the rate of interest is low or high.[221]

According to one observer, the reason for Pakistan's adoption of interest-free banking was due to the rise of the dictator Zia ul Haq (1924-1988), who became president of Pakistan in 1978. In order to garner the support of the populace, he decided to Islamize the country, his reasoning being, that "by supporting Islamic ideas and causes, he would get the support of the religious scholars who, in turn, would be able to tell their audiences to support Zia because he was trying to be [a] good Muslim ruler."[222] The Pakistani people were promised that, by removing interest, "the economic system would be fully purified [Islamized] with no unemployment, no inflation, and no income and wealth inequalities."[223]

---

[220]Tripp, 136.
[221]The Council of Islamic Ideology, "Elimination of Interest from the Economy," in *Money and Banking in Islam*, eds. Ziauddin Ahmed, Munawar Iqbal and M. Fahim Khan (Islamabad, Pakistan: Institute of Policy Studies, 1983), 106-107.
[222]Saleem, 28.
[223]Kazmi, 109.

In the Middle East, the rapid rise in the price of oil during the 1970s gave Middle Eastern nations both the financial capital and the political strength to advance *sharia*-compliant finance. In 1975, the Islamic Development Bank (IDB) was founded. In February 1976, Muslim academics came together to discuss and advance interest-free banking at the international "Islamic Economics Conference held in Mecca... under the auspices of King Abdul Aziz University, Jeddah."[224] Saudi Arabia's King Faisal was a proponent of *sharia*-compliant finance, and a network of Islamic banks were named after him.[225]

It should be noted that, from its earliest years, the IDB avoided the type of profit-and-loss sharing arrangements advocated by the proponents of *sharia*-compliant finance. Instead, it focused on financing oil purchases through *murabaha* contracts, which Badr-el-Din A. Ibrahim explained:

> In *murabaha* [contracts], the client applies to the bank for financing his purchases of specific raw materials or assets. The application is usually supported by invoices. The bank buys and resells the raw materials or assets at a price which covers the expenses and allows the bank a profit margin (*murabaha* margin) upon which the two parties agree. The price compensates the bank for the loss of the use of the money and the risk of non-repayment. The partner usually pays the bank in agreed installments.[226]

---

[224] Uzair, ii-iii.
[225] Warde, 93.
[226] Badr-el-Din A. Ibrahim, "Financing Challenges for Small Enterprises—The Experience of Sudanese Islamic Banks," in *Partnership Financing for Small Enterprise: Some lessons from Islamic credit systems*, ed. Malcolm Harper (London, UK: Intermediate Technology, 1997), 5.

(Author's note: It is my contention, based on my experience in corporate finance and investment banking, that *murabaha* contracts were favored because they essentially disguised interest as a markup on the price of the assets. Furthermore, the bank's risk was mitigated since it only owned the asset on paper and for just a short time before it was resold to the borrower. The term of the *murabaha* contract was also for less than a year, which further reduced the bank's risk.)

The prevalence of *murabaha* contracts influenced the operation of other "newly founded Islamic commercial banks, notably the Dubai Islamic Bank (founded 1975), the Kuwait Finance House (1977), the Faisal Banks of Egypt and the Sudan (1977), the Jordan Islamic Bank (1978), and the Bahrain (1979) and Qatar (1981) Islamic Banks."[227]

In more recent years, likely in response to criticism of their preference for *murabaha* contracts, Islamic banks have offered their clients longer-term lease financing, known as *ijara* contracts.[228] *Sharia*-compliant certificates (*sukuk*) have also been devised whereby Muslim governments and cities can sell certificates that "represent ownership of an underlying pool of assets, or the usufruct (manfaa) of such assets."[229] Both of these financial products are, in the author's opinion, attempts to disguise interest as either lease payments (*ijara* contracts) or as revenue-sharing arrangements (*sukuk* certificates).

In 2014, the British government became the first non-Muslim sovereign issuer of *sukuk* certificates when it sold 200 million pounds of *sukuk* to investors. Interestingly, the financial press reported the *sukuk* certificates as "bonds" and

---

[227] Wilson, *Islamic Economics*, 212.
[228] Ibid., 213.
[229] Warde, 150.

the interest rate as the "profit rate."[230] The opportunity to increase market share and increase their earnings by offering *sharia*-compliant securities has also attracted "a variety of conventional banks, many of them long-established pillars of American and European finance, such as Citibank, Union des Banques Suisses, HSBC, and Deutsche Bank."[231]

Assessment of Islamic Banking and Sharia-Compliant Finance

Proponents of interest-free banking have made the argument that "a system run on the PLS [profit-and-loss sharing] principle will unambiguously raise the rate of return on savings, thereby ensuring a more just distribution of the total profits to savers."[232] Drawing on the banking statistics of Pakistan, where interest-free banking has been instituted since 1983, a Muslim economist found that "The rate of return on the PLS deposits has consistently declined since 1983... [and], with a few exceptions, is lower than that on the non-PLS deposits."[233] It was also noted that the lower returns on PLS deposits hurt the least privileged in the society, who are characteristically risk-averse and who depended upon a stable return on their savings.[234] In fact, Naqvi acknowledged that the returns of interest-free banks will be more volatile because Islamic banks are actually replacing "capitalism based on interest-and-profit by a capitalism based only on profit."[235] Far from producing social justice (to use Qutb's term), the gap between the rich and poor will likely increase the longer interest-free banking is in

---

[230] Lyubov Pronina, "U.K. Sells Islamic Bonds in First Non-Muslim Sovereign Issue," Bloomberg, June 25, 2014, http://www.bloomberg.com/news/articles/2014-06-25/u-k-sells-200-million-pounds-of-debut-islamic-bonds (accessed 7/27/15).
[231] Tripp, 146.
[232] Naqvi, *Islam, Economics, and Society*, 141.
[233] Ibid.
[234] Ibid., 110.
[235] Ibid., 111.

place. This is due to the fact that borrowers are often wealthy individuals (e.g., property developers, business owners) who benefit if projects succeed but are bailed out in event the project fails, since the bank bears most, if not all, of the financial risk in a profit-and-loss sharing scenario.[236]

Early Muslim economists also spoke of an alliance between banking and industry. "As a result of the happy marriage between finance and industry, the onward march of economic progress will continue. Industry will flourish and national income will increase."[237] In the early years of Islamic finance, "Islamic bankers failed to act prudently and exercise the kind of due diligence expected of bankers.... In particular, forays into PLS activities proved to be disastrous.... They had trusted people who did not deserve their trust."[238] Khan further noted,

> The problem of deliberate misreporting by clients of Islamic banks is, perhaps, the most significant deterrent to Islamic financial institutions adopting PLS. The general standards of morality and integrity in present-day Muslim societies are quite low. Even if we assume that these standards are compatible with non-Muslim societies, the inborn greed and materialistic temptations create natural inclinations to hide and misreport real profits with a view to reducing the share of the financier.[239]

The *sharia* boards of Islamic banks have also come under sharp criticism. A common complaint is that Islamic finance is not built upon classical Islamic law, but rather has become a prohibition-driven industry[240] where Islamic jurists and

---

[236] Ibid., 126.
[237] Mannan, 229.
[238] Warde, 161-2.
[239] Khan, *What Is Wrong*, 275.
[240] El-Gamal, 8.

sharia experts, for a fee, will certify financial products as "Islamic." Rather than develop distinctively Islamic financial products, "the trend has been to scour the Islamic tradition—the basic sources of the *shari'ah*, as well as the writings of the *fuqaha'*—in order to find ways of legitimating financial transactions developed in the larger context of global finance capital."[241] *Sharia* bank officials, when faced with such criticism, maintain that "God is in the details [of the certifications]."[242] The independence of *sharia* boards has also been questioned since the board members are paid by the banks for their certifications.[243] It has been observed that Islamic banks have "challenged neither the idea nor the institution of the capital market which is at the heart of global capitalism. On the contrary, they have created a niche in that market for themselves."[244]

Islamic Economic Development

Islamic economists maintain that Western principles of economic development rooted in capitalism are not appropriate for Muslim societies; rather, Islamic economies should be developed using principles derived from Islam. The first section below will examine the Islamic critique of Western economic development principles and the proposed Islamic alternatives. The second section will highlight two early efforts to implement Islamic economic development principles. The third section will focus on modern Islamic business development. The final section will assess the arguments for Islamic economic development.

---

[241] Tripp, 143.
[242] El-Gamal, 2.
[243] Tripp, 144.
[244] Ibid., 146.

The Need for Islamic Economic Development

A traditional measure of a nation's economic development is its gross national product (GNP) per capita.[245] Based on such a measure, Islamic economists and development specialists realized there was an enormous disparity between developed nations and most Muslim economies. In the 1960s and 1970s, developed nations (both capitalist and communist), as part of their Cold War efforts, began to incorporate "the theme of [economic] development in their foreign policies. Each side competed with one another to win over 'devotees' of development ideologies that each advocated."[246] The results from foreign economic development programs, however, were disappointing. "The gap between the rich Western nations and the poorest Muslim economies increased significantly in the second half of the twentieth century."[247]

Arab socio-economic systems continued to be deficient in several measures of human development. Specifically, they had a low level of freedom as measured by political processes, rights, civil liberties and freedom of speech and free media. Arab countries also had a women's empowerment and a human capabilities/knowledge deficit.[248] Summarized by one scholar,

> Corruption and the concentration of wealth persisted as twin pillars of Muslim society while poverty, illiteracy, and overpopulation galloped along unchecked... [which resulted in] migration from the

---

[245] Aidit Ghazali, *Development: An Islamic Perspective* (Selangor, Malaysia: Pelanduk, 1990), 5.
[246] Ibid., 4.
[247] Wilson, *Islamic Economics*, 210.
[248] UN Development Programme, Arab Fund for Economic and Social Development, *Arab Human Development Report 2002*, (New York, NY: UN, 2002), 27.

villages and rapid urbanization of overcrowded cities with insufficient social support systems.[249]

Muslim responses to this situation varied. Some dismissed the lack of quantitative economic progress as unimportant, since what mattered was qualitative change. Others blamed the economic disparities on exploitation of the Muslim world; one Islamic scholar, for example, suggested that using Western development models meant that Muslim countries hadn't freed themselves from colonial domination.[250] "A third reaction was to blame internal factors, not least secularist governance, and the failure of any Muslim country to adopt an Islamic economic system."[251] One Muslim economist holding to the third view argued that the West, due to its embrace of positivism and logical empiricism, emphasized knowledge over values.[252]

Another economist argued that neoclassical Keynesian and socialist economic systems "disregard the role of moral values in individual and social reform and hence, in development, . . . overemphasize the role of the market or the state."[253] Yet another economist noted "value-free or ethically neutral decision rules as being both pointless and counter-productive."[254] In contrast to capitalism's "essentially materialistic and earthly worldview," Islam's worldview "consists of fulfilling one's covenant with Allah and of living out the worldly life in terms of divine guidance as preparation for a more beautiful life awaiting mankind."[255]

---

[249] John L. Esposito, *Voices of Resurgent Islam*, 12.
[250] Anne Eyre, "Religion, Politics and Development in Malaysia," in *Religion and the Transformations of Capitalism*, ed. Richard H. Roberts (London, UK: Routledge, 1995), 306.
[251] Wilson, *Islamic Economics*, 210.
[252] Ghazali, 14.
[253] Chapra, 149.
[254] Syed Nawab Haider Naqvi, *Development Economics: A New Paradigm* (New Delhi, India: Sage, 1993), 124.
[255] Khalid M. Ishaque, "The Islamic Approach to Economic Development," in *Voices of Resurgent Islam*, ed. John L. Esposito (New York, NY: Oxford University, 1983), 268.

Economic development was also linked to *jihad* or "striving in the cause of Allah" so that Muslim nations would no longer be "politically and economically subservient to the powers which stand for alien cultures."[256] It was stated, "Once that idea catches on [linking economic development with *jihad*] we can expect big results."[257]

The key elements of an Islamic economic development program varied among Muslim economists. Some placed man at the center of all development efforts—e.g., "Any development process must begin with the moral, spiritual, physical, and environmental development of man, who will be the agent of his own physical and socio-economic environment."[258] Others argued that Islamic development should focus on establishing a "just social order, in which the needs of the least-privileged sections in society are looked after in the best possible fashion."[259]

The means of achieving these ends also varied. Some noted that Muslims are commanded to worship (*ibadah*) Allah. Since poverty interfered with one's ability to properly worship, and since work (especially entrepreneurship) was a preferred source of livelihood, entrepreneurship in Islam was part of *ibadah*.[260] Others wanted to replace a market economy with a planned economy.[261] Still others focused on distributive justice where private assets, such as land that was not being cultivated by the owner, would be given to those who had no land to cultivate.[262] Among those economists who saw markets as being Islamic, there were calls for institutions to be established similar to the *hisbah* rules of the Islamic Golden Age. Such rules would ensure

---

[256] Siddiqi, *Muslim Economic Thinking*, 10.
[257] Ibid., 42.
[258] Ghazali, 23.
[259] Naqvi, *Development Economics*, 22.
[260] Rasem N. Kayed and M. Kabir Hassan, *Islamic Entrepreneurship* (London, UK: Routledge, 2011), 72.
[261] Mannan, 327.
[262] Naqvi, *Islam, Economics, and Society*, 100-1.

"that a high degree of public morality is attained and that the society is protected from fraud, exploitation and purposely-created inefficiencies such as uncontrolled monopolistic practices."[263]

Early Islamic Development Efforts

Two well-known early Islamic development initiatives were begun in Egypt. The first, which predates much of the Islamist movement and the call for interest-free banking, was begun in 1920 by Talaat Harb (1867-1941). He studied law and the French language at Pasha Muhammad Ali's School of Administration and Languages, where many of the professors were French and thus experts in the French civil code.[264] Harb was a member of the Egyptian intelligentsia and "a close associate of members of the Jewish upper class in Egypt . . . [from whom he] learned much about international capital."[265] He also was engaged as a *wakil* (agent) for many large Egyptian landowners.[266] In line with the rise of Egyptian nationalism after World War I, he established Bank Misr with the initial goal of applying technical and other innovations to modernize Egyptian agriculture.[267] Bank Misr also sought to fund a local entrepreneurs to compete with foreign enterprise, which was consistent with the desires of the bank's leading depositors and owners (wealthy landowners) to diversify their wealth.[268] To this end, the bank took equity stakes in, and sat on the boards of many of the industrial ventures it funded, which was in marked contrast to the British banks and the National Bank of Egypt.[269]

---

[263] Ghazali, 45.
[264] Davis, 87-8.
[265] Ibid., 94.
[266] Ibid., 97.
[267] Wilson, *Banking and Finance*, 33.
[268] Calvert, 77.
[269] Wilson, *Banking and Finance*, 34.

As its investments expanded across industries, Bank Misr entered into joint ventures with foreign companies. While one scholar maintained that the bank generally controlled these ventures,[270] another contended that it was generally the junior partner.[271] Until the advent of World War II, which proved catastrophic for the bank, it had become a dominant force in Egyptian manufacturing and played "a significant role in the country's trade, with *Société Misr pour l'Exportation du Coton* [as] the largest exporting concern."[272] One scholar credits the experience gained in the decades of Bank Misr's operation for Egypt's "subsequent development of manufacturing from the 1950s onwards."[273]

The establishment of Mit Ghamr Bank in Egypt in 1963 was, according to one scholar, a pivotal point in Islamic banking. Mit Ghamr was founded by Ahmed al-Najjar, who, while influenced by the Muslim Brotherhood's economic and social thought, had studied in Germany where he saw the success of German mutual savings banks.[274] Najjar promoted savings with the objective of investing in development projects in rural areas. He also organized a "Social Service Fund" to attract *zakat* donations.[275]

Mit Ghamr did not pay interest on deposits; but if depositors kept their money on deposit for at least one year, they were eligible for interest-free loans. Such loans could be used for "house building and repairs, the purchase of simple machinery for handicraft industries, such as hand looms for weaving textiles, or even simple sewing machines. Some loans helped finance the purchase of farm animals and basic improvements to the irrigation systems."[276] The loans were typically for one- to three-year terms. There were

---

[270] Ibid., 37.
[271] Calvert, 77.
[272] Wilson, *Banking and Finance*, 36.
[273] Ibid., 38.
[274] El-Gamal, 163.
[275] Siddiqi, *Muslim Economic Thinking*, 32-3.
[276] Wilson, *Banking and Finance*, 76.

"no grace periods on repayments. The emphasis was on keeping the funds circulating, following the Prophet's teaching on the evils of hoarding."[277] Mit Ghamr operated for five years, attracted a quarter million depositors, and was successful in loaning money to start numerous small businesses.[278] Because it only charged an administrative fee on its loans and did not share in the profits of businesses that it financed, the bank's limited profitability could not sustain its operations, resulting in it ultimately being acquired and nationalized under the regime of Gamal Abdul Nasser.[279] One scholar noted that Mit Ghamr was actually a microfinance initiative[280] (a topic discussed further in the following section).

Modern Islamic Business Development

Two of the primary means of developing new businesses are venture capital and the promotion of small businesses through small to medium enterprise (SME) development and microfinance. While these methodologies are largely of western origin, each will be examined from the Islamic perspective.

Among the prominent features of the Middle East in recent decades are Muslim-majority nations that have received substantial oil income. These revenues have allowed nations like Dubai, Abu Dhabi, and the United Arab Emirates, which are typically ruled by a royal family, to initiate major development projects in one or more urban centers in the hope of drawing investors and economic activity. Such top-down economic development, however, requires massive amounts of startup capital, which limits its

---

[277] Ibid.
[278] Tripp, 136.
[279] Wilson, *Banking and Finance*, 77.
[280] Hussam Sultan, "Islamic Microfinance: Between Commercial Viability and the Higher Objectives of Shari'a," in *Shari'a-compliant Microfinance*, ed. S. Nazim Ali (London, UK: Routledge, 2012), 49.

applicability to a narrow number of Muslim-majority nations and, hence, will not be addressed in this book.

Islamic Venture Capital

Attracting equity capital and the necessary management skills into the economies of developing nations is a proven success strategy. As one scholar noted, venture capital is vital "to build the economies of the developing countries through increases in employment and establishing small and strong businesses."[281] Several features of Islamic economies favor venture capital. The ownership and trading of common stock has been approved by numerous Islamic juristic counsels, who viewed common stock ownership as "partial ownership of the company's assets as a silent partner."[282] Even stock options were deemed Islamic since the employees who are offered such options "are directly responsible for increasing the value of such shares through their work efforts."[283] The general structure of venture capital funds, that of a limited partnership, where "the GP [general partner] receives a management fee and a percentage of profits, while the LPs [limited partners] receive income, capital gains and tax benefits . . . [is] strikingly similar in form and function to the traditional *muḍārabah* contract."[284] Even cases where multiple venture capital firms co-invest with an entrepreneur and co-manage the new business are similar to the Islamic form of partnership known as *musharakah*.[285]

Despite the fact that venture capital has been a key element in the growth of the United States and other developed nations, it has been noted that venture capital is

---

[281] Fara Madehah Ahmad Farid, *Shari'ah Compliant Private Equity and Islamic Venture Capital* (Edinburgh, UK: Edinburgh University, 2012), 110.
[282] El Gamal, 124.
[283] Rashid, 242.
[284] Ibid., 236.
[285] Farid, 64.

largely unknown in Muslim-majority nations.[286] Although a trade association—the Gulf Venture Capital Association—was formed in Bahrain in 2006 to facilitate venture investments, no significant transactions or company startups are apparent.[287] One reason for this lies in the fact that Islamic finance generally rejects the notion that preferred stockholders can receive preference (versus common stockholders) in the event a business fails and is liquidated.[288] Venture capital investors typically receive preferred shares to offset their lack of voting control in the companies they finance.[289] Some Muslim-majority nations have looked more favorably on preferred stock. For example, in Malaysia, a *Sharia* Advisory Council allowed the issuance of a preferred stock which received preference in liquidation but not with respect to accumulated earnings.[290]

Another barrier for venture capital investors in Muslim-majority nations has been the need to employ numerous *sharia* scholars and advisors on behalf of the fund and its investments. The role of these persons is to analyze each investment and its business operations for *sharia*-compliance and to issue various *sharia*-compliance documents and reports.[291] Hiring *sharia* scholars and advisors is both costly and time consuming.

---

[286]Rashid, 228.
[287]Bloomberg, "Company Overview of Gulf Venture Capital Association," http://www.bloomberg.com/research/ stocks/private/snapshot.asp?privcapId=114946893. (accessed August 13, 2015).
[288]Rashid, 229.
[289]If preferred stock could not be issued, venture capital investors would be subject to share dilution if additional common shares were issued at lower prices to subsequent investors—such as insiders. Owning preferred stock allows them to recoup their capital from any remaining assets (net of liabilities) before common stockholders are eligible to do so.
[290]Farid, 135.
[291]Ibid., 80.

Small to Medium Enterprise Development and Microfinance

While venture capital firms are focused on larger business opportunities, policymakers in Middle Eastern and North African nations have realized that small to medium enterprises (SMEs) are a key part "to improving competitiveness, raising incomes, and generating employment."[292] This is particularly the case wherever there is a surplus of labor and a scarcity of capital or technical expertise, which is a situation that exists in many Asian and African Muslim nations. SMEs "are usually run with family labour and use simple technology, and therefore they need less credit. They generate more output per unit of capital than large-scale enterprises."[293] In the view of one Islamic scholar, when SMEs are coupled with private equity and venture capital, they provide a pathway for employment or new enterprise.[294]

Despite the importance of SMEs in economic development, traditional commercial banks have largely ignored them in favor of larger-scale enterprises. The typical reasons for this disparity included SMEs' lack of collateral, their lack of bank accounts and financial accounting, and their inability to provide guarantors acceptable to the banks.[295] Others noted that lenders to SMEs considered them high risk and that there were very high managerial costs in dealing with small producers.[296]

Such objections were overcome, in part, by the Grameen Bank founded by Muhammad Yunus in Bangladesh in 1977. The loans made by Grameen focused on empowering the

---

[292]Ibid., 28.
[293]Muhammad Ramzan Akhtar, "Musharaka Financing for Small Enterprises in Pakistan," in *Partnership Financing for Small Enterprise: Some Lessons from Islamic Credit Systems*, ed. Malcolm Harper (London, UK Intermediate Technology, 1997), 35.
[294]Farid, 112.
[295]Mustafa Gamal-Eldin Abdalla, "Partnership Financing for Small Enterprise: Problems and Suggested Improvements," in *Partnership Financing for Small Enterprise: Some Lessons from Islamic Credit Systems*, ed. Malcolm Harper (London, UK: Intermediate Technology, 1997), 56-7.
[296]Ibrahim, 8.

poor by extending them small amounts of credit that they could use to establish micro enterprises and for personal purposes. The loans were typically for one year or less, and a flat interest rate of 20 percent was charged with repayments in equal installments due weekly. The loans were cross-guaranteed by a small group of borrowers, which increased the repayment rate. There was often a compulsory build-up of savings prior to any loan being extended.[297] Also, rebates were given for prepayments, and fees were charged if installments were missed.[298] The majority of the loans made by Grameen were to women.[299] Yunus labeled this form of lending the "Grameen Classic System."

By 2002, Yunus instituted the "Grameen Generalized System," which featured a flexible-term loan for borrowers who could not, for whatever reason, adhere to the terms of the original repayment schedule. He strongly maintained that the poor always pay back their loans—even if the repayments were sometimes delayed through difficult circumstances.[300] The financial effect of such a restructuring was to keep repayment rates high even though the repayment periods were extended.

Islamic banks have sought to develop SMEs by providing micro finance (MF) in ways that avoid the payment of interest and are *sharia*-compliant. Instead of lending money with interest, which the borrower uses to purchase an asset, the Islamic bank purchases the asset, and either enters into an agreement with the borrower to purchase the asset on installment (including a markup), or it simply leases the asset. The former is referred to as *murabaha* financing, the latter as *ijara* financing. While the interest rates associated

---

[297]Muhammad Yunus, *Banker to the Poor: Micro-Lending and the Battle Against World Poverty* (New York, NY: Public Affairs, 2003), chapter 5 passim.

[298]Saif I. Shah Mohammed, "Islamic Finance and Microfinance: An Insurmountable Gap?," in *Shari'a-compliant Microfinance*, ed. S. Nazim Ali (London, UK: Routledge, 2012), 36.

[299]Yunus, 73.

[300]Ibid., 237-8.

with MF are high, questions have been raised about the ultimate cost to borrowers after the costs of "purchasing, maintaining, selling, or leasing, and tracking a commodity" are added to a murabaha or *ijara* transaction.[301] Despite such concerns, *murabaha* financing constituted almost three-fourths of lending by such institutions as the Sudanese Islamic Bank to SMEs engaged in a "wide range of small urban enterprises such as tailoring, food processing, shoe- and soap-making, chalk, cheesemaking, goat and poultry keeping, petty retail trade and some informal sector activities, such as tea and *kisra* (local bread) making."[302]

Islamic financing of SMEs has also taken the form of *musharaka* contracts. As discussed in connection with venture capital financing, *musharaka* contracts are essentially joint ventures constructed around specific business projects. The profits of the joint venture are split between the borrower and the financial institution based on the capital and the amount of management expertise contributed by each party.[303] Such contracts are attractive to borrowers since they do not involve the collateral requirements of *murabaha* financing. Also, they provide the SME with a business partner who can assist in the production and sale of the product, which is the subject of the joint venture.[304] However, the cost and complexity of managing a *musharaka* contract (especially on a small scale) has limited its use.[305] Islamic micro finance providers have also discovered that, when *musharaka* contracts are used in

---

[301] Samer Badawi and Wafik Grais, "Meeting the Demand for Sustainable, Shari'a-Compliant Microfinance," in *Shari'a-compliant Microfinance*, ed. S. Nazim Ali (London, UK: Routledge, 2012), 12.

[302] Ibrahim, 8.

[303] Ibid., 3-4.

[304] Abdalla, 59.

[305] Asim Nourain, "ACORD Musharaka Credit Programmes in Sudan," in *Partnership Financing for Small Enterprise: Some Lessons from Islamic Credit Systems*, ed. Malcolm Harper (London, UK: Intermediate Technology, 1997), 33.

SMEs, a great deal of business training is required, which reduces the profitability of the loan.[306]

Indigenous savings programs have also proven to be successful in certain African Muslim countries in making finances available to poor communities. For instance, in Cameroon, the *njangi* saving system was instituted whereby "a group is formed and each member of the group regularly deposits a small amount of money into a central fund. The whole sum is then disbursed to each group member in a rotating manner. Lots might be drawn to determine the sequence of disbursements."[307] While such savings programs are not specifically targeted at developing micro enterprises, they do help to create economic conditions conducive to business development.

Assessment of Modern Islamic Business Development

Micro Finance

As it relates to the use of micro finance in Islamic development, one scholar stated, "Islamic finance, which has always envisioned a role for itself in development activity, has been strangely absent from the microfinance sector and microfinance debates."[308] There are a number of reasons for this absence. One area of controversy has arisen because of the emphasis of many micro finance institutions (beginning with the Grameen Bank) on empowering poor women. (Females account for about 80 percent of the clients at 34 of the largest micro-lenders.[309]) Many Islamic communities, including in Bangladesh, have often viewed this emphasis as

---

[306]Badawi, 14.
[307]Safaa Elagib Adam, "The Experience of Traditional Saving Groups and El Kifaya Bank in Financing Poor Women," in *Partnership Financing for Small Enterprise: Some Lessons from Islamic Credit Systems*, ed. Malcolm Harper (London, UK: Intermediate Technology, 1997), 24-5.
[308]Mohammed, 33.
[309]Sultan, 51.

an unbridgeable ideological gap.[310] A second area of controversy is the fact that micro finance programs are typically interest-based, and their interest rates are portrayed as extremely high.[311]

Also, the various Islamic forms of micro finance have had very limited success. "In many cases, the cost of maintaining an Islamic window at a microfinance institution has been much higher than expected. Moreover, the development and delivery of these products have generally been higher."[312] Another barrier to success has been the lack of consistency among *sharia* advisors, which has led to many communities to question whether or not the microfinance product was *sharia*-compliant.[313] A further problem is that borrowers generally prefer to "receive the cash and dispense of it as they see fit, rather than having assets purchased and sold to them at a mark-up, as in the case of *murabaha*, or leased to them over a period of time, as in the case of *ijara*."[314] Although some Islamic banks provide cash to the borrowers by allowing them to sell part of the assets received under *murabaha* loans back to the bank (a process known as *tawarruq*), this has been controversial as some s*haria* scholars view it as "a mere loophole device with little financial substance."[315]

Islamic Financial Institutions

Islamic financial institutions are also discovering that providing capital to develop Islamic communities, while religiously motivated, is no substitute for sound lending

---

[310] Mohammed, 42.
[311] Sultan, 51.
[312] Badawi, 9.
[313] Sultan, 53.
[314] Ibid., 53.
[315] Rodney Wilson, "Making Development Assistance Sustainable Through Islamic Microfinance," in *Shari'a-compliant Microfinance*, ed. S. Nazim Ali (London, UK: Routledge, 2012), 67.

practices. For example, it was discovered that proximity of the Islamic banks to their borrowers is important. One case study of an Islamic joint venture highlighted the need for close supervision and follow-up of the clients/partners in order to deter "any possible dishonesty . . . (e.g., unrecorded sale of the product or materials, or tampering with the records.)[316] Likewise, the Sudan Islamic Bank found that it needed to establish branches in residential areas to gauge the ability of its clients to repay their debts.[317] It was also noted that Islamic financial institutions needed to properly title and legally secure their asset-backed transactions, or disputes would occur and the loans would be left unpaid.[318]

A long-standing criticism of Islam, relevant in assessing the economic development of Muslim-majority nations, revolves around Islam's lack of separation between religion and politics. Max Weber noted that governments characterized by "sultanism" can exhibit a high degree of arbitrariness and discretion, "which distinguishes it from every form of rational authority."[319] Such rulers, Weber argued, place themselves "in a position to grant grace and favors" far beyond whatever could be considered normal or traditional.[320] Applying this observation to the modern Middle East, one scholar noted that capitalistic business has been negatively impacted since it is difficult "to deal with the discretionary powers of a single individual and his cadre of personal retainers."[321] Although Muslim-majority countries

---

[316] M.E.T. El-Bhasri and Nawal Abdalla Adam, "Examples of Partnership Financing for Microenterprise—The Case of Sudanese Islamic Bank," in *Partnership Financing for Small Enterprise: Some Lessons from Islamic Credit Systems*, ed. Malcolm Harper (London, UK: Intermediate Technology, 1997), 17.

[317] Ibrahim, 8.

[318] Kholoud Khaldi, "The Experience of Dawaimeh Self-help Group in Musharaka Financing," in *Partnership Financing for Small Enterprise: Some Lessons from Islamic Credit Systems*, ed. Malcolm Harper (London, UK: Intermediate Technology, 1997), 22.

[319] Max Weber, *Economy and Society: An Outline of Interpretive Sociology*, vol. 1, eds. Guenther Roth and Claus Wittich, trans. Ephraim Fischoff and others (Berkeley, CA: University of California, 1978), 232.

[320] Ibid.

[321] Swatos, 53.

today are no longer ruled by caliphs or sultans (Abu-Bakr al-Baghdadi's Islamic State notwithstanding), many are ruled by royal families or other leaders who possess totalitarian power. From the author's experience of living and doing business in such nations, Weber's observation and the negative impact on the business environment still ring true.

Sharia Law

Recent Islamic scholarship has focused on how certain aspects of *sharia* law have hampered economic development in Muslim-majority nations. The first area to be considered relates to the Islamic law regarding inheritance. The Qur'an and the *hadith* detailed how a decedent's estate is to be divided among the heirs and limited the total amount of a decedent's bequests to one-third of the estate. Since heirs included not only descendants but also agnatic heirs, "The bulk of the property, according to this law, went to the residuary heirs, whose number was in most cases considerable."[322] This made it very difficult to keep properties and businesses intact across generations. "Studies of pre-modern Anatolia, Syria, and Palestine show that fortunes often got fragmented. It was not uncommon for a dwelling or shop to have more than a dozen co-owners."[323]

In order to circumvent the inheritance laws, owners of property would endow *waqfs* with a large portion of their assets. "The founder [of a *waqf*] could appoint himself the waqf's caretaker (*mutawalli*), set his own salary, hire relatives to paid positions, and even designate his successor."[324] *Waqfs*, however, made poor business platforms in that they were irrevocable and unchangeable,

---

[322] Ashtor, 113.
[323] Kuran, *The Long Divergence*, 79.
[324] Ibid., 112.

the assets had to be used for charitable purposes, profit-making was frowned upon, any income the *waqf* did earn was not transferable, and the *waqf* lacked legal personhood by placing all liabilities on the caretaker.[325] Furthermore, since a *waqf* could only have one caretaker, it "precluded managerial innovations aimed at turning the family into an organization suitable to large-scale business in a dynamic economy."[326]

The second area of *sharia* law that came under scrutiny was Islam's limitation on the structure of business. As discussed in Chapter 4, Islamic law approved of only a few types of partnerships. According to Kohler, an Islamic legal historian, "The decline of Islamic commercial hegemony in the Middle Ages was due in a large part to the limitations placed by Islamic law on the development of associative relationships."[327] Among the problems of Islamic partnerships was their instability. Islamic jurists generally held that either partner could unilaterally dissolve partnerships and that they were automatically dissolved upon the death of any partner. Such conditions rendered these partnerships ill-equipped to hold the large amounts of capital needed to attain economies of scale or to compete with European stock companies in the industrial age.[328] One scholar noted that legal standing under Islamic law was limited to natural individuals and did not recognize the concept of a corporation until well into the 19th century, saying,

> The resulting lack of experience made it impossible to introduce the corporation into commerce when the need presented itself. Thus, when technologies of mass production raised the demand for large-scale financing, banks could not be established under

---

[325] Ibid., chapter 7 passim.
[326] Ibid., 137.
[327] Udovitch, 4.
[328] El-Gamal, 119.

Islamic law to mobilize the required resources. Nor could the new technologies be exploited through appropriately capitalized manufacturing enterprises.[329]

Islamic economic development was also negatively impacted because of the two-tier legal processes that emerged from the Capitulations (discussed in Chapter 5). Under this system, non-Muslims (primarily Middle Eastern Christians and Jews) "acquired western protection and moved their business dealings, usually in part, outside the Islamic legal system."[330] Because Muslims could not leave Islam, they were therefore excluded from commercial contacts that involved large and durable organizations, financial techniques, and litigation practices that enabled increasingly impersonal forms of exchange."[331] As Kuran noted (with more than a touch of irony), "Imposed initially to benefit Muslims, the Pact of Umar, and specifically its provision that gave the *kadi* sole jurisdiction over cases involving Muslims, thus had the unintended effect, more than a millennium later, of seriously harming Muslim economic opportunities."[332] Perhaps the call of Islamists for a return to the *sharia* of Islam's Golden Age will also have grave unintended consequences.

---

[329]Kuran, *The Long Divergence*, 282.
[330]Ibid., 171.
[331]Ibid., 200.
[332]Ibid., 208.

CHAPTER 7

Business and Christian Mission

The objective of this chapter is to survey and categorize the ways in which business has been a part of Christian missions. (The various business and mission strategies will not be critiqued or judged as to their missiological strengths and weaknesses.) The chapter begins with a historical overview of business and Christian mission, after which the current forms of both business and Christian mission are categorized and defined. The resulting framework will set the stage for Chapter 8, which focuses on the challenges faced by those engaging in business and Christian mission in its various forms as they seek to properly contextualize their activities in Muslim majority nations.

Historical Overview

The book of Acts, along with some of the epistles, provide an account of the spread of the Gospel after Jesus' resurrection and ascension. While the activities of the apostles occupy center stage, there are also many references to the role of businesspeople in spreading the Gospel. Among the list of self-supporting witnesses "Zacchaeus was a tax collector; Nicodemus and Joseph of Arimathea were supreme-court councilors; Barnabas was a landowner; Cornelius was an officer; Luke was a doctor; Priscilla, Aquila, and Paul were tentmakers; Lydia, a purple-dye seller; Zenas was a lawyer; and Erastus was a city treasurer."[1]

Early Christian church history continued to highlight the importance of business in the spread of the Gospel. One scholar noted that merchants were effective in transmitting ideas because "traveling businessmen do not simply convey, sell, and acquire goods, and move on. They socialize, interact, and observe while on the road, and they take their impressions home with them."[2]

The role of the merchant/missionary was especially significant in the eastward expansion of Christianity out from Jerusalem. "The size of the church in Europe paled in comparison to the breadth of the church in Asia."[3] Writing of the Sogdian merchants in Persia, who engaged in trade with Asia and became converts to Manichaeism or Nestorian Christianity, Foltz recorded that the Sogdians "were like cultural bees, cross-pollinating ideas and traditions from one civilization to another."[4] He further noted that, "Among the early Christians, the Syriac word for merchant, *tgr'*, was often used as a metaphor for those who spread the Gospel."[5] This was especially significant because Syriac was both the *lingua franca* (common language) of West Asian trade and the liturgical language of the Eastern church.[6]

The seriousness with which merchants took their roles as disseminators of the Gospel was shown by the fact that Nestorian Christian merchants were required to attend one of two Nestorian monasteries "to study the Psalms, the New Testament, and to attend courses of lectures before entering

---

[1] J. Christy Wilson, *Today's Tentmakers: Self-Support—An Alternative Model for Worldwide Witness* (Wheaton, IL: Tyndale House, 1979), 21.

[2] Richard C. Foltz, *Religions of the Silk Road: Overland Trade and Cultural Exchange from Antiquity to the Fifteenth Century* (New York, NY: St. Martin's Griffin, 1999), 6-7.

[3] Howard Owens, "Nestorian Merchant Missionaries and Today's Unreached People Groups," in *Business as Mission: From Impoverished to Empowered,* ed. Tom Steffen and Mike Barnett (Pasadena, CA: William Carey Library, 2006), 133.

[4] Foltz, 13.

[5] Ibid., 62.

[6] Ibid.

on a business career."[7] The effectiveness of these Nestorian merchant/missionaries was seen in the fact that, when the first Catholic missionaries arrived in China, they discovered Nestorian Christianity "comfortably entrenched there as the recognized resident Christianity of the East."[8]

A similar pattern was observed in Europe, where the early church "was a predominantly urban phenomenon that moved along the trade routes from city to city."[9] For example, in southern Gaul, churches were established in cities such as Marseilles, Aries, and Lyon where flax, linen, wool, and clothing were traded.[10] In the Middle Ages, there were also accounts of Waldensians who became itinerant peddlers in order to travel freely about Europe. An inquisitor during the 14th century described the activities of one Waldensian as follows:

> It seems that upon his arrival at the local manor all the townspeople, including masters and servants, would gather around while he showed his various wares—fabrics, jewelry and artifacts which he displayed artfully and offered for sale. But even as he sold he would make allusion to more precious goods in his possession, to jewels of inestimable value he was in a position to offer.[11]

When European Christians embraced the need to spread the Gospel to foreign nations and peoples in the wake of the Reformation, artisans were among the first to respond, most

---

[7] Owens, 138-9.
[8] Foltz, 8.
[9] Heinz A. Suter, "Starting Kingdom Companies: A Biblical and Historical Overview," in *On Kingdom Business: Transforming Missions Through Entrepreneurial Strategies,* ed. Tetsunao Yamamori and Kenneth A. Eldred (Wheaton, IL: Crossway, 2003), 183.
[10] Ibid.
[11] Giorgio Tourn, *The Waldensians: The First 800 Years (1174-1974),* trans. Camillo P. Merlino, ed. Charles W. Arbuthnot (Torino, Italy: Claudiana, 1980), 37.

notably those associated with the Moravian community, which was founded on the estate of Count Zinzendorf. In planning their overseas missions, the Moravian artisans reasoned, "What was more natural than that where possible they should continue their crafts overseas rather than rely wholly on the over-strained exchequer of the tiny supporting groups?"[12] Zinzendorf supported the idea of sending independent artisan/missionaries because they were free to manage their time while on the mission field.[13] Certain crafts, such as blacksmithing and shoemaking, were favored over other crafts like bricklaying and carpentry, which required the missionaries to work at job sites, away from the mission station.[14] In Britain, Quakers were active in melding business with mission. The teachings of George Fox, the founder of the Society of Friends, "motivated many Quakers to try to make the world a better place through business."[15]

One of the most well known artisan/missionaries was William Carey, a pioneer missionary to India, who, "next to the Apostle Paul, ... was perhaps the greatest self-supporting missionary who ever lived."[16] According to one scholar, he represented "a type bred among the English Dissenters and the Scots seceders . . . [who] had practiced trades or crafts before their call; and some might, as Carey had for some time done with his cobbling, continue with them thereafter."[17] Carey wrote in his treatise, *An Inquiry Into the Obligation of Christians to Use Means for the Conversion of the Heathens*, that it is "an essential principle in the conduct of missions, that whenever it is practicable, missionaries should support themselves in whole or in part through their own

---

[12]William J. Danker, *Profit for the Lord: Economic Activities in Moravian Missions and the Basel Mission Trading Company* (Eugene, OR: Wipf and Stock, 1971), 28.

[13]Ibid., 32.

[14]Ibid., 35.

[15]Bridget Adams and Manoj Raithatha, *Building the Kingdom Through Business: A Mission Strategy for the 21st Century World* (Watford, UK: Instant Apostle, 2012), 19.

[16]Wilson, 19.

[17]Andrew F. Walls, *The Missionary Movement in Christian History: Studies in the Transmission of Faith* (Maryknoll, NY: Orbis, 1996), 161.

exertions."[18] His views were largely accepted by the mission societies of his time. Thomas Haweis, a prominent early supporter of the London Missionary Society, wrote,

> A plain man—with a good natural understanding,—well read in the Bible,—full of faith, and of the Holy Ghost,—though he comes from the forge or the shop, would, I own, in my view, as a missionary to the heathen, be infinitely preferable to all the learning of the schools; and would possess, in the skill and labour of his hands, advantages which barren science would never compensate.[19]

The missionary profile advocated by Haweis largely came to fruition. One mission historian noted, "The typical missionary long remained, as he had been in the first generation, a man of humble background and modest attainments . . . it was the journeymen, artisans, and clerks who came to the mission field from England."[20]

There were also early mission societies that established business firms as part of their strategy. For example, in conducting its mission in Africa, the Basel Mission Society in 1859 established the Mission Trading Company as a separate entity, which "was organized with 100 shares at 2000 francs each. The shareholders were to receive 6 percent interest from the profits. Any remaining profit was to be divided equally between the shareholders and the mission. However, any loss was to be borne by the shareholders alone."[21] The trading company worked closely with the society's mission stations. For example, it

---

[18] Wilson, 32.
[19] Walls, 162-3.
[20] Walls, 171.
[21] Danker, 103.

was able to use its economic leverage at times to persuade African chieftains to keep the peace, thus creating the prerequisites for the coming of a missionary. Sometimes, too, when the Basel Mission Society could not afford to open a mission station, the company could open a trading post, where its *Missionskaufmann* [salesmen] would witness to the gospel.[22]

Christian mission and British economic interests were also often linked with English mission societies. John Philip of the London Missionary Society wrote, "While our missionaries . . . are everywhere scattering the seeds of civilization, social order, and happiness, they are, by the most unexceptionable means, extending British interests, British influence, and the British empire."[23] Christianity thus became part of "the 'three C's of colonialism'—Christianity, commerce, and civilization."[24]

Although colonialism came to an end after World War II, one missions historian noted that, because of colonialism, "All that the West has done tends to be interpreted in terms of aggression."[25] Mission work, in particular, came under criticism since it directly threatened native religious culture, which was at "the heart of the nations and endangers their very existence as peoples with a history and a destiny."[26] Mission societies and missionaries that enthusiastically embrace strategies of business and mission without careful contextualization may well run the risk of being regarded as some form of neo-colonialist.

---

[22]Ibid., 107.
[23]David J. Bosch, *Transforming Mission: Paradigm Shifts in Theology of Mission* (Maryknoll, NY: Orbis, 1991), 305.
[24]Ibid.
[25]Stephen Neill, *Colonialism and Christian Missions* (New York: McGraw-Hill, 1966), 12.
[26]Ibid.

Missiological Framework for Business and Christian Mission

Numerous events in recent decades (discussed below) have prompted a renewed interest in various forms of business and mission. The missiological framework presented in this chapter (see Appendix 3 for a summary of that framework) will place modern business and mission strategies into context with other, more traditional ways business and mission have interacted. In the sections to follow, the key characteristics of each part of the missiological framework are discussed. Understanding these characteristics will be important when, in Chapter 8, business and mission in Muslim-majority nations are contextualized. The framework will include only those aspects of business and mission that are cross-cultural.

The missiological framework of business and Christian mission as presented in this chapter is divided into two major categories—mission-driven and business-driven. This is not to say that projects listed under one category do not contain elements of both. For example, if people are self-employed tentmakers, which is listed under business-driven, this does not mean there are not legitimate missional elements in their tentmaking activities. Placing a particular business and mission strategy under one or the other category of "drivenness" only signifies emphasis.

The Mission-Driven Category

Business for Mission

Business-for-mission projects either directly support the work of the mission or they facilitate or support the missionary. Examples of such projects that support the mission include printing and publishing enterprises; radio and television broadcasting stations; creation and maintenance of websites and social media sites; establishment of medical clinics, hospitals, schools, community development, and non-governmental organizations; and provision of individual economic assistance through handicraft sales or other means. While all of these activities may entail registering a business, or engaging in some type of business activity, the core of the business is closely tied to the mission. Business for mission is well documented in mission history. For example, one of the first enterprises established by the Basel Mission Society was a printshop and bindery.[27] The archives of many mission societies include photos of missionaries and national employees standing in front of printshops, printing presses, and other buildings and/or equipment that was dedicated to the dissemination of Christian literature or to other ministry.

Business-for-mission projects that facilitate or support the missionary include guest houses and other types of short-term missionary accommodations, schools (both non-residential and boarding) serving the children of missionaries, and training centers for language or culture acquisition to equip new missionaries. Such businesses may also serve the broader community; for example, a school established for missionary kids may enroll the children of non-missionaries (often for a higher fee), or a missionary guest house may rent rooms to non-missionaries if there is availability. However, the main purpose of the particular business is clear—serving the missionary community.

Business Funding Mission

Another type of mission-driven project consists of businesses established or acquired with the intent to support the mission financially. In the missiological framework, these are known as business-funding-mission

---

[27]Danker, 86.

projects. One mission executive referred to these businesses as endowment enterprises, which he defined as "commercial activity solely for financial support of social programs... [where] the businesses are managed as completely separate units."[28] Often, such projects were attractive since income-producing assets in developing nations could be acquired by mission organizations or their missionaries somewhat inexpensively. This was especially the case for missionaries receiving support from the United States, where the U.S. dollar exchange rate has often been favorable when compared to local currencies.

Business-funding-mission projects were quite common in the past. "Religious orders such as the Franciscans, Jesuits, and Benedictines utilized productive economic activity to finance their programs, and gave a very important place to the concept of work."[29] Another example is found in the general store of the Moravian community, which, in 1747, was placed by Count Zinzendorf under the management of Abraham Dürninger. Danker reported that "Under Dürninger's skillful and devoted hands, the little general store grew to an international business complex in textiles, especially linen, tobacco, and the wholesale and retail trade, manufacturing and export-import business."[30] Over 25 years, it contributed 131,715 *thalers* (several million dollars in current value) to the Moravian community and to the cause of missions.[31] Danker also noted that Dürninger remitted only some of the profits to the Moravian community, reinvesting the remainder back into the business, which no doubt at least partially accounts for its longevity.[32]

---

[28]David R. Befus, *Where There Are No Jobs: Enterprise Solutions for Employment and "Public Goods" for the Poor* (Miami, FL: LAM, 2005), 29-30.

[29]David Befus, "Economic Development and Holistic Mission," in *Business as Mission: From Impoverished to Empowered,* ed. Tom Steffen and Mike Barnett (Pasadena, CA: William Carey Library, 2006), 104.

[30]Danker, 23.
[31]Ibid.
[32]Ibid.

A more recent example is Assemblies of God missionary Florence Steidel, founder of a ministry to hundreds of African lepers in post-World War II Liberia. She established a farm that consisted of about 4,000 rubber-producing trees, plus palm trees, cocoa plants, and coffee plants—all for the express purpose of generating cash to support the leprosarium.[33]

Business for Entry

One of the reasons business-for-entry projects became an important mission strategy was due to the Lausanne conferences in the 1970s and 1980s, where the "evangelical missions community focused on reaching the world's 'hidden' or 'unreached people groups.'"[34] With this renewed vision, missionaries faced obstacles of how to reach the "unreached," because an increasing number of countries were changing their attitudes toward religious workers, particularly Christian missionaries. Many countries began to restrict the number of entry visas granted to religious workers or even prevented them from entering. One missiologist wrote,

> Long gone were the days of going only where professional missionaries with missionary visas were welcomed or invited. How could we access the world's unreached peoples if professional missionaries were not allowed to live among them? How were we to preach and teach the gospel behind the iron and bamboo curtains of communism? How could we plant churches in the heart of the Islamic world?[35]

---

[33] Paul Lewis, "Assemblies of God World Missions: A History of BAM" (presentation, Orlando, FL, July 31, 2015).

[34] Mike Barnett, "Creative Access Platforms: What Are They and Do We Need Them?" in *Evangelical Missions Quarterly* 41 (January 2005): 89-90.

[35] Ibid., 90.

One answer to these questions arose from the fact that many nations, despite being closed to religious workers, were issuing business visas that allowed the recipients to live in the country. Taking advantage of this opportunity, companies (often with little or no capitalization) would register in the foreign country to do business and act as the "employer" for missionaries who would work for the company and receive a business visa. Examples of such companies were consulting firms engaged in such activities as business management or agriculture. Although they provided access into a country, these companies were (and still are) controversial since the actual amount of business conducted varies widely. At stake are issues of truthfulness and integrity, particularly if the business is only a "front" and generates little or no revenue from local customers or clients.

The Business-Driven Category

Poverty Alleviation and Empowerment

In the mid-20th century, a branch of economics emerged that focused on development. The claim of development economists was that, if the economy of a developing nation was altered with respect to certain fundamental characteristics (including political and legal factors) and if capital or aid money was added to its economy, that nation could be "jumpstarted" and move to a higher level of growth.[36] The goals of development economists were focused on material measures, such as gross national product per capita and other monetary standards of living.

The initial thrust of economic development in the post-World War II period was on large projects. It was thought

---

[36] Richard Starcher, "Development: A Term in Need of Transformation," in *Evangelical Missions Quarterly* 42 (January 2006): 55.

that by increasing the size and scope of development projects, the economic benefits would be larger and come sooner. However, the hoped-for outcomes generally were disappointing. "Despite an estimated $2.3 trillion in foreign aid dispensed from Western nations during the post-World War II era, more than 2.5 billion people, approximately 40 percent of the world's population, still live on less than two dollars per day."[37] In the view of one expert, the problem is that economic development requires decades and centuries and is best stimulated and fostered from below.[38]

Many Muslims have argued that Christians are concerned with only the spiritual life. Yet Christian history is filled with efforts to relieve the material suffering and deprivations experienced by mankind in a spiritually fallen world.[39] Thus, when it came to economic development, Christians generally viewed it from a broader perspective, coupling it with relief efforts. Carl F. H. Henry saw relief and development activities as part of being our "brother's keeper."[40] Others saw them in the light of Jesus' incarnation and identification with humanity.[41] Christians have also raised the concern that growth in material goods does not automatically result in quality of life.[42] Rather, it was argued that true development must involve the spiritual,

---

[37] Steve Corbett and Brian Fikkert, *When Helping Hurts: How to Alleviate Poverty Without Hurting the Poor . . . and Yourself* (Chicago, IL: Moody Publishers, 2009), 141-2.

[38] Thomas W. Dichter, *Despite Good Intentions: Why Development Assistance to the Third World Has Failed* (Amherst, MA: University of Massachusetts, 2003), 6-7.

[39] Alvin J. Schmidt, *Under the Influence: How Christianity Transformed Civilization* (Grand Rapids, MI: Zondervan, 2001), 11.

[40] Carl F.H. Henry, "The Genesis of a Movement," in *The Ministry of Development in Evangelical Perspective: A Symposium on the Social and Spiritual Mandate*, conv. Carl F.H. Henry, ed. Robert L. Hancock (Pasadena, CA: William Carey Library, 1979), 1.

[41] Mans Ramstad, "Relief Work and Development Work: Complement or Conflict?," in *Evangelical Missions Quarterly* 39 (January 2003): 80.

[42] Wayne G. Bragg, "Theological Reflections on Assisting the Vulnerable," in *Christian Relief and Development: Developing Workers for Effective Ministry*, ed. Edgar J. Elliston (Dallas: Word, 1989), 56.

intellectual, and physical realms, in addition to the economic.[43]

Much current Christian thought regarding development views it from a transformational perspective. One missiologist wrote, "Development is based on relationships, but its goal is transformation—the creation of new communities in which people live in harmony under God and enjoy the basic necessities of life."[44] The opinion that development involves transforming communities has become a major theme in Christian development activities. Another scholar noted, "The differences in Christian social transformation [versus government agencies] appear principally in its goals, motives, and methods as they relate to spiritual, social, and/or physical or environmental issues."[45] For example, a ministry known as Community Health Evangelism "has the expressed purpose of helping people prevent disease, promoting good health, and living an abundant Christian life.[46] Service businesses have also been established to meet community needs. One mission leader described such businesses as

> subsidized projects begun in response to a specific need for promoting health (clinics, hospitals, etc.), education (schools, literature distribution, etc.), or other social outreach such as camp programs and radio stations. . . . In many cases, a two-tier fee

---

[43]George W. Peters, "The Church and Development: A Historical View," in *The Ministry of Development in Evangelical Perspective: A Symposium on the Social and Spiritual Mandate*, conv. Carl F H. Henry, ed. Robert L. Hancock (Pasadena, CA: William Carey Library, 1979), 7.

[44]Paul E. Hiebert, "Anthropological Insights for Whole Ministries," in *Christian Relief and Development: Developing Workers for Effective Ministry*, ed. Edgar J. Elliston (Dallas, TX: Word, 1989), 85.

[45]Edgar J. Elliston, "Christian Social Transformational Distinctives," in *Christian Relief and Development: Developing Workers for Effective Ministry*, ed. Edgar J. Elliston (Dallas, TX: Word, 1989), 167.

[46]Stanley Rowland, "Training for Community Health Evangelism," in *Christian Relief and Development: Developing Workers for Effective Ministry*, ed. Edgar J. Elliston (Dallas, TX: Word, 1989), 285.

structure allows organizations to charge commercial rates to clients who are able to pay, thus allowing the program to subsidize services to poorer target groups.[47]

Focusing specifically on economic development, Christian mission organizations have assisted the poor using a variety of approaches. One of the most basic forms of assistance has involved helping the poor with periodic large expenses. Rutherford said,

> Just because you're poor doesn't mean that all your expenditure will be in small sums. Much of it may be ... [that] you may buy only a little food or clothing at a time. But from time to time you need to spend large sums. We can list these times in three main categories: "life-cycle" events, emergency needs, and investment opportunities.[48]

Micro-finance programs of various forms were instituted to address such needs. According to Fikkert, micro-finance "refers to the provision of financial services, such as savings, credit, or insurance, to low-income people to enable them to prepare [for] and cope with emergencies, to meet life-cycle needs, or to pursue opportunities to invest in their businesses, education, etc."[49] Some such programs also assisted the poor in establishing small businesses, commonly known as "micro-enterprises." The two types of activities—micro-finance and micro-enterprise development (MED)—are distinct in that MED typically requires "an

---

[47]Befus, *Where There Are No Jobs*, 27.
[48]Stuart Rutherford, "The Poor and Their Money: An Essay About Financial Services for Poor People" (paper, Institute for Development Policy and Management, University of Manchester, Manchester, UK, January 1999).
[49]Brian Fikkert, "Economists, Practitioners and the Attack on Poverty: Toward Christian Collaboration" (paper, Association of Christian Economists 20th Anniversary Conference, Washington D.C., January 5-6, 2003).

administrative unit capable of organizing basic paperwork, evaluating loan proposals, disbursing loans, providing training, collecting loans, and financial reporting."[50] Secular MED has become an increasingly popular activity only since the 1990s. In addition to the Grameen Bank, organizations such as Association for Social Advancement (ASA) and Bangladesh Rural Advancement Committee (BRAC), were reaching millions of clients, while other entities like ACCION International and Foundation for International Community Assistance (FINCA) reach tens of thousands of clients in Latin America.[51]

MED projects (although not referred to by that name) can be found throughout mission history. For example, in the late 1800s, the Basel Mission Trading Company "played an important role in the introduction of cocoa into Ghana. Cocoa was indigenous not to Africa, but to South America. Three Swiss farmers, members of the Basel Mission, were the first to plant cocoa in what is now Ghana."[52] Also, early Mennonite missions commonly featured industrial work and training schools designed to make the society they were evangelizing more productive.[53] Missiologists have described the goal of MED as

> [helping] the world's poorest people bootstrap themselves out of poverty by helping them create a business. . . . These are the smallest of businesses, designed to help poverty-stricken families become

---

[50]Befus, *Where There Are No Jobs*, 34.

[51]David Bussau and Russell Mask, *Christian Microenterprise Development: An Introduction* (Oxford, UK: Regnum, 2003), 1.

[52]Danker, 97.

[53]Richard A. Yoder, Calvin W. Redekop, and Vernon E. Jantzi, *Development to a Different Drummer: Anabaptist/Mennonite Experience and Perspectives* (Intercourse, PA: Good Books, 2004), 44.

economically productive, but generally too small to employ others in the community.[54]

Enterprise development has typically included "capital investment, loans, equipment, expertise, prayer, encouragement, business training, one-on-one mentorship, hands-on business consulting and counseling, and perhaps partnerships or alliances."[55] The size of Christian MED projects have also grown. One Christian practitioner noted that MED "seeks to serve a spectrum of people ranging from the sidewalk vendor requiring US$5 of working capital to the furniture maker with 10 employees and perhaps $50,000 in working capital."[56] Development programs focused on larger enterprises are often referred to as SME programs.

Tentmaking

The term "tentmaking" is derived from Scripture. Christy Wilson, a missiologist who wrote one of the first books on the topic, stated,

> Scriptures say that there are two types of cross-cultural witnesses. The first are those who receive full support from churches. This is the way the Apostle Peter was supported. On the other hand, the Apostle Paul earned his own salary by making tents. Even today, cross-cultural witnesses or "missionaries" fall into these two categories.[57]

---

[54]Neal Johnson and Steve Rundle, "Distinctives and Challenges of Business as Mission," in *Business as Mission: From Impoverished to Empowered*, ed. Tom Steffen and Mike Barnett (Pasadena. CA: William Carey Library, 2006), 23.

[55]C. Neal Johnson, *Business as Mission: A Comprehensive Guide to Theory and Practice* (Downers Grove, IL: IVP Academic, 2009), 62.

[56]Bussau, 2.

[57]Wilson, *Today's Tentmakers*, 15.

An early advocate of tentmaking wrote, "Successful tentmakers realize their jobs are not 'necessary evils' that get in the way of ministry. Rather, they are means to an end, strategic resources to be used for accomplishing God's purposes—purposes that might not otherwise be fulfilled."[58] A more recent advocate claimed that focusing primarily on financial self-support misses the point, saying, "Tentmaking is not about money; it is about God. Tentmaking is about a way of revealing God's glory to the ends of the earth."[59]

As a modern mission strategy, tentmaking began in the 1970s, which was a difficult time for the United States. The dramatic rise in oil prices sent shock waves throughout the economy; and growth was negatively impacted which, when combined with high inflation and high interest rates, resulted in "stagflation." These factors, which made it more difficult for mission organizations to raise the needed funding to send fully-supported traditional missionaries to foreign lands, helped spur a renewed interest in tentmaking, where some or all of the financial support could be provided by one's employment. Educator Harold Ockenga wrote that tentmaking was the biblical answer to the high cost of missions.[60]

While the cost of sending missionaries overseas was a contributing factor in the number of tentmakers, certainly the desire to "reach the unreached" was as great, or even greater, in importance. One missiologist, who used the term "new envoys" to describe tentmakers, stated,

> In contrast to the church growth movement's strategy of "winning the winnable," the New Envoys will take for their harvesting target the groups that often have

---

[58]Don Hamilton, *Tentmakers Speak: Practical Advice from Over 400 Missionary Tentmakers* (Duarte, CA: TMQ Research, 1987), 10.

[59]Patrick Lai, *Tentmaking: Business as Missions* (Waynesboro, GA: Authentic Media, 2005), 3.

[60]Wilson, *Today's Tentmaking*, 9.

proved the least winnable—yielding the greatest dangers, the most frustrations, and the lowest conversion rates.[61]

Tentmakers responded to the willingness of even "closed nations" to issue visas if the recipients possessed certain needed skills, such as teachers of English or other subjects and consultants of various types (e.g., business, agriculture). Early proponents of tentmaking described their jobs in those closed places as "the hidden highway" for ministry.[62] The key was for them to be competent in their fields. "Overseas as well as here at home, your knowledge of your profession and your ability on the job becomes known. If you want to command respect it is important to do your job well and to be perceived as competent by others."[63] They also needed to be able to integrate their work and ministry. Tentmaking was described as being particularly important for ministry to Muslims, one tentmaker to the Muslim world commenting, "Nearly all 'missionaries' in the Middle East have a tentmaker guise . . . regardless of their funding sources."[64]

Business as Mission

The term "business as mission" came into widespread usage in the late 1980s and roughly paralleled the rise of "marketplace ministries" in the church in America. Marketplace ministries typically focused on how Christians might better represent Christ in their workplace and emphasized the doctrine of the priesthood of all believers and the doctrine of vocation. The result was that Christian business persons reassessed not only their role in the workplace, but also their role in missions. Whereas many

---

[61]Tetsunao Yamamori, *God's New Envoys: A Bold Strategy for Penetrating "Closed Countries"* (Portland, OR: Multnomah, 1987), 57.
[62]Wilson, *Today's Tentmaking*, 47
[63]Hamilton, 70.
[64]Ibid., 69.

business people had viewed their role as being limited to providing financial support, they now saw that their talents—and their businesses—could be used in foreign missions. Hence, the rise of business as mission as a distinct mission strategy.

Comparing business as mission to other strategies and terminology used to describe the relationship of business and mission helps to clarify the differences. As discussed previously, tentmaking refers to

> Christian professionals who support themselves financially by working as employees or by engaging in business. . . . Business as mission sees business both as the medium and the message. Business as mission most often involves "job-making" as an integral part of its mission. Tentmaking may involve this but is more often simply about "job-taking"—taking up employment somewhere in order to facilitate ministry.[65]

Business as mission (BAM) is also distinct from business funding mission. The latter often limits "business and business people to a role of funding the 'real ministry.' While funding is an important function, business as mission is about for-profit businesses that have a kingdom focus."[66] BAM companies are sometimes referred to as "kingdom businesses" or "kingdom companies." One missiologist has noted that, when the term "kingdom" is used, it often refers to "a Christian-led company, usually in a mono-cultural setting, whose CEO is intentionally integrating the Christian faith into his company's DNA and attempting to operate his

---

[65] Lausanne Committee for World Evangelization, *Business as Mission: Lausanne Occasional Paper No. 59*, ed. Mats Tunehag, Wayne McGee, and Josie Plummer (n.p.: Lausanne Committee for World Evangelization, 2005), 6.
[66] Ibid.

company by biblical principles."[67] While BAM companies also seek to integrate the Christian faith into the fabric of the business, their focus is cross-cultural. Business as mission is also distinct from enterprise development in that the latter promotes local entrepreneurship whereas the former typically uses expatriate entrepreneurs to launch and manage a business which then employs local people.[68]

Rundle and Steffen have popularized the term "Great Commission companies," leading some to use that term to describe BAM companies. However, as the authors stated, "Most missionary-run businesses continue to be small, almost mom-and-pop operations that rarely become financially self-sustaining or grow to any meaningful size."[69] What they are referring to are "relatively larger businesses [that] are often more effective because they are generally more respected in the community and able to minister in ways that are impossible for individuals or smaller companies."[70] From my perspective, these larger businesses need to be funded by different means than BAM companies, which will result in different ownership and management structures and, hence, a different missiological focus. A final comparison is between social enterprise and business as mission. A recent article by Wismer noted that a BAM company should also be "a socially responsible business," which the article's author defined as "business is mission."[71]

A number of definitions have been proposed for business as mission. One of the broadest is "the utilization [by Christian businesspeople] of for-profit businesses as instruments for global mission."[72] Another describes it as operating "crossculturally, whose CEO engages the company

---

[67]Johnson, *Business as Mission*, 61.
[68]Johnson and Rundle, 25.
[69]Steve Rundle and Tom Steffen, *Great Commission Companies: The Emerging Role of Business in Missions*, rvd. and exp. (Downers Grove, IL: IVP, 2011), 9.
[70]Ibid.
[71]Ron Wismer, "Business Is Mission: An Integrated Model," in *Evangelical Missions Quarterly* 51 (July 2015): 270.
[72]Johnson and Rundle, 25.

in holistic community development projects that have kingdom impact.[73] Still another defined it as

> a socially responsible, income-producing business managed by kingdom professionals and created for the specific purpose of glorifying God and promoting the growth and multiplication of local churches in the least evangelized and least developed parts of the world.[74]

Notwithstanding the various definitions, business as mission has certain distinctive elements. Contrary to most traditional missions, BAM makes financial sustainability a high priority. "Differences notwithstanding, most BAM advocates agree that what is most distinctive about BAM is its for-profit approach to mission."[75] It is also focused on cross-cultural mission, "in particular in those areas where the gospel has yet to be received... [and] to areas of endemic poverty"[76] The business aspect of BAM is not viewed "as a distraction from ministry but rather as the *necessary context* through which relationships can be built and Christ can be revealed."[77] BAM practitioners also recognize that, in the Great Commission, "the Greek uses the imperative voice for the verb *to make disciples.*"[78] The focus of BAM companies is, therefore, on discipleship.[79] At the same time, BAM companies seek to be 'holistic,' which the Lausanne Committee defined as

---

[73] Johnson, *Business as Mission*, 61.
[74] Rundle and Steffen, *Great Commission Companies*, 45.
[75] Johnson and Rundle, 27.
[76] Lausanne Committee, 5.
[77] Rundle and Steffen, 41.
[78] Ralph A. Miller, "Key Concepts and Lessons Learned," in *On Kingdom Business: Transforming Missions Through Entrepreneurial Strategies*, ed. Tetsunao Yamamori and Kenneth A. Eldred (Wheaton, IL: Crossway, 2003), 284.
[79] Michael R. Baer, *Business as Mission: The Power of Business in the Kingdom of God* (Seattle, WA: YWAM, 2006), 14.

[bringing] all aspects of life and godliness into an organic biblical whole. This includes God's concerns for such business related issues as economic development, employment and unemployment, economic justice and the use and distribution of natural and creative resources among the human family.[80]

In order to keep these multiple objectives balanced, many BAM companies have adopted the concept of multiple bottom lines composed of social, economic and spiritual measures.[81] Recently, BAM companies have been described as being "missional," which includes a concern for church planting and evangelism, but also include "actions [that] produce real change for the sake of His mission of love and reconciliation to a broken world."[82] As observed by William Danker, the long-term hope is that contemporary BAM projects will assist local people with employment, thereby providing the base and nucleus of large and strong congregations.[83]

---

[80]Lausanne Committee, 5.
[81]Johnson and Rundle, 28.
[82]Mark L. Russell, *The Missional Entrepreneur: Principles and Practices for Business as Mission* (Birmingham, AL: New Hope, 2010), 21.
[83]Wilson, *Today's Tentmakers*, 73.

CHAPTER 8

Contextualization, Research Findings, Approaches, and Conclusion

This chapter begins with a discussion of the importance of contextualization, both as it relates to business and mission projects, and use of the Qur'an and other Islamic texts. The following section summarizes the research that was presented in the previous chapters. The findings of that research will inform the various approaches to contextualization, which is the subject of the third section. The last section focuses on recommendations for future research.

Contextualization

Contextualizing Business and Christian Mission

The subject of contextualization in Christian mission can take many directions. For the purposes of this book, the focus is on how Christians operating business-and-mission companies can best contextualize themselves and their business within Muslim-majority nations (MMNs). The argument has been made that, when conducted from a business base, Christian mission requires a further degree of contextualization from what would normally be considered as necessary to minister cross-culturally. Such contextualization goes beyond understanding business concepts as they would be taught at universities. Missionaries have found advanced training in such fields as "cultural anthropology, sociology, linguistics, translation theory, and communication science . . .

[to] have changed evangelical attitudes toward culture and non-Christian religions and have revolutionized the evangelical missionary enterprise through the infusion of new ideas."[1] Could it be that an understanding of the business, and economic underpinnings, of a culture may also prove valuable?

Practitioners and scholars in the arena of business and mission have consistently written about the need for specialized training to meet the challenges of doing business cross-culturally. In the 1970s and 1980s, much of that writing was directed at tentmakers—although it is certainly relevant for modern business and mission companies. One Christian leader who specializes in international job placement feels strongly that tentmakers "must have specialized orientation" and training "for cultural sensitivity."[2] Further, Yamamori wrote of the need for ministries that are "symbiotic," by which he meant they were "in accordance with contextual factors."[3]

When the concept of "business as mission" took root as a mission strategy, so did calls for greater training and the need for contextualization. Scholars noted that

> At present, most business people lack any meaningful training in cross-cultural ministry, and most missionaries are inadequately trained in the ways of business. For example, somewhere between 10 and 40 percent of American business professionals return early from extended assignments abroad because of difficulties associated with adjusting to a foreign country.[4]

---

[1] Sam Schlorff, *Missiological Models in Ministry to Muslims* (Upper Darby, PA: Middle East Resources, 2006), 25.
[2] J. Christy Wilson, 103.
[3] Yamamori, 141.
[4] Johnson and Rundle, 32.

One scholar and practitioner of BAM included, in a list of training requirements for BAMers, "contextual issues relevant to doing business and living in their particular foreign country . . . [including] its own peculiar culture, traditions, religions, language, power centers, markets, government, laws, corruption, security issues, and infrastructure."[5]

The ministry effectiveness of a BAM project is dependent upon the project's acceptance within the local community, which, in turn, depends upon how contextually appropriate the project is. Without community acceptance, the business may fail and "with the business's demise, the opportunity for mission both within the business and within the community will also be lost."[6] Another missiologist noted that, if contexts are disregarded, dysfunction will be the result, saying, "Context serves to condition what can and should be done. . . . Rural contexts in Kansas or Kenya, or urban slums in Sao Paulo or Jakarta will each require a different balance."[7]

There is also a growing awareness that a variety of factors (including economic) shape beliefs within a culture. For example, Priest wrote, "Economic and psychological and political dynamics can also be independent variables contributing to larger sociocultural patterns, with belief sometimes a dependent variable influenced by other factors."[8] In Muslim contexts, Cheong noted that money, finance, and economics, because of their foundations in the Qur'an, are part of a spiritual economy. As such, "Any witness of Christian mission that touches upon the material and

---

[5] C. Neal Johnson, 208.
[6] Ibid., 47.
[7] Edgar J. Elliston, "Contextualized Christian Social Transformation," in *The Word Among Us: Contextualizing Theology for Mission Today*, ed. Dean S. Gilliland (Eugene, OR: Wipf & Stock, 1989), 199.
[8] Robert J. Priest, introduction to *Christian Mission & Economic Systems: A Critical Survey of the Cultural and Religious Dimensions of Economies*, ed. John Cheong and Eloise Meneses (Pasadena, CA: William Carey, 2015), xxiv.

economic aspects of Islam . . . must consider what Muslims conceive to be the normative good."⁹

Contextualization Using the Qur'an and the *Hadith*

Utilizing the Qur'an and the *hadith* as a means to communicate the Gospel to Muslims has a long and complicated history. In his book, *Missiological Models in Ministry to Muslims*, Schlorff has traced this history from the highly polemical uses of the Qur'an in the 19th century to modern uses of the Qur'an, which regard it as containing some measure of truth that merely need to be fulfilled by a more complete witness of the Gospel. While I affirm Biblical revelation as truth, the question of whether or not the Qur'an or other Islamic texts contain elements of truth is not a subject of this book.

Here I propose to use passages in the Qur'an and the *hadith* as "points of contact." This term also has a long and controversial history, so additional clarification is needed. "Points of contact" do not connote "points of agreement." When points of contact are referred to in this book, it is for the purpose of comparing and contrasting the Christian meaning with the Islamic meaning—giving full respect to cultural and historical factors. The objective is to use points of contact to enhance the communication of the Gospel to Muslims in the marketplace.

From such points of contact the hope is that "stepping stones" will emerge having eternal significance. In the words of one missiologist, "Good contextualized communication is, in essence, an understanding of the audience and its context, and an adaptation of the message to fit the needs of people

---

⁹John Cheong, "Islamic Banking and Economics: A Mirror for Christian Practices and Mission in Muslim Contexts," in *Christian Mission & Economic Systems: A Critical Survey of the Cultural and Religious Dimensions of Economies*, ed. John Cheong and Eloise Meneses (Pasadena, CA: William Carey, 2015), 70.

in that context."[10] Using the points of contact provided by the Qur'an is also timely since the Qur'an is at the center of many Muslims' search for identity, particularly in the post-colonial world. McCurry noted, "We can no longer ignore Muslims or their book. It is becoming a 'must read' for all who would seek to understand what in the world is going on in our day."[11]

Research Findings

While numerous observations about business in Islam can be made from the various areas of Islamic doctrine, history, and thought that were examined, many of these observations fall into four broad categories. The first two are positive, in the sense that Islam presents points of contact that can be helpful to Christians engaging in business and mission. The last two are more apologetic in nature but nevertheless useful to Christians in that they refute arguments advanced by certain Muslim scholars, particularly by Islamists. Each of these categories will be described in separate sub-sections below.

Business in Islam and Capitalism are Highly Compatible

There are many verses in the Qur'an (as shown in Chapter 2 and Appendix 1), that address various aspects of trade and commerce and indicate their importance and acceptance in early Islam. The Qur'an refers to *tijarah* (trade and the act of trading) numerous times, and the passages are concerned with how *tijarah* is to be conducted. As noted in Chapter 2, there is a distinct business atmosphere in the Qur'an. This should not be surprising since Muhammad was

---

[10]Viggo Sogaard, "Dimensions of Approach to Contextual Communication," in *The Word Among Us: Contextualizing Theology for Mission Today*, ed. Dean S. Gilliland (Eugene, OR: Wipf & Stock, 1989), 168.

[11]Don McCurry, *Stepping Stones to Eternity: Jesus from the Quran to the Bible* (Colorado Springs, CO: Ministries to Muslims, 2012), 4.

integrally involved in trade and commerce as a young man and in the early years of his marriage to Khadijah. In the *hadith*, merchants are spoken of as being seated in places of honor next to martyrs. The Qur'an speaks in glowing terms of such trade being carried out over long distances from ships cutting through the seas. Allah is said to clearly distinguish trade from usury, permitting the former and prohibiting the later.

Restrictions on the types of trade and commerce that can be engaged in (activities identified as *haram*) are mainly religious and moral ones and have little impact on most economic activity. It was noted in Chapter 6 that *falah* (well-being or success) was at the core of Islamic economics. One scholar has even argued that the call of Islam is, in essence, a call to success, writing, "This call to success is proclaimed in the *adhan*, or call to worship (*salat*), which sounds forth to Muslims five times a day. . . . Come to success. Come to success."[12]

One of the hallmarks of capitalism is free markets for goods and services. Based on the Qur'an, the *hadith*, and Islamic thought and history, it can be shown that Islam is supportive of free markets. In the golden era of Islam, great importance was given to the smooth functioning of the marketplaces, as evidenced by passages from the *hadith* and later by the *hisbah* manuals. The fact that the marketplace was governed by the *muhtasib* (a person tasked with both religious and civil authority) is an indication of the close relationship between Islam and the marketplace. That close connection is also seen in Islamic history. Under the Fatimids, for example, the *muhtasib* was the third highest ranking religious figure, just below the chief *qadi* (judge) and the chief religious scholar. Even under the rule of Saladin, despite his many battles against European Crusaders, he

---

[12]Durie, 17.

expanded the marketplaces of Egypt when he opened them to trade with the Venetians and Pisans.

Notwithstanding the regulatory activities of the *muhtasib*, marketplaces in the early centuries of Islam were relatively free—i.e., supply and demand could function without interference. In the *hadith*, Muhammad specifically refrained from controlling the price of a certain commodity and stated that prices were from Allah. The underlying marketplace motives of self-interest and profit-making were also not restricted. Such freedom is seen in Islamic history when the Fatimids adopted *laissez-faire* market policies— another hallmark of capitalism.

Another hallmark is the right to private property. The Qur'an and the *hadith* clearly teach that possessions can be private and that an unequal distribution of them is permitted by Allah. The *hadith* even condones the defense of one's property to the point of death. In Fatimid Egypt, private property, private profit, and private capital were integrated into a form of capitalistic economy. As noted in Chapter 6, the affirmation of the private ownership of property in the Qur'an and in *sharia* (including the private ownership of land) was conceded even by Mawdudi—a man influential among the Islamists.

Participants in capitalist economic systems are incentivized to lower their costs in order to compete more effectively in the marketplace. Raw materials, labor, and other products are sourced wherever in the world they can be advantageously obtained and resold in other markets, hopefully at a higher price. This leads to a feature of capitalism that is highly noticeable and often criticized— globalism. Islamists have criticized Western capitalism for such activities, yet globalism was practiced in Muslim societies. As shown in Chapter 5, the Egyptian transit trade (i.e., importing and exporting the same product) was an important feature of its economy. The fact that *wakalas* and *funduqs* dominated the townscapes of such cities as Cairo attests to the importance of this global form of trade.

Islamists who decry Western industrialism made possible by globalism should take note that Egypt's rise to dominance in textiles in the Middle Ages benefited greatly from its participation in the Mediterranean transit trade. And its dominance did not stop with textiles, as evidenced by the Geniza Documents, which reference a highly diversified economy with dozens of industries operating in numerous industrial centers. Globalism in Islam also extended across religious lines. Even during the time of the Crusades, trade with Europe (particularly the Venetians) continued.

Many of the trappings of capitalist economic systems were also found in Islamic societies. The development of currencies to facilitate trade was an accepted feature of Islamic rule. As early as the Abbasids, regional mints were established. Modern scholars have also noted the similarities between Western capitalist economies and Islamic economies as it pertains to forms of commerce. For example, the *hadith* and *sharia* both evidence the development and acceptance of various forms of partnerships. The purpose of these partnerships was to allow Muslims to combine their resources, which permitted them to participate in global trading ventures. Fatimid Egypt was replete with such partnerships. There were even trading partnerships between Muslims and Jews

Although Islamists often rail against Western banks, Islam allowed Muslim merchant banks to finance the commercial transactions of others, and to accept deposits and take in capital from new investors. As noted in Chapter 5, detailed commercial contracts (often in triplicate) were drafted and conformed to the religious requirements of Muslims and others. There is also evidence that rudimentary double-entry bookkeeping was in use in Fatimid Egypt, which is certainly consistent with the argument that capitalism, involving multiple participants in scattered locations, was flourishing within Islam.

Business Provides Numerous Points of Contact Between Islam and Christianity

"Possessions and wealth" is a topic containing several points of contact. Islam identifies Allah as the creator, owner, and sustainer of the earth. All earthly possessions belong to Allah, and Allah distributes them to mankind in accordance with his will. Islam's doctrine of *tawhid*, (all human existence is submitted to the will of Allah) governs the distribution and use of possessions and wealth. In Islam, there is a sense that wealth and poverty are pre-ordained, which can result in fatalism. In the *hadith*, wealth and possessions are portrayed as temporal and a test, thus being ostentatious with one's possessions is prohibited. Muslims are to act as *khalifas* (trustees) under Allah with regard to their possessions.

Several Christian doctrines seem to be echoed in the Islamic view of possessions and wealth. For example, Christians would agree that both are owned by God and are distributed in God's providence. Christians also regard wealth and possessions as temporal and that one's role as a steward resembles, to some degree, the Muslim's role as *khalifah*. However, many Christians would differ with Muslims in such areas as the origin of poverty, Christians being more likely to view it as resulting from a web of factors that include human action (or inaction), as opposed to being completely pre-ordained by God.

A profound difference in the Christian view of wealth and possessions versus the Muslim view can be seen in the early centuries of Islam's history, where much of its growth and the increase in the wealth and possessions of Muslim adherents were provided by the booty gained through military conquest. The distribution of booty was also a subject of numerous passages in the Qur'an and the *hadith*.

Essentially, Islam condoned the acquisition of possessions and wealth through *jihad*. There is nothing analogous to this in the teaching and life of Jesus or in the doctrines of the Christian church.

Notwithstanding the connection between *jihad* and possessions and wealth, both the Qur'an and the *hadith* contain numerous teachings on work as a means of obtaining possessions and wealth. Allah prepared a Muslim's work, and the *hadith* teaches that one's livelihood (i.e., occupation) was pre-ordained. Manual labor was especially commended in the *hadith*, although in later Islamic history, trades came to be regarded as either "base" or "raised." During Islam's Golden Age, many Arab Muslims even eschewed the hard work of the marketplace, preferring rather to join the warrior class to receive booty and military pensions. In fact, later on, Muslims in Fatimid Egypt considered it degrading to be employed by others.

In any case, a good Muslim was to persevere in his livelihood and thereby gain the bounty of Allah. Earning a living through work enabled one (by virtue of having time and finances) to worship properly. It is interesting to note that the Islamist, Sayyid Qutb, affirmed work—even wage labor. He also accepted that, due to individual differences in talents and circumstances, some will be wealthier than others and some will inevitably serve others. Nevertheless, Qutb wrote that it was essential for Muslims to work and earn a living.

Christians would agree on the value of work, especially considering the apostle Paul's admonition that, if Christians want to eat, they should work (2 Thessalonians 3:10). Considering that Jesus was a carpenter, the dignity of manual labor is certainly affirmed by Christians. Although Roman Catholicism distinguishes between sacred and secular work, the Reformation reestablished the spiritual significance of all forms of work, Martin Luther's doctrine of vocation being seminal in this regard. Most Christians would reject the

Islamic doctrine of earning the bounty of Allah through work. While material wealth is not regarded by them as sinful, it is not the motivation underlying work. Rather, work is done to the glory of God and, in that sense, becomes a form of worship. Some Christians also connect work to a personal calling from God, a concept not found in Islamic teaching on work.

One's work conduct and business must be governed by a set of ethics. On this point, Muslims and Christians largely agree. While this book is being written at a time of heightened tensions between many MMNs and the West, I am reminded of an event several years prior when I missed a late-night connecting flight and was forced to stay overnight in Istanbul. Unbeknownst to me, a wallet containing a significant amount of cash plus credit cards fell from my coat pocket while in a taxi. The hotel concierge awakened me shortly before dawn to inform me that a taxi driver and his father were in the lobby desiring to return a wallet to someone with my name. The Muslim man and his father had, over several hours, retraced the taxi's stops. No cash was missing, the credit cards were not used, and the man and his father would accept no payment for their time and effort—let alone a reward. They were simply being good Muslims. As discussed in Chapters 2 and 3, the Qur'an and the *hadith* stress the need for honesty and fair dealing—e.g., using fair weights and measures, honoring transactions and written contracts, and exercising magnanimity with competitors. Greed is condemned. There would be many similar ethical exhortations in the Bible. It is important to remember that *sharia* in Islam is the supreme authority in determining the ethical behavior of Muslims, whereas Christians, because of the Biblical doctrine of separation of church and state, are commanded to respect civil authority as long as their conscience or the Gospel is not compromised.

In the *hadith* it is taught that merchants redeem their profits from work through almsgiving to the poor. Two of the most discussed forms of almsgiving in Islam are *zakat* and *sadaqa*, which represent important points of contact with Judeo-Christian teachings. One missiologist noted that *zakat* is an Aramaic loan word "for virtue . . . [which] came to be used by the rabbis for charitable gifts," and *sadaqa* is a loan word "from the Hebrew *sedaqa* or *sedeq*, meaning 'honesty' or 'righteousness,' . . . [which] was used by the rabbis of 'almsgiving.'"[13] Woodberry further noted that both Old Testament and New Testament passages clearly demonstrate concern that alms should be given to the poor. He also noted that both the Qur'an and the Bible lauded secret giving and giving with the proper attitudes.[14]

One of the more controversial points of contact between Islam and Christianity is the topic of usury. The seeming parity, however, masks the fact that Christians and Muslims are concerned with different things. For Muslims, *riba* is the focus. "Usury" was the word used in several early English translations of the Qur'an to translate *riba*. When Christians use the term "usury," they usually mean excessive interest. As discussed in Chapters 2 and 6, the term *riba* was not specifically connected with interest, rather it was more associated with transactions involving undue risk and chance where one party could be exploited. That the Qur'an would ban transactions involving *riba* as a means of protecting poorer Muslims from exploitation by the wealthy Meccan trading class casts a different light on the concerns that were being addressed.

That both Muslims and Christians desire to prohibit oppressive and exploitive transactions may move beyond a point of contact to a point of agreement. To regard Islam's

---

[13] J. Dudley Woodberry, "Contextualization Among Muslims: Reusing Common Pillars," in *The Word Among Us: Contextualizing Theology for Mission Today*, ed. Dean S. Gilliland (Eugene, OR: Wipf & Stock, 1989), 299.

[14] Ibid., 299-300.

prohibition of *riba* (especially the Islamist assertion that all interest should be prohibited) as somehow equivalent to Christianity's concerns about usury is not warranted and, in my view, is dangerous from an economic standpoint. The Islamist advocacy of interest-free banking and the dangers inherent in such action will be addressed in a separate section below.

Islam and Christianity have each criticized certain aspects of capitalism. Since the 1800s, Muslims have criticized numerous aspects of the Western capitalistic system. For example, in Egypt, whenever cotton prices dropped, Western-controlled markets and globalism were blamed by *fellahs*, who bore the brunt of the price decreases.[15] The worldwide depression of the 1930s was also blamed upon capitalist excesses. Early Islamists, such as al-Banna and Qutb, criticized Western capitalism for its materialism, especially compared to the hardships of the laboring classes. During Qutb's travels in the United States, he frequently attacked the busyness and pace of the West, which he viewed as being directed toward materialistic goals.

The extremes of wealth troubled both al-Banna and Qutb, with Qutb criticizing Adam Smith's "invisible hand" of the marketplace observing that such an idea only resulted in empowering "capitalist freebooters" who trampled on the poor.[16] Both Islamists and Muslim economists called for a middle way, where markets and capitalism would be tempered by Islamist moral principles and inequities remedied through *zakat* and *sadaqa*. A point of contact with Christianity arises since Christians have also criticized excessive materialism and argued for greater ethics in business.

---

[15] Yet, Egyptian rulers routinely skimmed the market when prices rose, thereby keeping producers from reaping excess profits that could have cushioned them during declines.

[16] Calvert, 134.

While the marketplace in Western capitalist systems is not specifically identified with any religion, numerous businesspeople hold to Christian ideals in the conduct of their business. The legal systems in the U.S. have traditionally upheld the right of individuals, and businesses owned by them, to operate by such principles. The fact that such rights have, in recent years, come under attack only added another point of contact between Muslims and Christians. Christian businesspeople have also used their wealth for the benefit of both Christians and non-Christians. One need only review the history of many foundations and non-profit organizations to see this phenomenon validated many times over.

Underdevelopment in MMNs is not Explained by Western Capitalism and Colonial Domination

Christians doing business in MMNs will at some time face resentment and possibly hostility from those Muslims who are of the opinion that the economic gap between rich Western nations and the poorest Muslim countries is due to exploitation and historical domination. One missiologist has also noted that Muslims tend to view Christian missions (even humanitarian efforts) with suspicion, writing,

> They assume that such activities are funded by Western governments, with a view to extending Western political control over the Muslim world. They typically charge Christian missions with being "imperialistic" and "immoral and despicable," and that we "take advantage of" the poor and needy in Muslim countries by "inducements to change religions." . . . In a word, Muslims assume that

Christianity is at bottom political in nature, and even territorial.[17]

This book sheds a different light on the real causes of underdevelopment in MMNs. While European colonial activities were admittedly at times arbitrary and discriminatory, they also left behind beneficial effects. Far more lasting and detrimental were the negative impacts of errors in governance by Muslim rulers, who often exercised power in a totalitarian manner, created massive bureaucracies, raised taxes, and expropriated private property. From a missiological standpoint, it is likely true that debates seldom win converts; however, being able to defend the moral ground upon which one is treading (daily) in the case of business and mission certainly seems justifiable. A summary of the key findings related to economic underdevelopment in MMNs is provided below.

While a comprehensive analysis of European colonial actions within Muslim countries is beyond the scope of this book, nonetheless the actions of the French and the British in Egypt, which were discussed at some length, will serve as the basis for the summary findings. The French conquest and occupation of Egypt at the end of the 18th century lasted only a few years, yet in that brief time Egypt's economy was certainly dramatically expanded. As noted in Chapter 5, Napoleon's experts laid the groundwork for large irrigation projects, which greatly increased Egypt's agricultural output. Also, a Frenchman was responsible for developing the strain of cotton that catapulted Egypt into the top ranks of producers of high-quality cotton. Although intended to supply their occupation troops, the French initiated some of the first factories in Egypt for the production of military supplies and windmills to make flour. It is likely more than coincidence that Muhammad Ali, who ruled Egypt after the

---

[17]Schlorff, 97.

French withdrawal, developed Egypt along the lines laid out by the French (i.e., through agricultural expansion and industrialization) and almost succeeded in toppling Ottoman hegemony by the 1840s.

The British occupation of Egypt, which lasted several decades, was resented by many classes within Egyptian society, and inequities resulted particularly in the area of land ownership. Early Islamists, such as al-Banna and Qutb, were motivated in part by their experiences in Egypt during the British occupation. Yet, the modernization of Egypt's agriculture, infrastructure, and industry continued under the British, which (by the way) also lowered the taxes on the peasants and abolished the Egyptian practice of forced labor. Under the British, government corruption was substantially eliminated and a new legal system was implemented, modeled after those in Europe. These structural changes led to sharply increased capital investment in Egypt by foreign investors. During the years of British occupation, Egypt's stock market thrived, although not without boom-and-bust cycles. Depicting European involvement in Egypt as producing nothing but oppression and exploitation is certainly an incomplete and unbalanced characterization.

A common theme of Islamic history was the emergence of strong leaders who established centralized governmental structures to carry out their wishes. This was not surprising since Muhammad set the pattern when he assumed both religious and civil authority and then selected a caliph to succeed him. However, authoritarian governance often has deleterious effects upon the business environment since individual freedoms are curbed, individual property rights restricted, and heavy taxes imposed to fund centralized institutions and bureaucracy.

While Muhammad did not accumulate wealth personally, many of his close associates did. As the caliphate shifted to the Umayyads, then to the Abbasids, so did increasing amounts of wealth and power. Toward the end of

Islam's Golden Age, the wealth of the ruling court was so great that even eminent Muslim scholars like Ibn Khaldun commented about it negatively. Ultimately, the Abbasids lost touch with the needs of their empire and did not administer the territories under their control efficiently. Economic strength shifted west to Egypt, and the Mongols ultimately conquered the Abbasids.

In Egypt, power was concentrated in the Fatimids. Although the leadership at times included non-Muslims (mainly as *viziers*), the Fatimids nevertheless saw themselves as successors to the caliphate. While marketplaces were allowed to function relatively freely, the Fatimids instituted various forms of taxes and often participated financially in the trade and businesses that were flourishing. (One might even refer to this as an early form of "crony capitalism.") When the Fatimids were replaced by the Ayyubids, the level of control and taxation continued to increase. The Ayyubids established a new system of land taxes (the *iqta*) to finance its military and the Sultanate (its form of government). The Mamluks, who succeeded the Ayyubids, took over ownership of the land; and by the time the Ottomans conquered Egypt, the Mamluks were the dominant landowners and had nationalized the trade of spice, sugar, and other goods. Egypt's agricultural output had fallen dramatically and production of textiles had also dwindled. All of the above occurred under the governance of Muslims.

After the Ottomans conquered Egypt, the level of taxation did not diminish. In fact, there is evidence that the tax rates levied on Egyptian peasants rose to 33 percent. Agricultural lands were turned into "tax-farms," which were auctioned off to officials and wealthy local families. In an effort to induce foreigners to do business in the Ottoman Empire, Suleiman the Magnificent in 1535 instituted the Capitulations, which exempted foreigners from local taxes and laws. These Capitulations were expanded over the centuries and by the time of the British occupation had become a major source of anger and resentment toward foreigners. That the Capitulations placed Muslims at a competitive disadvantage *vis-à-vis* foreigners is not in question; but it was Suleiman who initiated them, not the foreigners who benefited from them.

As discussed in Chapter 6, underdeveloped Muslim nations are also often characterized by corruption. It is important to note that the centralized governance of many MMNs makes them very prone to corruption. The reason is that centralized government becomes highly personal. Laws are not impartially adjudicated, rather they are interpreted by officials. Hence, a payment-for-service mentality arises, and it is not long before corruption is endemic. One example from Islamic history are the Janissaries who, under the Ottomans, entered into partnerships with Cairo businesses in exchange for protection. Later in Egyptian history, the successors to Muhammad Ali became deeply indebted as they borrowed to fund lavish life styles. Because they ruled Egypt through "hereditary right," many of Egypt's assets were sold to bidders who also paid monies to Muhammad Ali's family members. Even in current times, the author has encountered this form of corruption in many business contexts in MMNs.

Islamist Economic Arguments are Unproven

In response to a number of factors, as discussed in Chapter 6, Islamist thought gained in popularity in many MMNs in the 20th century. Although Islamist writings dealt with many factors outside of business and economics, several of their arguments are relevant to the conduct and structure of businesses operating in MMNs. One of the foundational arguments Islamists advanced was the need to return to a strict adherence of *sharia*. Growing out of this argument was the view that all banking should be *sharia*-compliant (i.e., interest-free). This is still a common theme, and some in the West are sympathetic to them. One eminent Christian missiologist has written that Islamic banking and economic ideas might help not only missionaries, but also "earnest Christians serving within the power structures of Western financial institutions and businesses . . . to repent and get our banking practices back in line with biblical ethics."[18] Yet, my findings would not support such an assertion. Conducting business under *sharia* and eliminating all interest would likely be harmful, not helpful.

Recent research by Muslim scholars (again as discussed in Chapter 6) has highlighted the cumulative negative impact of restrictive business practices and structures mandated by *sharia*. While Islam in its Golden Age proved to be accommodating when trade was between individuals or between small groups, due to its acceptance of various partnership structures, it had little ability to accommodate larger-scale trading operations or manufacturing operations, which required significant amounts of capital. Islamic partnerships had no legal standing apart from the individuals who formed them. These partnerships lacked continuity and lasted only as long as the partners lived. Muslim societies could not create new legal entities and legal concepts since the Qur'an and the *hadith* essentially placed outer boundaries on what was acceptable.

The joint stock company that evolved into the modern corporation had no rival in the Islamic world. The corporate structure could aggregate capital from an unlimited number of investors and could exist into perpetuity unless certain actions were taken. Ownership interests could be transferred or sold to others without the consent of the other owners. No Islamic business structure could rival these features within the legal framework of Islam until very late

---

[18] Jonathan J. Bonk, foreword to *Christian Mission & Economic Systems: A Critical Survey of the Cultural and Religious Dimensions of Economies*, ed. John Cheong and Eloise Meneses (Pasadena, CA: William Carey, 2015), xii.

into the rule of the Ottomans. Furthermore, Islamic inheritance laws had the continual effect of breaking up businesses and landholdings into smaller and smaller pieces. Attempts to circumvent those laws through putting assets into *waqfs* only served to freeze capital in structures that were inherently unsuitable to the conduct of business. While Islamic inheritance laws seemed egalitarian in early Islam, as economies of scale became a prerequisite for success in the industrialized world, Muslim societies found they could not compete effectively. When Islamists call for a return to pure Islam (including a return to *sharia*), one wonders how this would be beneficial to Muslims economically—let alone what Christians would find to lead them to repentance.

By far the most visible element of the call for *sharia*-compliant finance is the call to eliminate all interest. Equating the Qur'an's ban on *riba* with a ban on interest disregards much of Islamic history. As demonstrated in Chapter 6, there has always been debate over what constitutes *riba*, along with the recognition that interest (in some form) was needed in order to carry out trade. The Islamist position on interest has only gained traction since the 1970s, when Arab Muslim nations received an economic windfall due to the rise in oil prices. Within a few years, sovereign wealth funds controlled by oil-rich Arab nations had ballooned to unprecedented levels.

Based on my extensive experience in global capital markets, I am of the opinion that much of the enthusiasm about *sharia*-compliant banking stems from the desire of banks and financial institutions to structure products that will attract these pools of capital—along with the fees derived from them. Many *sharia*-compliant finance instruments are interest-free in name only—i.e., the returns to investors and purchasers of these instruments are paid in ways other than a stated interest rate. The returns may be lease payments or a certain amount of revenue from a specified asset. This corresponds with the conclusions of Chapter 6 where Islamic banks, by a wide margin, preferred to loan money on asset-based terms as opposed to the profit-and-loss system that is so touted by proponents of *sharia*-compliant finance.

Eliminating interest in favor of lending on the basis of profit-and-loss sharing (PLS) also appears to be harmful to depositors. As discussed in Chapter 6, returns to depositors decreased where returns were based on PLS as opposed to interest. Again, drawing upon the author's experience in performing corporate due diligence, the phenomenon of lower returns to depositors under PLS is quite understandable. In the absence of highly sophisticated accounting systems and internal control procedures, PLS lending will always favor the borrower. If the venture funded by the bank is profitable, the borrower (being closer to the cash flows) will normally find ways to siphon off cash flow before it is shared with the bank. Not surprisingly, the bank's losses will be magnified by this same phenomenon if the venture is unprofitable. In either case, the depositor's return will be reduced. Eliminating interest and substituting PLS would likely increase the overall financial risk of countries engaging in this practice, thereby reducing the value of businesses in those nations, which will ultimately lead to capital flight. The history of Islamic banking demonstrates that even devout Muslims will diversify their holdings and deposit funds with Western financial institutions in order to earn a more attractive return.

Approaches to Contextualization

Contextualization in missions is often concerned with how the message of the Gospel can best be communicated to a particular people group. In the case of business and missions conducted in Muslim-majority nations, contextualizing the Gospel message for Muslim businesspeople with whom we come into contact in the marketplace would be appropriate. This is but one facet of contextualization. Rundle and Steffen noted, "Since many people take an interest in the message of Jesus Christ only after seeing the Gospel in action, this means that the *messenger*, as well as the *message*, is important."[19] Every person engaged in business and mission cross-culturally is faced with the challenge of contextualizing his own words and deeds, beginning with the question raised in Chapter 1, which was, "Why are you here?" Contextualizing the message and the messenger is not the end of the story—at least for business and mission. In the modern world, business is seldom accomplished without a legal, financial, and business plan. How the business looks and operates on the ground is very noticeable in the local community and by authorities. Hence, there is also need to contextualize the method used in business and mission. Each of these three areas of contextualization will be addressed below.

Contextualizing the Messenger

The tentmaker, or missionary, who adopts a business and mission strategy in an MMN steps into two roles simultaneously—missionary and businessperson. The traditional missionary or mission organization knows little of this tension. The reason is that mission has historically been conducted from a Christian platform, such as a church, ministry, Bible school, or (in recent decades) from a non-governmental organization or some form of relief and development entity. Shifting the center of mission to a for-profit business requires that missionaries embrace a new role—that of businesspeople—while retaining their former role of missionary.

---

[19]Rundle and Steffen, *Great Commission Companies*, 43.

Mission organizations will often manage the tension by prioritizing mission over business. This does little to help business and mission practitioners deal with the ethical challenges and the day-to-day time demands emanating from the business. Dissolving the tension entirely by condoning the use of business fronts may remove the business challenges, but it exacerbates other pressures upon the missionary since his business will soon be recognized in the community as a sham. Thus, the question—"Why are you here?"—will be asked more insistently and with more suspicion.

Acting simultaneously as a businessperson and missionary often places the missionary in a paradox—to borrow a concept from H. Richard Niebuhr's *Christ and Culture*. Coming from a Pentecostal tradition, paradoxes provide opportunities for prayer and for the Holy Spirit to work. Paradoxes also provide opportunity to theologize more deeply. One such theologian was the reformer Martin Luther, who not only elevated the spiritual significance of everyday work by linking it with God's calling, but also developed a doctrine of vocation that provided guidelines on how Christians are to perform their work at the same time as the Gospel is being advanced. Studying Luther in this area would reward business and mission practitioners. Many of the current books and teachings on work and marketplace ministry owe much to Luther.

Once the messenger of the Gospel takes on the business role spiritually, intellectually, and emotionally, bridges with local business people can be built. For example, I befriended a Muslim businessman who was learning English. When I displayed an interest in his business (e.g., how it started, where his equipment came from, whether his children were involved in the business, etc.), he was motivated to communicate and talking became easy.

In a Muslim context, some approaches for contextualizing the messenger and establishing stepping stones for further relationship are as follows. If messengers of the Gospel working in MMNs speak to Muslims about the significance and value of work, they would likely meet with a positive response. Recall that the Qur'an and the *hadith* praise work, even manual labor. Thus, if these messengers were engaged in trade and commerce in the marketplace, they would likely meet with even greater acceptance since merchants are spoken of by Muhammad as having the same status as *jihad* martyrs. Likewise, if messengers of the Gospel come to an MMN from another part of the world having traveled great distances to engage in trade, this would also resonate with Muslims since the Qur'an speaks glowingly of merchants traveling long distances in order to pursue bounty.

Depending on a Muslim's background and education, business and mission practitioners should not be surprised if Muslims are puzzled by businesspeople who are also Christian, since there is a relatively long history of Muslims regarding Christians as being unconcerned with the affairs of this world. For example, Al-Din maintained that Christianity aimed at happiness only in the next world, and Qutb wrote that Christianity doesn't have much influence on the capitalist system since it left "Caesar to Caesar."

Thus, Christian businesspeople will need to convince Muslims that Christian doctrine is not opposed to business and supports many of the foundational components of business, including the right to private property. Furthermore, Christianity is not opposed to working in business and many Christians have been successful businesspeople and have used their businesses for good. Pointing out examples of businesses that are active in the region where the BAM project is located would be helpful. Citing Christian businesspeople who have instituted principles of service, honesty, fair dealing, etc. that correspond to the highest ethical standards of the Qur'an and the *hadith* would also be positive. In the event that Islamists concede there may be a few such businesses but then proceed to argue that the bulk of Western business has no moral concern and is only materialistic, one may make the following point. Even where there are dishonest and unscrupulous businesspeople, their competitors will hold them in check. For any business to operate for any length of time, they must treat customers fairly or those customers will not spend money a second time at a business that cheats them.

Contextualizing the Method

It may be stating the obvious, but the most effective means of contextualizing the method of any business and mission project is to actually perform a service, or produce and sell a product, that meets a need of the local community where the business is located. This calls for market research and business planning focused on that community. Often mission organizations and missionaries become enamored with a particular type of business or service (cafes and coffee shops, for example), and seek to replicate it wherever they wish to place a missionary. A one-size-fits-all approach to business startups is seldom possible without the benefit of a substantial marketing campaign, along with commensurate financial expenditures, to build brand awareness and demand (think Coca-Cola or Starbucks). Without such capabilities, businesses are typically built "one satisfied customer at a time," amplified through word of mouth (or social media), plus advertising and marketing efforts (often personal), directed at likely users of the company's products and services. Obviously, this poses a problem for substantially all businesses located under the mission-driven side of the missiological framework discussed in Chapter 7 and shown in Appendix 3. This is not to say such businesses should not be undertaken; but they will likely always be viewed as "foreign creations," and the expectation will be that foreigners will financially support them. The only business and mission companies that are truly contextualized as to their methodology are those that exchange goods and services for money with members of the local community and do so profitably—i.e., covering all their costs (even those of the missionaries involved). Anything short of this and the business is still foreign in the eyes of the local community and authorities, making it more likely to be closed in the event authorities in the MMN choose to do so.

In addition to the business basics discussed above, business and mission companies also need to be mindful of certain other constraints of operating in MMNs. The Islamic distinction between *halal* and *haram* activities represents a clear demarcation of the types of businesses that would be unacceptable. *Haram* activities, for the most part, do not pose a significant limitation upon business and mission companies since many of the prohibited activities would be questionable for Christians as well. Mission teams contemplating business and mission strategies should also include women, since in many MMNs only women are permitted to work with women. This is especially important because, as noted in Chapter 6, women are often more engaged in entrepreneurial activities than are men.

One area that impacts the methodology of business and mission companies is the Islamic restrictions on *riba*, specifically where *riba* restrictions are interpreted as prohibiting the payment of interest. As was discussed in Chapter 6, this directly affects many micro-finance projects, which provide financing in the form of loans (after the model of the Grameen Bank) and stipulate the payment of interest along with a return of the capital. An approach here would be to copy what many Islamic banks do—i.e., structure the loan as an asset purchase or lease arrangement, thereby replacing interest payments with installment or lease payments. If the borrower already has a business, the new monies could be structured as a joint venture, which would resemble Islamic *musharaka* financing. Avoiding interest entirely by first establishing indigenous savings programs, which then become sources of capital for micro enterprises, would also be a viable approach in MMNs.

Interest restrictions may also impact the manner in which BAM companies are capitalized. In the West, businesses are capitalized via a mixture of debt and equity. In an MMN, the solution may well require that funding plans substitute equity investments of various types in place of debt. The ownership of the BAM company would resemble a limited partnership in that returns would vary inversely with the amount of management contributed to the business—even if it was organized as a corporation with several classes of stock. The point is that the investors would be sharing risk, hence conforming to the Islamic ideal of profit-and-loss sharing.

A variation on this theme would be a venture-capital company whose purpose is to assist in the startup of new businesses by providing training and capital, which would be repaid through the profits of the businesses. This author has been involved in the establishment of such a venture company within an MMN. The authorities accepted the legitimacy of the entity and allowed it to operate in multiple MMNs. From the perspective of Islamic finance, it was not receiving interest and was sharing in the risks of each business it funded. It also resembled the highly regarded Bank Misr, which was discussed in Chapter 6.

While the previous paragraphs focused on certain big-picture contextual aspects of business and mission projects, it is important to note (due perhaps to the author's experience in global investment banking) that contextualizing the method needs to extend to a business' financial profile. A business must integrate all its financial transfers internally within the nation and externally with foreign entities into its operations and rationale. If the history of financial transactions of the business and mission company are not plausible given the nature of the business, this will be a red flag signaling danger for its longevity and providing the tax authorities in the MMN ample reason to close the business. Gone are the days when well-meaning missionaries can carry currency into nations and think that good will come of it. Due to the digital nature of the world's records, a dossier can rapidly and inexpensively be compiled on any company operating within any given nation. Also, recent U.S. laws, such as the Foreign Account Tax Compliance Act, require foreign financial institutions to provide a higher level of information to the IRS about the financial transactions of U.S. citizens. This higher level of scrutiny further complicates the situation for business and mission practitioners.

Contextualizing the Message

While the bulk of this sub-section will be devoted to specific approaches regarding how the Gospel message can be contextualized, there is one overarching issue that should be highlighted. The first two research findings described, (a) the parallels between business in Islam and capitalism, and (b) the points of contact between business in Islam and Christianity. The confluence of these two findings necessitates that the objective of the Christian message be carefully distinguished from Islam. While both Islam and Christianity address business topics, the reasons the topics are addressed and the conclusions reached are very different.

It has been noted by one scholar that Islam has an "underlying commercial spirit" that holds every man to a final reckoning where "their actions are read from the account-book, weighed in the balances; each is paid his exact due, no one is defrauded. Believer and unbeliever receive their wages."[20] Islam maintains that man is perfectly suited for his final accounting by Allah; he merely needs proper guidance to achieve *falah* (success). While the Bible also addresses business topics, such as private property, and links abundant possessions to diligent labor, such material blessings have no eternal value nor are they a measure of spiritual success. Man is rescued from sin only through Jesus' death on the cross. Herein is a fundamental difference between Islam and Christianity:

> A rescued person is not the same as a successful person. A rescued person is humbled by their experience, but a successful person will tend to feel superior and proud of their success. From the perspective of Islam, the losers are the humiliated ones; but from the perspective of Christianity, the saved are the humbled ones.[21]

Having highlighted this fundamental difference between Christianity and Islam, there is nevertheless an opportunity in the marketplace to use the points of contact between business in Islam and business in Christianity to communicate the Gospel.

Regarding Property and Wealth

In Islam, Allah is portrayed as creator, sustainer, and provider. Allah is also portrayed as the sole decider of who receives wealth and possessions. As was noted in Chapter 2, there is a strong sense that Allah pre-ordains wealth along with the status and position in society accorded with such wealth. Piety is also rewarded with material blessing, although the Qur'an teaches that some who are evil will also

---

[20]Torrey, 48.
[21]Durie, 19.

receive wealth. However, the pious are told that evil ones cannot be assured of retaining wealth and that disbelievers will be punished. While Allah owns everything, Muslims are given the right to possess and use property (as *khalifa*) in accordance with *sharia*. Among the obligatory items are the *zakat* poor tax, spending on one's family, leaving an inheritance, and not being wasteful in one's spending but rather keeping a proper balance.

While Christians can agree about much in the previous paragraph, there are some important distinctions. First, the Christian doctrine of stewardship varies from the Muslim *khalifa*. Since God created man in His image, man works creatively (like God) with the delegated authority he has received. Man was given an open-ended command to "fill the earth and subdue it, and have dominion" (Genesis 1:28, ESV). This is a mandate that's creative. The *khalifa* acts as a servant carrying out a set of duties, whereas Christians carry out their role of steward with great freedom, being led by the Holy Spirit and walking in His ways. There is no analogous pneumatology in Islam.

Second, as opposed to a predetermination of wealth, there is no fatalism in Christianity as it pertains to wealth and possessions. Man is not consigned to live in poverty, for if believers are in need, God promises to help them. The economic uplift often associated with Christianity is a testimony to the veracity of this promise. While the Qur'an has numerous passages related to the increase of wealth and possessions through the distribution of booty gained by military conquest, this is not so in Christianity. War, if condoned by Christians at all, must be "just"—personal enrichment never being regarded as justifying war.

Regarding Trade and Commerce

In Islam, the Qur'an affirms the value of work, both in this life and in eternity, and Allah has even ordained man for various livelihoods. Man is to pursue the bounty of Allah. Trading is clearly approved of in Islam and the merchant accorded high status. Marketplace ethics are primarily governed by what is lawful and unlawful. People are responsible for their own actions. There should be honesty and mutual consent in business transactions. Contracts and oaths should be kept. Employees should be paid for their labor. Competition is permitted but never to the point of unjustified aggression. *Riba* is clearly prohibited, but financing a business by entering into partnerships is permitted.

Many of the above business ethical standards contained in Islam would not pose a problem to Christian businesspeople, and Christian theologians could likewise make an affirmative Biblical case for business.[22] However, there are some profound differences. First, Islam often mixes the pursuit of business success with spirituality—e.g., pursuing Allah's bounty, Islam's preferential treatment of merchants in the afterlife, and earning rewards through giving. While Christians also pursue success in business, their motivation is to give glory to God, to give to others and to support the spread of the Gospel, not to gain God's wealth or earn spiritual rewards. It is true that some Christians adhere to a "prosperity Gospel," which regards wealth as part of what man receives from God through faith in Jesus, but only a minority of Christians hold such an understanding. Second, in Christianity there is a distinction between the kingdom of God and the affairs of this earth. While Islamists, such as Qutb, state that Christianity has no impact upon business, this is incorrect since it ignores the Christians' duty to live out their faith through their vocations.

There are certainly other approaches to contextualization for messenger, method, and message that could be mentioned. The following section will discuss the framework

---

[22] See, for example, Wayne Grudem, *Business for the Glory of God*.

of a more comprehensive comparison of business in Islam and business in Christianity, along with additional suggestions.

Suggestions for Further Research

As was mentioned earlier in this chapter, business-and-mission strategies—whether carried out in a Muslim setting or not—move the center of mission to a for-profit business. These are largely uncharted waters for modern mission agencies and missionaries. It requires learning another language (e.g., financial accounting, business terminology), learning new skills (e.g., analyzing markets, preparing business plans), and navigating complex laws, both U.S. and foreign—in addition to actually starting up and operating a business in an often-challenging business environment. Resources in these areas are readily available, although they would likely need to be tailored to the educational backgrounds and experiences of missionaries and other potential business and mission practitioners.

However, there are theological and missiological gaps that need to be filled for those seeking to engage in business and mission. For example, is their understanding of "business in Christ" at least as good as their understanding of "business in Islam?" It would be extremely helpful for business and mission practitioners to understand how business had been treated throughout Christian history and in Christian thought (from its various traditions), along with the various Christian responses to modern business issues.

One such issue often mentioned by Muslims relates to the longstanding Christian concerns about usury, which is interpreted by Muslims as supporting the Islamic call for interest-free banking. Yet, there is considerable variance in how the church has interpreted usury over the centuries. There are also tremendous differences between modern economies and those of Biblical times and the medieval period. These differences impact the discussion on what is usurious. While there are scholarly works available that analyze usury in various times and places, a concise survey and summary would be helpful to Christians doing business and mission in MMNs.

In dialogue between Muslim and Christian businesspeople, there is also a need for Christians to distinguish themselves from capitalism. While there are many areas in which Christianity is compatible with capitalism, there are also areas where Christianity will operate on a moral plane different from capitalism's emphasis on monetary and economic tools of analysis. Most research and writing in the Christianity/capitalism arena has been either by business people and non-Christian scholars or (in a few cases) by Biblical scholars and theologians who venture into the business and economics arena. Often, neither group possesses significant knowledge (let alone work experience) in the other group's field of expertise. Thus, interdisciplinary efforts are needed to forge theologies related to possessions and wealth, to stewardship, and to such real-world business issues as negotiation, tax minimization strategies, corruption, and security measures.[23] How should Christian ethics operate where business ethics are largely governed by family and clan loyalties as is the case in many MMNs?

While not directly connected to business, there is yet another area that impacts how BAM projects are contextualized. Most Christians would agree that for-profit businesses, which are regulated by governmental authorities and pay taxes to these authorities, operate as part of the world system. At best, institutions and structures of the world system are spiritually neutral, but they can also be

---

[23] I recount another discussion centered on how to protect a business and mission company's assets from the threat of armed robbery. Should it hire guards or should its people be armed? This raises the much larger issue of whether those seeking to advance the kingdom of God should use deadly force.

vehicles that oppress and corrupt. A business and mission company seeks to advance the kingdom of God, yet its environment and its continued existence are controlled by government authorities. Theologians have wrestled with the relationship of church and state for centuries. Therefore, would it not be appropriate to develop a theology for how business and mission companies should relate to state authorities while also advancing the kingdom of God? Also, in nations where law and order is not enforced, should business and mission companies seek protection from quasi-governmental groups or from local mafia groups? Such questions become even more difficult when the group is either unstable or corrupt. What theological frameworks can be developed to help business and mission practitioners answer such questions? And are there limits on how far a business and mission project can be contextualized? Does there come a point where business and mission simply cannot be contemplated?

Claims by Islamists and others that Islam represents a more community-based and less materialistic approach to organizing the economies of a global society need to be carefully assessed. One Christian scholar noted that

> if Islamic banking and economics can be used as a mirror in which to understand Christian mission and its relationship to the economic dimensions of life, it can open up new spaces to rediscover the practice of mission in more biblically faithful and holistic ways, in both Muslim and Christian settings.[24]

Based on the early returns from *sharia*-compliant finance efforts (discussed in Chapter 6), it is premature to give Islamic banking and economics the preeminent seat at the table. Nevertheless, high-quality academic research

---

[24]Cheong, 70-1.

should be conducted to test the outcomes of Islamic banking practices (e.g., interest-free banking) and *sharia*-derived requirements (e.g., nationwide *zakat* transfer payments), which claim to eliminate poverty.

Conclusion

There is little doubt that, at the present time, much mistrust exists toward Muslims, largely as a result of targeted attacks against non-Muslims by Islamic *jihadists*. Although *jihadist* attacks in the West have received global media coverage, such attacks are occurring with even greater regularity against non-Muslims living in many other parts of the world. With each attack, it is understandable that suspicion and fear of Muslims grows.

Yet as Christians, we cannot let our emotions overshadow the Great Commission of our Lord to "Go therefore and make disciples of all nations" (Matthew 28:19, ESV). Business has historically crossed many national and ethnic boundaries. As services are provided, and goods and money are exchanged, trust grows. Eventually, those who do business together form relationships. It is out of these relationships that opportunities will emerge to "walk on stepping stones of understanding" toward the truth of Jesus Christ.

APPENDIX ONE

BUSINESS IN THE QUR'AN

Topics Surah: Verse

I. Possessions and Wealth
   A. Allah's Role
      1. As Creator
         2:29; 3:190; 10:3; 11:7; 13:3; 14:32-34; 15:19-21; 16:5-6; 16:12; 25:48-50; 27:60; 36:34-36; 38:27; 42:11; 50:38; 91:5.

      2. As Owner
         1:2; 2:22; 2:106-107; 3:109; 3:189; 3:191; 4:131-132; 5:17-18; 5:120; 9:111; 16:52; 53:31; 63:7; 67:1; 85:8-9; 85:40.

      3. As Sustainer
         6:95; 6:141; 7:57; 15:19-21; 16:10-11; 16:65-70; 26:7; 32:27; 34:2; 35:9; 35:27; 36:33; 39:21; 50:9-11; 55:10; 56:63-73; 67:15; 80:24-32.

      4. As Provider/Rewarder
         2:2-5; 2:189; 3:174; 4:130; 4:134; 5:114; 6:44; 6:151; 7:32; 7:96; 11:6; 14:7; 16:53; 16:80-81; 16:97; 17:20; 17:31; 17:70; 19:77-80; 23:5; 24:32-33; 26:131-134; 28:60-61; 28:78; 29:17; 31:20; 34:4; 38:49-51; 38:54; 51:58; 53:31; 53:48; 57:10; 64:11; 65:2-3; 68:34; 71:12; 74:11-15; 87:14; 93:5-8; 96:6-7.

B. Distributed Unequally
> 2:212; 2:245; 3:26-27; 3:37; 3:73-74; 4:32; 5:64; 6:165; 7:37; 7:128; 10:107; 11:3; 11:9; 15:21; 15:88; 16:71; 17:21; 17:30; 20:131; 24:38; 29:62; 30:37; 34:39; 35:2; 39:52; 41:10; 42:12; 43:32.

C. Ownership (Private vs. Public)
> 2:205; 2:220; 3:49; 4:2; 4:5-6; 4:10; 4:29; 5:38; 6:142; 11:87; 16:71; 16:80; 17:34; 24:27; 24:61; 36:71-73; 38:24; 59:8; 61:11

D. Man as Khalifa
> 2:30; 2:155-157; 2:254; 2:261; 2:284; 3:14-15; 3:142; 3:186; 6:165; 8:28; 8:36; 9:24; 9:35; 9:75-76; 10:14; 17:16; 18:17; 18:34-36; 18:46; 21:35; 22:65; 23:64; 24:33; 27:62; 29:2; 33:72; 34:34-37; 35:39; 39:49; 40:4; 42:36; 43:23; 43:33; 45:12; 49:15; 57:7; 57:20; 61:11; 64:15; 68:14-20; 68:26-29; 69:28; 72:16-17; 73:11; 89:14-20; 90:5-7; 102:1-2; 113:5.

E. Spending and Use of

1. Right vs. Wrong
> 2:83; 2:179-180; 2:188; 2:195; 2:215; 2:219; 2:245; 2:261-267; 2:271-274; 3:92; 3:129; 3:180-181; 4:2; 4:5; 4:7; 4:36-39; 4:53; 4:176; 5:87; 7:31; 7:45-49; 9:35; 9:55; 17:26-27; 17:29; 24:22; 25:67; 28:76-77; 36:47; 42:23; 47:38; 51:19; 56:45; 57:20; 57:24; 59:7; 61:10; 63:9-10; 64:16; 65:7; 70:15-25; 76:8; 89:17-20; 92:8-11; 92:17-21; 98:5; 100:8; 103:1-3; 104:1-4; 107:2.

2. Zakat/Sadaqa
    2:3; 2:177; 2:219; 2:254; 2:261-277;
    6:141-142; 9:44; 9:53; 9:58-60; 9:79;
    9:103; 13:22; 30:39; 35:29; 36:47; 57:7;
    59:7-8; 70:24-25.

3. Giving to Allah
    2:58; 2:177; 2:245; 2:261-262; 3:181;
    3:199; 4:36; 5:12; 14:7; 8:41; 8:60; 9:20;
    9:24; 9:34; 9:41; 9:103; 22:40-41; 22:77;
    35:29-30; 47:7; 47:36-38; 48:11; 57:10-11;
    57:18; 64:17; 73:20.

II. Trade and Commerce

A. Allah's View of Trading
    2:16; 2:164; 2:184; 2:197-198; 2:254;
    2:273; 2:275-276; 3:196; 4:29; 10:22;
    14:31-32; 16:7; 16:14; 17:66; 17:70; 22:65;
    23:21-22; 24:36-37; 25:7; 28:57-58; 30:46;
    31:31; 35:12; 35:29; 40:79-80; 45:12-13;
    61:10-11; 62:9-11; 67:15; 73:20; 106:1-2.

B. Work and Success
    2:198; 3:136; 3:145; 4:32; 6:164; 7:10;
    9:24; 9:28; 17:12; 24:32; 30:23; 30:45;
    31:22; 34:12; 43:32; 45:13; 46:19; 53:39-
    41; 56:77; 56:81-82; 57:27; 61:10-11;
    62:10; 65:3; 67:15; 90:4; 94:6-8.

C. Halal vs. Haram Activities
    2:173; 2:219; 2:268; 5:87; 5:90; 7:33;
    10:59; 16:116; 31:6.

D. Marketplace Ethics
    2:188; 2:195; 2:205; 2:282-283; 3:75-77;
    3:104; 3:112-115; 3:161; 4:29; 4:58; 4:135;

5:1; 5:38-40; 5:89; 6:141; 6:152; 7:33;
7:85; 8:27-28; 11:84-85; 11:116; 13:20-22;
16:90-92; 16:93; 17:34-37; 18:77; 23:1-11;
26:176-177; 26:182-183; 28:25-26; 36:20;
38:24; 42:38; 43:32; 49:12-13; 50:24-26;
52:21; 55:7-10; 57:25; 58:11; 73:20; 83:1-3; 99:7-8.

E. Prohibition of Usury

2:188; 2:275-276; 2:278-280; 2:282-283;
3:13; 3:130; 4:160-161; 5:51; 30:39.

The assignment of verses to specific topics is based on the author's judgment. Certain verses appear in more than one topical category.

APPENDIX TWO

BUSINESS IN THE HADITH

The two major *hadith* traditions, *Sahîh Al-Bukhâri* and *Sahîh Muslim* are placed at the beginning of each topical analysis. The remaining *hadith* traditions are listed alphabetically by their abbreviation.

<u>Topics</u>   <u>Hadith- Book: Verse</u>

I. Possessions and Wealth (P&W)

   A. Allah's Role

        Bu- 15:28; 59:2; 97:35, 56
        Mus- 1:10, 44; 12:100, 144; 22:16; 38:5
        Maj- 37:14
        Nas- 23:64
        Muw- 13:1-3
        Tir- 34:18, 33

   B. Nature of P&W

        Bu- 77:31; 81:7, 10-11; 92:25
        Mus- 1:36; 12:34-35, 75-77, 113-115, 116-118, 120, 121-123, 124; 45:34; 50:55
        Maj- 34:3; 36:18; 37:3, 8, 9
        Nas- 44:2, 3; 50:26
        Tir- 12:42; 34:13-15, 19, 28, 31-32, 34-35, 40, 43, 44; 35:28-29, 30

   C. Distributed Unequally

        Tir- 25:24; 34:37

   D. Ownership (Private vs. Public)

        Bu- 36:1; 41:15; 45:8; 46:13, 33, 34

Mus- 22:136-143; 29:8-11; 31:13
Daw- 15:1215; 16:1278; 17:1335-1337;
33:1615-1625; 35:1708; 36:1845-1850
Maj- 12:67-68; 16:13; 17:3; 20:21; 36:2
Nas- 37:21-23; 41:1-6; 45:47-48; 46:1,15
Muw- 35:1-2; 36:24, 38
Tir- 12:54, 60; 13:29, 38-39; 31:2

E. Spoils of Battle
Bu- 2:40; 42:14-15; 47:3, 16; 56:186, 189, 191;
57:1-2, 6-7, 8-11, 17, 20; 72:36
Mus- 1:23, 182-183; 12:137-141; 17:35; 32:29-
30, 32, 33-40, 41-45, 47-50, 57, 72-3; 33:24-25,
153-154
Daw- 8:883, 977, 984-1007
Maj- 15:12; 24:34-36, 46; 36:3
Muw- 21:6-13, 20
Nas- 25:14, 15; 35:38; 38[1]; 44:78-79; 47:25
Tir- 15:28; 19:5, 8, 10, 12, 13, 14, 21, 32, 39, 40

F. Payment of Jizya
Bu- 58:1, 3, 5, 8
Daw- 13:1118-1122
Tir- 5:11; 19:31

G. Lost and Found
Bu- 28:9, 10; 45:2-4, 5-6, 9; 78:75
Mus- 31:1-10, 11-12
Maj- 18:1, 2, 4
Nas- 23:28
Tir- 13:35

H. Inheritances
Bu- 25:44; 51:12; 55:1-2, 3, 6; 85:6-16

---

[1]The book is concerned with the distribution of *al-Fay* which is the wealth taken from non-Muslims without fighting. The book has no chapters.

Mus- 12:51; 23:1, 2-4, 5-6, 14-17; 24:13, 18, 25, 31; 25:5-8
Daw- 11:1054-1065; 12:1071-1088
Maj- 14:1-2, 3; 22:3, 5, 6; 23:6, 10
Muw- 27:1-15; 37:1-10
Nas- 30:1, 3; 31:1
Tir- 8:6; 13:30; 27:7, 15-16; 28:1

I. Man as Khalifa
Bu- 81:3, 17
Mus- 33:42; 45:69
Tir- 34:19, 25, 27, 29, 30, 31, 38

J. Spending and Use of P&W

1. Right vs. Wrong
Bu- 23:2; 24:5; 34:40; 43:19; 51:27-29; 56:37, 177; 69:1, 9, 11; 70:29; 74:27-28; 75:4; 77:12, 25, 27, 36, 45, 46, 93; 78:66
Mus- 12:36-50, 57, 88-89; 30:12; 31:18; 37:1-5, 6-9, 13, 15-16, 23, 27, 31-32, 41, 42-50, 51-53
Daw- 27:1511-1514, 1530
Maj- 12:64-65; 24:4; 30:17; 32:3, 16, 17, 18, 19, 44, 45-46
Nas- 12:61; 21:53; 48:95; 49:31; 50:6
Tir- 5:34; 22:1, 2, 5, 13; 24:10; 34:26; 41:45-52

2. Zakat/Sadaqa/Charitable Giving
Bu- 2:2, 17, 20, 34, 40-45; 3:6, 25; 9:2; 24:1-4, 6-9, 10-30, 31-38, 46-49, 54-59, 63-66, 70; 34:12; 51:14, 15, 30; 52:26; 56:137; 69:2; 70:1; 79:9; 83:24; 88:3; 90:3, 14; 97:23
Mus- 1:8, 10, 12, 14-15, 19-22, 29, 32; 12:1-30, 32, 52-56, 58-62, 66-71, 72-75, 78, 80-81, 85-87, 92-93, 94-97, 110-112, 131-132, 160-161; 24:1, 9; 25:11; 31:19; 45:69
Daw- 3:519-567

Maj- 8:1-3, 4, 5, 6, 7, 9-13, 15-18, 19, 20, 24, 26-27, 28; 14:2, 5, 6; 15:1; 22:4; 23:5; 37:22, 23
Muw- 17:1-30; 21:5; 36:36, 41
Nas- 5:4, 10; 22:1; 23:1, 2-4, 5-11, 16-19, 20, 21-25, 28-30, 39-43, 46, 47, 53, 57, 58, 60, 61, 62-63, 64, 67, 68, 71, 76, 78, 82, 87, 89, 90, 93; 25:7-8, 45-46; 32:2-4; 33:2; 34:1-4; 35:37
Tir- 5:1-2, 3-5, 6, 7-9, 10, 12-13, 22, 27, 28, 36, 37; 12:62; 20:4, 6; 25:37, 40; 29:7; 34:17, 31; 38:1, 3, 5, 8

3. Waqfs
Bu- 40:12; 41:14; 55:12, 14
Mus- 25:15, 20
Daw- 11:1066
Maj- 15:4
Tir- 13:36

K. Poverty Alleviation/Economic Development
Bu- 24:50-53
Mus- 1:44; 12:69, 98-99, 101-102, 103-107, 109, 124-125; 53:50
Maj- 8:25; 16:17; 37:5-7
Nas- 23:80, 83, 85-89, 92-93; 50:14, 16, 29
Tir- 5:22, 23, 25, 38; 12:67; 13:38; 25:44

II. Trade and Commerce
A. Allah's View of Trading
Bu- 11:40; 25:150; 34:1, 6, 8-11, 13, 35, 49; 65:2
Mus- 5:288; 44:100
Daw- 3:572; 9:1025-1026
Maj- 12:3, 40, 41; 24:23
Nas- 44:7
Tir- 12:4, 34, 76; 45:36

B. Work and Success
> Bu- 34:1; 41:15; 59:6; 82:1
> Mus- 12:63-65
> Maj- 12:1-2, 4, 5, 64; 37:14
> Nas- 14:9; 23:48; 44:1; 50:33
> Tir- 12:6; 30:4

C. Halal vs. Haram Activities
> Bu- 8:73; 34:7, 39, 102-106, 112; 74:1; 86:1, 20
> Mus- 20:19; 22:38, 41, 67-70, 71-74
> Maj- 12:2, 5, 9-11; 16:18, 19; 30:6
> Nas- 44:2, 88-94
> Tir- 12:44, 46-48, 51, 52, 58-59, 61

D. Marketplace Ethics

  1. General
> Bu- 24:9; 34:2, 19, 22, 27, 48, 50, 51-52, 64-65, 95; 43:19; 44:3; 52:22; 78:58; 90:7; 93:48
> Mus- 1:107, 164, 186, 252; 21:23-28, 47-48; 22:14; 27:7; 33:21; 45:74-76
> Daw- 16:1251-1253; 36:1715-1719, 1795
> Maj- 12:34-35, 36, 39, 42, 45; 13:8-9; 24:42
> Muw- 22:9; 47:1-3; 56:1-8
> Nas- 35:22-23; 44:4-6, 12, 13-14, 30, 53-54
> Tir- 12:1, 3, 5, 9, 28-29, 32, 38, 55, 66, 69, 74; 25:46; 37:13

  2. Prices
> Bu- 34:41, 59, 68-72; 54:8, 11
> Mus- 21:11-13, 18-22; 22:129-130
> Daw- 17:1290-1296
> Maj- 12:6, 14, 15, 16, 27-28, 29
> Muw- 31:22-24, 45
> Nas- 26:20; 44:16, 17-18, 60-63
> Tir- 12:10, 12, 13, 40, 65, 73

3. Contracts
    Bu- 34:42-47, 57-58; 35:1-8; 37:22
    Mus- 21:7-10, 34, 44-46; 22:127-128
    Daw- 17:1297-1304, 1314-1326
    Maj- 12:17, 18, 21, 22, 26, 59-60, 61-62
    Muw- 31:1, 3, 7-15, 46
    Nas- 44:8-11, 30, 81-82, 95-96
    Tir- 12:8, 26-27, 30, 43, 53, 70

4. Competition
    Bu- 54:8, 11
    Mus- 45:31, 32-33
    Daw- 3:566
    Maj- 12:13
    Nas- 44:16, 19-21
    Tir- 12:57

5. Authorities, Corruption
    Bu- 24:41, 57, 67, 69; 51:7, 17; 90:15; 93:24, 41
    Mus- 12:177; 33:26-30, 48-50
    Daw- 18:1338-1368
    Maj- 8:14; 13:2
    Muw- 36:2
    Nas- 23:12, 14-15, 26, 95, 97-98
    Tir- 5:20; 13:4, 8, 9

E. Labor Practices
    Bu- 34:15; 37:1, 3, 4-8, 10, 14-15, 18; 49:15, 16, 18; 70:55
    Mus- 27:38-41, 58-59; 33:22
    Daw- 17:1282-1285
    Maj- 12:7-8; 16:4-6; 29:19; 33:10
    Tir- 23:44; 25:29-31

F. Ownership and Finance

1. Prohibition of Usury
	Bu- 34:23-26, 54-56, 60-63, 74-79, 89; 68:51;
	77:86, 96; 96:20
	Mus- 21:29-41, 57-69, 82, 121-122; 22:75-78,
	79-85, 93-104, 105-106
	Daw- 16:1249-1250
	Maj- 12:12, 20, 23, 32-33, 37-38, 48-50, 53-55,
	58
	Muw- 31:30-31, 33-34, 39
	Nas- 44:23-26, 27-29, 31-35, 36-44, 55-57, 73
	Tir- 12:2, 14-16, 17, 18-19, 23-24

2. Money vs. Barter
	Bu- 34:20
	Maj- 12:52
	Muw- 31:16-22
	Nas- 44:45-52
	Tir- 12:21, 37

3. Debts Allowed
	Bu- 8:71; 34:14, 16-18, 88; 38:1-3; 39:1, 3, 5;
	40:5-6; 43:1-5, 7-10, 12-13, 16-18; 44:9; 48:1-3,
	5; 51:23, 25; 53:14; 69:15; 80:39; 85:4
	Mus- 12:41-42, 96-97; 22:18-21, 22, 26-32, 39,
	118-122, 124-126, 142; 23:16-17
	Daw- 11:1070; 16:1254-1256
	Maj- 15:8, 9, 10, 11, 15-16, 18, 19, 20-21; 16:1,
	3; 22:7; 23:9
	Muw- 31:40, 42-44; 36:5, 10-14, 31
	Nas- 30:4; 44:57-59, 83, 97-104; 50:22-25
	Tir- 12:7, 31, 36, 39, 68

4. Partnerships
	Bu- 34:96; 36:2; 47:2, 5, 11

Mus- 22:133-135
Daw- 16:1272-1275
Maj- 12:63; 17:1, 3, 4
Muw- 31:36, 41; 32:1-15
Nas- 44:80, 106-109
Tir- 12:71; 13:31-32, 33, 34

5. Sharecropping
Bu- 41:8-12, 17; 51:35; 54:5, 7, 14
Mus- 21:86-112, 118-119, 120-123; 22:1-6
Daw- 16:1276-1277, 1279-1280
Maj- 16:7-9, 11,12
Muw- 33:1-2; 34:1
Nas- 35:45, 46
Tir- 13:41-42

APPENDIX THREE

BUSINESS AND CHRISTIAN MISSION: MISSIOLOGICAL FRAMEWORK

MISSION DRIVEN	BUSINESS DRIVEN
<ul><li>Business for Mission<ul><li>Facilitating the Mission<ul><li>Printing/publishing</li><li>Radio/TV/Internet</li><li>Medical clinics/hospitals</li><li>Schools</li><li>Community development</li><li>Handicraft sales</li><li>Individual economic assistance</li></ul></li><li>Facilitating the Missionary<ul><li>Guest houses</li><li>MK boarding schools</li><li>Language/culture training</li></ul></li></ul></li><li>Business funding Mission<ul><li>Income to support the mission</li><li>Income to support the missionary or mission agency</li></ul></li><li>Business for Entry</li></ul>	<ul><li>Poverty Alleviation/Empowerment<ul><li>Micro-savings and micro-credit</li><li>Micro-finance (Grameen)</li><li>Micro-enterprise</li><li>Small to medium size enterprise development</li></ul></li><li>Tentmaking<ul><li>As an owner (Apostle Paul)</li><li>As an employee</li></ul></li><li>Business as Mission<ul><li>Mission-owned</li><li>Investor-owned (Kingdom Business; Great Commission Companies)</li></ul></li></ul>

BIBLIOGRAPHY

Abdalla, Mustafa Gamal-Eldin. "Partnership Financing for Small Enterprise: Problems and Suggested Improvements." In *Partnership Financing for Small Enterprise: Some Lessons from Islamic Credit Systems*. Edited by Malcolm Harper, 56-61. London, UK: Intermediate Technology, 1997.

Abu-Lughod, Janet L. *Before European Hegemony: The World System A.D. 1250-1350*. New York, NY: Oxford University, 1989.

_____. *Cairo: 1001 Years of the City Victorious*. Princeton, NJ: Princeton University, 1971.

Abu-Rabi', Ibrahim M. *Intellectual Origins of Islamic Resurgence in the Modern Arab World*. Albany, NY: State University of New York, 1996.

Ackerman-Lieberman, Phillip I. *The Business of Identity: Jews, Muslims, and Economic Life in Medieval Egypt*. Stanford, CA: Stanford University, 2014.

Adam, Safaa Elagib. "The Experience of Traditional Saving Groups and El Kifaya Bank in Financing Poor Women." In *Partnership Financing for Small Enterprise: Some Lessons from Islamic Credit Systems*. Edited by Malcolm Harper, 24-29. London, UK: Intermediate Technology, 1997.

Adams, Bridget and Manoj Raithatha. *Building the Kingdom Through Business: A Mission Strategy for the 21st Century World*. Watford, UK: Instant Apostle, 2012.

Adams, Charles J. "Mawdudi and the Islamic State." In *Voices of Resurgent Islam*. Edited by John L. Esposito, 99-133. New York, NY: Oxford University, 1983.

Ahmad, Mushtāq. "Business Ethics in the Qur'an: A Synthetic Exposition of the Qur'anic Teachings Pertaining to Business." Ph.D. diss., Temple University, 1984.

Akhtar, Muhammad Ramzan. "Musharaka Financing for Small Enterprises in Pakistan." In *Partnership Financing for Small Enterprise: Some Lessons from Islamic Credit Systems*. Edited by Malcolm Harper, 35-41. London, UK: Intermediate Technology, 1997.

'Alī, 'Abdullah Yūsuf. *The Meaning of the Holy Qur'ān*. 10th ed. Beltsville, MD: Amana, 1999.

Ali, Maulana Muhammad. *A Manual of Hadith*. 2d ed. Lahore, Pakistan: Ahmadiyya Ishaat Islam, 2001.

Amin, Osman. "The Modernist Movement in Egypt." In *Islam and the West: Proceedings of the Harvard Summer School Conference on the Middle East, July 25-27, 1955*. Edited by Richard N. Frye, 165-178. The Hague, Netherlands: Mouton, 1956.

Asad, Muhammad. *The Message of The Qur'ān*. London, UK: The Book Foundation, 2003.

Ashtor, E. *A Social and Economic History of the Near East in the Middle Ages*. London, UK: Collins, 1976.

Badawi, Samer and Wafik Grais. "Meeting the Demand for Sustainable, Shari'a-compliant Microfinance." In *Shari'a-compliant Microfinance*. Edited by S. Nazim Ali, 9-16. London, UK: Routledge, 2012.

Baeck, Louis. *The Mediterranean Tradition in Economic Thought*. London, UK: Routledge, 1994.

Baer, Gabriel. "Guilds in Middle Eastern History." In *Studies in the Economic History of the Middle East from the Rise of Islam to the Present Day*. Edited by M. A. Cook, 11-30. New York, NY: Oxford University, 1970.

Baer, Michael R. *Business as Mission: The Power of Business in the Kingdom of God.* Seattle, WA: YWAM, 2006.

al-Banna, Hasan. "Toward the Light." In *Princeton Readings in Islamist Thought: Texts and Contexts from al-Banna to Bin Laden.* Edited by Roxanne L. Euben and Muhammad Qasim Zaman, 56-78. Princeton, NJ: Princeton University, 2009.

Barnett, Mike. "Creative Access Platforms: What Are They and Do We Need Them?" *Evangelical Missions Quarterly* 41 (January 2005): 88-96.

Befus, David R. "Economic Development and Holistic Mission." In *Business as Mission: From Impoverished to Empowered.* Edited by Tom Steffen and Mike Barnett, 101-113. Pasadena, CA: William Carey Library, 2006.

———. *Where There Are No Jobs: Enterprise Solutions for Employment and 'Public Goods' for the Poor.* Miami, FL: LAM, 2005.

Bloomberg. "Company Overview of Gulf Venture Capital Association." http://www.bloomberg.com/research/stocks/private/snapshot.asp?privcapId=114946893.

Bonk, Jonathan J. Foreword to *Christian Mission & Economic Systems: A Critical Survey of the Cultural and Religious Dimensions of Economies.* Edited by John Cheong and Eloise Meneses, xi-xiii. Pasadena, CA: William Carey, 2015.

Bosch, David J. *Transforming Mission: Paradigm Shifts in Theology of Mission.* Maryknoll, NY: Orbis, 1991.

Bragg, Wayne G. "Theological Reflections on Assisting the Vulnerable." In *Christian Relief and Development: Developing Workers for Effective Ministry.* Edited by Edgar J. Elliston, 49-73. Dallas, TX: Word, 1989.

Brunschvig, Robert. "Base Trades in Islam." In *Manufacturing and Labor*. Edited by Michael G. Morony, 151-166. Hampshire, UK: Ashgate, 2003.

Bulliet, Richard W. *Cotton, Climate, and Camels in Early Islamic Iran: A Moment in World History*. New York, NY: Columbia University, 2009.

Burton, John. *The Sources of Islamic Law: Islamic Theories of Abrogation*. Edinburgh, UK: Edinburgh University, 1990.

Bussau, David and Russell Mask, *Christian Microenterprise Development: An Introduction*. Oxford, UK: Regnum, 2003.

Calvert, John. *Sayyid Qutb and the Origins of Radical Islamism*. New York, NY: Columbia University, 2010.

Carré, Olivier. *Mysticism and Politics: A Critical Reading of* Fī Ẓilāl al-Qur'an *by Sayyid Qutb (1906-1966)*. Translated by Carol Artigues and revised by W. Shepard. Leiden, Netherlands: Brill, 2003.

Chapra, M. Umer. *Islam and the Economic Challenge*. Leicester, UK: The Islamic Foundation, 1992.

Chaudhuri, K. N. *Trade and Civilization in the Indian Ocean: An Economic History from the Rise of Islam to 1750*. Cambridge, UK: Cambridge University, 1985.

Cheong, John. "Islamic Banking and Economics: A Mirror for Christian Practices and Mission in Muslim Contexts." In *Christian Mission & Economic Systems: A Critical Survey of the Cultural and Religious Dimensions of Economies*. Edited by John Cheong and Eloise Meneses, 43-85. Pasadena, CA: William Carey, 2015.

Çizakça, Murat. *Islamic Capitalism and Finance: Origins, Evolution and the Future*. Cheltenham, UK: Edward Elgar, 2011.

Constable, Olivia Remie. *Trade and Traders in Muslim Spain: The Commercial Realignment of the Iberian Peninsula, 900-1500.* Cambridge, UK: Cambridge University, 1994.

Corbett, Steve and Brian Fikkert. *When Helping Hurts: How to Alleviate Poverty Without Hurting the Poor ... and Yourself.* Chicago, IL: Moody Publishers, 2009.

Coulson, N. J. *A History of Islamic Law.* Edinburgh, UK: Edinburgh University, 1964.

The Council of Islamic Ideology. "Elimination of Interest from the Economy." In *Money and Banking in Islam.* Edited by Ziauddin Ahmed, Munawar Iqbal and M. Fahim Khan, 103-257. Islamabad, Pakistan: Institute of Policy Studies, 1983.

Cragg, Kenneth. *Counsels in Contemporary Islam.* Edinburgh, UK: Edinburgh University, 1965.

———. "The Modernist Movement in Egypt." In *Islam and the West: Proceedings of the Harvard Summer School Conference on the Middle East, July 25-27, 1955.* Edited by Richard N. Frye, 149-164. The Hague, Netherlands: Mouton, 1956.

Crone, Patricia. *Meccan Trade and the Rise of Islam.* Piscataway, NJ: Gorgias, 2004.

Cummings, John Thomas, Hossein Askari, and Ahmad Mustafa. "Islam and Modern Economic Change." In *Islam and Development: Religion and Sociopolitical Change.* Edited by John L. Esposito, 25-47. Syracuse, NY: Syracuse University, 1980.

Cuno, Kenneth M. *The Pasha's Peasants: Land, Society, and Economy in Lower Egypt, 1740-1858.* Cambridge, UK: Cambridge University, 1992.

Daftary, Farhad. *The Ismāʿīlīs: Their History and Doctrines.* 2d ed. Cambridge, UK: Cambridge University, 2007.

Danker, William J. *Profit for the Lord: Economic Activities in Moravian Missions and the Basel Mission Trading Company.* Eugene, OR: Wipf and Stock, 1971.

Dashti, 'Ali. *Twenty Three Years: A Study of the Prophetic Career of Mohammad.* Translated by F. R. C. Bagley. Costa Mesa, CA: Mazda, 1994.

Davis, Eric. *Challenging Colonialism: Bank Miṣr and Egyptian Industrialization, 1920-1941.* Princeton, NJ: Princeton University, 1983.

Debs, Richard A. *Islamic Law and Civil Code: The Law of Property in Egypt.* New York, NY: Columbia University, 2010.

Dermenghem, Émile. *The Life of Mahomet.* Translated by Arabella York. New York, NY: Lincoln MacVeagh, 1930.

Dichter, Thomas W. *Despite Good Intentions: Why Development Assistance to the Third World Has Failed.* Amherst, MA: University of Massachusetts, 2003.

Dodwell, Henry. *The Founder of Modern Egypt: A Study of Muhammad 'Ali.* 1931. Reprint, Cambridge, UK: Cambridge University, 1967.

Durant, Will. *The Age of Faith: A History of Medieval Civilization—Christian, Islamic, and Judaic—from Constantine to Dante: A.D. 325-1300.* New York, NY: Simon and Schuster, 1950.

Durie, Mark. *The Third Choice: Islam, Dhimmitude and Freedom.* N.p.: Deror, 2010.

Ehrenkreutz, Andrew S. "Monetary Aspects of Medieval Near Eastern Economic History." In *Studies in the Economic History of the Middle East from the Rise of Islam to the Present Day.* Edited by M. A. Cook, 37-50. New York, NY: Oxford University, 1970.

El-Bhasri, M.E.T. and Nawal Abdalla Adam. "Examples of Partnership Financing for Microenterprise—The Case of Sudanese Islamic Bank." In *Partnership Financing for Small Enterprise: Some Lessons from Islamic Credit Systems*. Edited by Malcolm Harper, 13-18. London, UK: Intermediate Technology, 1997.

El-Gamal, Mahmoud A. *Islamic Finance: Law, Economics, and Practice*. Cambridge, UK: Cambridge University, 2006.

Elliston, Edgar J. "Christian Social Transformational Distinctives." In *Christian Relief and Development: Developing Workers for Effective Ministry*. Edited by Edgar J. Elliston, 167-177. Dallas, TX: Word, 1989.

———. "Contextualized Christian Social Transformation." In *The Word Among Us: Contextualizing Theology for Mission Today*. Edited by Dean S. Gilliland, 199-218. Eugene, OR: Wipf and Stock, 1989.

The Encyclopaedia of Islam. CD-ROM ed. Leiden, Netherlands: Brill, 2002.

Esposito, John L., ed. *Voices of Resurgent Islam*. New York, NY: Oxford University, 1983.

Essid, Yassine. *A Critique of the Origins of Islamic Economic Thought*. Leiden, Netherlands: E. J. Brill, 1995.

———. "Islamic Economic Thought." In *Pre-Classical Economic Thought: From the Greeks to the Scottish Enlightenment*. Edited by S. Todd Lowry, 77-102. Boston, MA: Kluwer Academic, 1987.

Euben, Roxanne L. and Muhammad Qasim Zaman, eds. *Princeton Readings in Islamist Thought: Texts and Contexts from al-Banna to Bin Laden*. Princeton, NJ: Princeton University, 2009.

Eyre, Anne. "Religion, Politics and Development in Malaysia." In *Religion and the Transformations of*

Capitalism. Edited by Richard H. Roberts, 301-309. London, UK: Routledge, 1995.

Farid, Fara Madehah Ahmad. *Shari'ah Compliant Private Equity and Islamic Venture Capital.* Edinburgh, UK: Edinburgh University, 2012.

Faroqhi, Suraiya. "Crisis and Change, 1590-1699." In *An Economic and Social History of the Ottoman Empire, 1300-1914.* Edited by Halil İnalcik and Donald Quataert, 411-636. Cambridge, UK: Cambridge University, 1994.

Fikkert, Brian. "Economists, Practitioners and the Attack on Poverty: Toward Christian Collaboration." Paper, Association of Christian Economists 20th Anniversary Conference, Washington DC, January 5-6, 2003.

Foltz, Richard C. *Religions of the Silk Road: Overland Trade and Cultural Exchange from Antiquity to the Fifteenth Century.* New York, NY: St. Martin's Griffin, 1999.

Frantz-Murphy, Gladys. "A New Interpretation of the Economic History of Medieval Egypt: The Role of the Textile Industry 254-567/868-1171." In *Manufacturing and Labor.* Edited by Michael G. Morony, 119-142. Hampshire, UK: Ashgate, 2003.

Gabriel, Richard A. *Muhammad: Islam's First Great General.* Normal, OK: University of Oklahoma, 2007.

Ghazali, Aidit. *Development: An Islamic Perspective.* Selangor, Malaysia: Pelanduk, 1990.

Goitein, S. D. *Economic Foundations.* Vol. 1 of *A Mediterranean Society: The Jewish Communities of the Arab World as Portrayed in the Documents of the Cairo Geniza.* Berkeley, CA: University of California, 1967.

———. "Mediterranean Trade in the Eleventh Century: Some Facts and Problems." In *Studies in the Economic History of the Middle East from the Rise of Islam to the Present Day.* Edited by M. A. Cook, 51-62. New York, NY: Oxford University, 1970.

———. "The Working People of the Mediterranean Area During the High Middle Ages." In *Manufacturing and Labor.* Edited by Michael G. Morony, 211-234. Hampshire, UK: Ashgate, 2003.

Goldberg, Jessica L. *Trade and Institutions in the Medieval Mediterranean: The Geniza Merchants and Their Business World.* Cambridge, UK: Cambridge University, 2012.

Goldschmidt, Arthur Jr. *Modern Egypt: The Formation Of a Nation-State.* 2nd ed. Boulder, CO: Westview, 2004.

Goldziher, Ignaz. "The Crafts Among the Arabs." In *Manufacturing and Labor.* Edited by Michael G. Morony, 145-150. Hampshire, UK: Ashgate, 2003.

———. *Introduction to Islamic Theology and Law.* Translated by Andras and Ruth Hamori. Princeton, NJ: Princeton University, 1981.

Gran, Peter. *Islamic Roots of Capitalism: Egypt, 1760-1840.* Syracuse, NY: Syracuse University, 1998.

Haddad, Yvonne Y. "Sayyid Qutb: Idealogue of Islamic Revival." In *Voices of Resurgent Islam.* Edited by John L. Esposito, 67-98. New York, NY: Oxford University, 1983.

Hallaq, Wael B. *A History of Islamic Legal Theories: An Introduction to Sunnī Uṣūl al-Fiqh.* Cambridge, UK: Cambridge University, 1997.

Hamilton, Don. *Tentmakers Speak: Practical Advice from Over 400 Missionary Tentmakers.* Duarte, CA: TMQ Research, 1987.

Hanna, Nelly. *Artisan Entrepreneurs in Cairo and Early Modern Capitalism: 1600-1800.* Syracuse, NY: Syracuse University, 2011.

Hathaway, Jane. "Egypt in the Seventeenth Century." In *Modern Egypt, from 1517 to the End of the Twentieth Century,* vol. 2. Edited by M. W. Daly, The Cambridge History of Egypt, 34-58. Cambridge, UK: Cambridge University, 1998.

Heck, Gene W. *Charlemagne, Muhammad, and the Arab Roots of Capitalism.* Berlin, Germany: Walter de Gruyter, 2006.

———. "Gold Mining in Arabia and the Rise of the Islamic State." *Journal of the Economic and Social History of the Orient* 42, no. 3 (1999): 364-395.

Henry, Carl F. H. "The Genesis of a Movement." In *The Ministry of Development in Evangelical Perspective: A Symposium on the Social and Spiritual Mandate.* Convened by Carl F. H. Henry, edited by Robert L. Hancock, 1-2. Pasadena, CA: William Carey Library, 1979.

Hiebert, Paul E. "Anthropological Insights for Whole Ministries." In *Christian Relief and Development: Developing Workers for Effective Ministry.* Edited by Edgar J. Elliston, 75-92. Dallas, TX: Word, 1989.

Al-Hilali, Muhammad Taqi-ud-Din and Muhammad Muhsin Khan. *Interpretation of the Meanings of The Noble Qur'ān in the English Language.* Riyadh, Saudi Arabia: Darussalam, 2000.

Hirszowicz, Lukasz. *The Third Reich and the Arab East.* London, UK: Routledge & Kegan Paul, 1966.

Hitti, Philip K. *History of the Arabs: From the Earliest Times to the Present.* 10th ed. Hampshire, UK: Palgrave Macmillan, 2002.

Hodgson, Marshall G. S. *The Classical Age of Islam.* Vol. 1 of *The Venture of Islam: Conscience and History in a World Civilization.* Chicago, IL: University of Chicago, 1974.

Homoud, Sami Hassan. *Islamic Banking: The Adaptation of Banking Practice to Conform with Islamic Law.* London: Arabian Information, 1985.

Hourani, Albert. *A History of the Arab Peoples.* New York, NY: MJF Books, 1991.

———. *Arabic Thought in the Liberal Age: 1798-1939.* Cambridge, UK: Cambridge University, 1983.

Hourani, George F. *Arab Seafaring: In the Indian Ocean in Ancient and Early Medieval Times.* Rev. exp. ed. Edited by John Carswell. Princeton, NJ: Princeton University, 1995.

Hoyland, Robert G. *Arabia and the Arabs: From the Bronze Age to the Coming of Islam.* Oxon, Canada: Routledge, 2001.

Ibn Khaldûn. *The Muqaddimah: An Introduction to History.* Abr. ed. Translated by Franz Rosenthal, abridged and edited by N. J. Dawood. Princeton, NJ: Princeton University, 2005.

Ibn Rushd. *The Distinguished Jurist's Primer.* Vol. 2. Translated by Imran Khan Nyazee. Reading, UK: Garnet Publishing, 1996.

Ibn Taymīya. *Public Duties in Islam: The Institution of the Ḥisba.* Translated by Muhtar Holland. Leicester, UK: The Islamic Foundation, 1982.

Ibrahim, Badr-el-Din A. "Financing Challenges for Small Enterprises—The Experience of Sudanese Islamic Banks." In *Partnership Financing for Small Enterprise: Some Lessons from Islamic Credit*

Systems. Edited by Malcolm Harper, 3-12. London, UK: Intermediate Technology, 1997.

Ibrahim, Mahmood. *Merchant Capital and Islam*. Austin, TX: University of Texas, 1990.

İnalcik, Halil. "The Ottoman State: Economy and Society, 1300-1600." In *An Economic and Social History of the Ottoman Empire, 1300-1914*. Edited by Halil İnalcik and Donald Quataert, 9-410. Cambridge, UK: Cambridge University, 1994.

Ishaq, Ibn. *The Life of Muhammad: A Translation of Isḥāq's Sīrat Rasūl Allāh*. Translated by Alfred Guillaume. Karachi, Pakistan: Oxford University, 1967.

Ishaque, Khalid M. "The Islamic Approach to Economic Development." In *Voices of Resurgent Islam*. Edited by John L. Esposito, 268-276. New York, NY: Oxford University, 1983.

Islahi, Abdul Azim. *Economic Concepts of Ibn Taimīyah*. Leicester, UK: Islamic Foundation, 1988.

———. "Economic Concepts of Ibn Taimiyyah." In *Readings in Islamic Economic Thought*. Edited by Abul Hasan M. Sadeq and Aidit Ghazali, 183-238. Dhaka, Bangladesh: Islamic Foundation, 2006.

Issawi, Charles. "Ibn Khaldun's Analysis of Economic Issues." In *Readings in Islamic Economic Thought*. Edited by Abul Hasan M. Sadeq and Aidit Ghazali, 332-355. Dhaka, Bangladesh: Islamic Foundation, 2006.

Jāmi' At-Tirmidhi. 6 volumes. Translated by Abu Khaliyl, edited by Hāfiz Abu Tāhir Zubair 'Ali Za'i. Riyadh, Saudi Arabia: Darussalam, 2007.

Jihad Watch, "Pakistan: Armed Muslims attack Christians, collect *jizya* from Christian merchants," http://www.jihadwatch.org/2012/09/pakistan-armed-muslims-attack-christians-collect-jizya-from-christian-merchants.html (accessed September 3, 2012).

Jihad Watch, "Sharia in action in Pakistan: Women's clothing store blown up after Islamic supremacists warned it not to sell women clothes, shoes, and bangles," http://www.jihadwatch.org/2012/08/sharia-in-action-in-pakistan-womens-clothing-store-blown-up-after-islamic-supremacists-warned-it-not.html (accessed August 24, 2012).

Johnson, C. Neal. *Business as Mission: A Comprehensive Guide to Theory and Practice*. Downers Grove, IL: IVP Academic, 2009.

Johnson, Neal and Steve Rundle. "Distinctives and Challenges of Business as Mission." In *Business as Mission: From Impoverished to Empowered*. Edited by Tom Steffen and Mike Barnett, 19-36. Pasadena, CA: William Carey Library, 2006.

Judah, Jamal. "The Economic Conditions of the Mawālī in Early Islamic Times." In *Manufacturing and Labor*. Edited by Michael G. Morony, 167-197. Hampshire, UK: Ashgate, 2003.

Kassis, Hanna E. *A Concordance of the Qur'an*. Berkeley, CA: University of California, 1983.

Kayed, Rasem N. and M. Kabir Hassan. *Islamic Entrepreneurship*. London, UK: Routledge, 2011.

Kazmi, Aqdas Ali. "A Window to the Unexplained: The mythology of Islamic banking is being propagated as a new science while the real questions about *riba* remain largely unaddressed," *Hamdard Islamicus* 29, no. 3 (July-September 2006): 108-109.

Khaldi, Kholoud. "The experience of Dawaimeh self-help group in musharaka financing." In *Partnership Financing for Small Enterprise: Some Lessons from*

Islamic Credit Systems. Edited by Malcolm Harper, 22-23. London: Intermediate Technology, 1997.

Khalil, Emad H. "An Overview of the Sharia'a Prohibition of Riba." In *Interest in Islamic Economics: Understanding Riba.* Edited by Abdulkader Thomas, 55-68. London, UK: Routledge, 2006.

Khan, Muhammad Akram. *Economic Teachings of Prophet Muhammad: A Select Anthology of Hadith Literature on Economics.* New Delhi, India: Oriental Publications, 1989.

———. "*Al-Ḥisba* and the Islamic Economy." Appendix in *Public Duties in Islam: The Institution of the Ḥisba."* Ibn Taymiya, translated by Muhtar Holland, 135-151. Leicester, UK: The Islamic Foundation, 1982.

———. *What is Wrong with Islamic Economics? Analyzing the Present State and Future Agenda.* Cheltenham, UK: Edward Elgar, 2013.

Kister, M. J. "The Market of the Prophet," *Journal of Economic and Social History of the Orient* 8 (1965): 272-276.

Kuran, Timur. *Islam and Mammon: The Economic Predicaments of Islamism.* Princeton, NJ: Princeton University, 2004.

———. *The Long Divergence: How Islamic Law Held Back the Middle East.* Princeton, NJ: Princeton University, 2011.

Labib, Subhi. "Egyptian Commercial Policy in the Middle Ages." In *Studies in the Economic History of the Middle East from the Rise of Islam to the Present Day.* Edited by M. A. Cook, 63-77. New York, NY: Oxford University, 1970.

Lai, Patrick. *Tentmaking: Business as Missions.* Waynesboro, GA: Authentic Media, 2005.

Landes, David S. *Bankers and Pashas: International Finance and Economic Imperialism in Egypt.* Cambridge, MA: Harvard University, 1958.

Lapidus, Ira M. *Muslim Cities in the Later Middle Ages,* student ed. Cambridge, UK: Cambridge University, 1984.

Lausanne Committee for World Evangelization. *Business as Mission: Lausanne Occasional Paper No. 59.* Edited by Mats Tunehag, Wayne McGee and Josie Plummer. N.p.: Lausanne Committee for World Evangelization, 2005.

Lewis, Bernard. *The Middle East: A Brief History of the Last 2,000 Years.* New York, NY: Scribner, 1995.

Lewis, Paul. "Assemblies of God World Missions: A History of BAM." Presentation, Business as Mission Consultation, Orlando, Florida, July 31, 2015.

Lings, Martin. *Muhammad: His Life Based on the Earliest Sources.* Rochester, VT: Inner Traditions, 2006.

Lombard, Maurice. *The Golden Age of Islam.* Translated by Joan Spencer. Princeton, NJ: Markus Wiener, 2003.

Lopez, Robert S. *The Commercial Revolution of the Middle Ages 950-1350.* Cambridge, UK: Cambridge University, 1976.

Lopez, Robert, Harry Miskimin, and Abraham Udovitch. "England to Egypt, 1350-1500: Long-term Trends and Long-distance Trade." In *Studies in the Economic History of the Middle East from the Rise of Islam to the Present Day.* Edited by M. A. Cook, 93-128. New York, NY: Oxford University, 1970.

Lopez, Robert S. and Irving W. Raymond. *Medieval Trade in the Mediterranean World: Illustrative Documents Translated with Introductions and Notes.* New York, NY: Columbia University, 2001.

Al-Mahalli, Jalalu'd-Din and Jalalu'd-Din As-Suyuti, *Tafsir Al-Jalalayn.* Translated by Aisha Bewley. London, UK: Dar Al Taqwa, 2007.

Mannan, M. A. *Islamic Economics: Theory and Practice (A Comparative Study).* Lahore, Pakistan: Sh. Muhammad Ashraf, 1983.

Al-Marghinani, Burhan al-Din. *The Hedaya, or Guide: A Commentary on the Mussulman Laws.* 4 vols. Translated by Charles Hamilton. London, UK: T. Bensley, 1791; reprint, Cambridge, UK: Cambridge University, 2013.

Marsot, Afaf Lutfi al-Sayyid. *Egypt in the Reign of Muhammad Ali.* Cambridge, UK: Cambridge University, 1984.

Al-Mawardi, Abu'l-Hasan. *Al-Ahkam As-Sultaniyyah: The Laws of Islamic Governance.* Translated by Asadullah Yate. London, UK: Ta-Ha Publishers, 1966.

Mawdūdī, Sayyid Abul A'lā. *First Principles of Islamic Economics.* Edited by Khurshid Ahmad, translated by Ahmad Imam Shafaq Hashemi. Leicestershire, UK: The Islamic Foundation, 2011.

McCurry, Don. *Stepping Stones to Eternity: Jesus from the Quran to the Bible.* Colorado Springs, CO: Ministries to Muslims, 2012.

McGowan, Bruce. "The Age of the *Ayans,* 1699-1812." In *An Economic and Social History of the Ottoman Empire, 1300-1914.* Edited by Halil İnalcik and Donald Quataert, 637-758. Cambridge, UK: Cambridge University, 1994.

Miller, Ralph A. "Key Concepts and Lessons Learned." In *On Kingdom Business: Transforming Missions Through Entrepreneurial Strategies.* Edited by Tetsunao

Yamamori and Kenneth A. Eldred. Wheaton, IL: Crossway, 2003.

Al-Misri, Ahmad ibn Naqib. *Reliance of the Traveller.* Rvd. ed. Edited and translated by Nuh Ha Mim Keller. Beltsville, MD: Amana Publications, 1994.

Mitchell, Richard P. *The Society of the Muslim Brothers.* New York, NY: Oxford University, 1993.

Mohammed, Saif I. Shah. "Islamic finance and microfinance: An insurmountable gap?" In *Shari'a-compliant Microfinance.* Edited by S. Nazim Ali, 33-45. London, UK: Routledge, 2012.

Al-Muwatta of Imam Malik ibn Anas: The First Formulation of Islamic Law. Revised and translated by Aisha Abdurrahman Bewley. Inverness, Scotland: Madinah Press, 2004.

Nafi, Basheer M. "The Rise of Islamic Reformist Thought and its Challenge to Traditional Islam." In *Islamic Thought in the Twentieth Century.* Edited by Suha Taji-Farouki and Basheer M. Nafi, 28-60. London: I.B. Tauris, 2004.

Naqvi, Syed Nawab Haider. *Development Economics: A New Paradigm.* New Delhi, India: Sage, 1993.

_____. *Islam, Economics, and Society.* London: Kegan Paul International, 1994; reprint, London: Routledge, 2013.

Navdi, Muhammad Junaid. "Understanding Economic Philosophy of the Holy Qur'ān," *Hamdard Islamicus* vol. 29, no. 3 (July-September 2006): 35-56.

Neill, Stephen. *Colonialism and Christian Missions.* New York, NY: McGraw-Hill, 1966.

Nourain, Asim. "ACORD Musharaka Credit Programmes in Sudan." In *Partnership Financing for Small Enterprise: Some Lessons from Islamic Credit Systems*. Edited by Malcolm Harper, 30-34. London, UK: Intermediate Technology, 1997.

Owen, E. R. J. "The Attitudes of British Officials to the Development of the Egyptian Economy, 1882-1922." In *Studies in the Economic History of the Middle East from the Rise of Islam to the Present Day*. Edited by M. A. Cook, 485-500. New York, NY: Oxford University, 1970.

Owen, Roger. *The Middle East in the World Economy: 1800-1914*. London, UK: I. B. Tauris, 2002.

Owens, Howard. "Nestorian Merchant Missionaries and Today's Unreached People Groups." In *Business as Mission: From Impoverished to Empowered*. Edited by Tom Steffen and Mike Barnett, 133-146. Pasadena, CA: William Carey Library, 2006.

Peters, George W. "The Church and Development: A Historical View." In *The Ministry of Development in Evangelical Perspective: A Symposium on the Social and Spiritual Mandate*. Convened by Carl F. H. Henry, edited by Robert L. Hancock, 3-30. Pasadena, CA: William Carey Library, 1979.

Priest, Robert J. "Christian Mission and Economic Realities." In *Christian Mission & Economic Systems: A Critical Survey of the Cultural and Religious Dimensions of Economies*. Edited by John Cheong and Eloise Meneses, xxi-xxxi. Pasadena, CA: William Carey, 2015.

Pronina, Lyubov. "U.K. Sells Islamic Bonds in First Non-Muslim Sovereign Issue." *Bloomberg*, June 25, 2014. http://www.bloomberg.com/news/articles/2014-06-

25/u-k-sells-200-million-pounds-of-debut-islamic-bonds (accessed 7/27/15).

The Qur'an. Translated by M. A. S. Abdel Haleem. Oxford, UK: Oxford University, 2005.

Qutb, Sayyid. *In the Shade of the Qur'ān.* Edited and translated by Adil Salahi and Ashur Shamis. 18 vols. Leicester, UK: The Islamic Foundation, 2000-2009.

Ramstad, Mans. "Relief Work and Development Work: Complement or Conflict?" *Evangelical Missions Quarterly* 39 (January 2003): 76-87.

Rashid, Saqib. "Islamic Finance and Venture Capital: A Practical Approach." In *Islamic Perspectives on Wealth Creation.* Edited by Munawar Iqbal and Rodney Wilson, 228-248. Edinburgh, UK: Edinburgh University, 2005.

Reilly, Robert R. *The Closing of the Muslim Mind: How Intellectual Suicide Created the Modern Islamist Crisis.* Wilmington, DE: ISI Books, 2010.

Risso, Patricia. *Merchants and Faith: Muslim Commerce and Culture in the Indian Ocean.* Boulder, CO: Westview, 1995.

Roberts, Robert. *The Social Laws of the Qorân.* London, UK: Curzon, 1971.

Rodinson, Maxime. *Islam and Capitalism.* Translated by Brian Pearce. London, UK: Saqi, 2007.

Rowland, Stanley. "Training for Community Health Evangelism." In *Christian Relief and Development: Developing Workers for Effective Ministry.* Edited by Edgar J. Elliston, 283-296. Dallas, TX: Word, 1989.

Rundle, Steve and Tom Steffen. *Great Commission Companies: The Emerging Role of Business in Missions.* Rvd. and exp. ed. Downers Grove, IL: IVP, 2011.

Russell, Mark L. *The Missional Entrepreneur: Principles and Practices for Business as Mission.* Birmingham, AL: New Hope, 2010.

Rutherford, Stuart. "The Poor and Their Money: An Essay About Financial Services for Poor People." Paper, Institute for Development Policy and Management, University of Manchester, Manchester, UK, January 1999.

Sadeq, Abul Hasan M. "Al-Ghazali on Economic Issues and Some Ethico-Juristic Matters Having Implications for Economic Behavior." In *Readings in Islamic Economic Thought.* Edited by Abul Hasan M. Sadeq, 138-171. Dhaka, Bangladesh: Islamic Foundation, 2006.

Sahîh Al-Bukhâri. 9 volumes. Translated by Muhammad Muhsin Khan. Riyadh, Saudi Arabia: Darussalam, 1997.

Sahîh Muslim. 7 volumes. Edited by Hâfiz Abu Tâhir Zubair 'Ali Za'i, Huda Khattab and Abu Khaliyl, translated by Nasiruddin al-Khattab. Riyadh, Saudi Arabia, 2007.

Sait, Siraj and Hilary Lim. *Land, Law & Islam: Property and Human Rights in the Muslim World.* London, UK: Zed Books, 2006.

Saleem, Muhammad. *Islamic Banking—A $300 Billion Deception: Observations and Arguments on Ribā (Interest or Usury), Islamic Banking Practices, Venture Capital and Enlightenment.* N.p.: Xlibris, 2005.

Schacht, Joseph. *The Origins of Muhammadan Jurisprudence.* Oxford, UK: Clarendon Press, 1953.

Schlorff, Sam. *Missiological Models in Ministry to Muslims.* Upper Darby, PA: Middle East Resources, 2006.

Schmidt, Alvin J. *Under the Influence: How Christianity Transformed Civilization.* Grand Rapids, MI: Zondervan, 2001.

Shepard, William. "The Diversity of Islamic Thought: Towards a Typology." In *Islamic Thought in the Twentieth Century.* Edited by Suha Taji-Farouki and Basheer M. Nafi, 61-103. London, UK: I.B. Tauris, 2004.

———. *Sayyid Qutb and Islamic Activism: A Translation and Critical Analysis of Social Justice in Islam.* Leiden, Netherlands: E.J. Brill, 1996.

Siddiqi, Muhammad Nejatullah. "Islamic Economic Thought: Foundations, Evolution and Needed Direction." In *Readings in Islamic Economic Thought.* Edited by Abul Hasan M. Sadeq and Aidit Ghazali, 29-56. Dhaka, Bangladesh: Islamic Foundation, 2006.

———. *Muslim Economic Thinking: A Survey of Contemporary Literature.* Leicester, UK: The Islamic Foundation, 1981.

Smith, Wilfred Cantwell. *Islam in Modern History.* Princeton, UK: Princeton University, 1957.

Sogaard, Viggo. "Dimensions of Approach to Contextual Communication." In *The Word Among Us: Contextualizing Theology for Mission Today.* Edited by Dean S. Gilliland, 160-182. Eugene, OR: Wipf and Stock, 1989.

Starcher, Richard. "Development: A Term in Need of Transformation." *Evangelical Missions Quarterly* 42 (January 2006): 52-58.

Sultan, Hussam. "Islamic Microfinance: Between Commercial Viability and the Higher Objectives of Shari'a." In *Shari'a-compliant Microfinance.* Edited by S. Nazim Ali, 46-59. London, UK: Routledge, 2012.

Sunan Abu Dawud, 11th ed. 3 volumes. Translated by Ahmad Hasan. New Delhi, India: Kitab Bhavan, 2012.

Sunan An-Nasâ'i. 6 volumes. Edited by Hâfiz Abu Tâhir Zubair 'Ali Za'i, Huda Khattab and Abu Khaliyl, translated by Nasiruddin al-Khattab. Riyadh, Saudi Arabia, 2007.

Sunan Ibn Mâjah. 5 volumes. Edited by Hâfiz Abu Tâhir Zubair 'Ali Za'i, Huda Khattab and Abu Khaliyl, translated by Nasiruddin al-Khattab. Riyadh, Saudi Arabia, 2007.

Suter, Heinz A. "Starting Kingdom Companies: A Biblical and Historical Overview." In *On Kingdom Business: Transforming Missions Through Entrepreneurial Strategies.* Edited by Tetsunao Yamamori and Kenneth A. Eldred, 181-194. Wheaton, IL: Crossway, 2003.

Swarup, Ram. *Understanding the Hadith: The Sacred Traditions of Islam.* Amherst, NY: Prometheus Books, 2002.

Swatos, William H. "Islam and Capitalism: A Weberian Perspective on Resurgence." In *Religion and the Transformations of Capitalism: Comparative Approaches.* Edited by Richard H. Roberts, 47-62. London, UK: Routledge, 1995.

Tafsir Ibn Kathir. Abr. ed. Riyadh, Saudi Arabia: Darussalam, 2003.

Taji-Farouki, Suha and Basheer M. Nafi, eds. *Islamic Thought in the Twentieth Century.* London, UK: I. B. Tauris, 2004.

Tignor, Robert L. *Modernization and British Colonial Rule in Egypt, 1882-1914.* Princeton, NJ: Princeton University, 1966.

Torrey, Charles Cutler. *The Commercial-Theological Terms in the Koran.* Leyden, Netherlands: E. J. Brill, 1892; reprint, n.p.: Kessinger, n.d.

Toth, James. *Sayyid Qutb: The Life and Legacy of a Radical Islamic Intellectual.* New York, NY: Oxford University, 2013.

Tourn, Giorgio. *The Waldensians: The First 800 Years (1174-1974).* Translated by Camillo P. Merlino, edited by Charles W. Arbuthnot. Torino, Italy: Claudiana, 1980.

Tripp, Charles. *Islam and the Moral Economy: The Challenge of Capitalism.* Cambridge, UK: Cambridge University, 2006.

'Ubayd, Abu. *The Book of Finance.* Translated by Noor Mohammad Ghiffari. New Delhi, India: Adam Publishers, 2012.

Udovitch, Abraham L. *Partnership and Profit in Medieval Islam.* Princeton, NJ: Princeton University, 1970.

UN Development Programme, Arab Fund for Economic and Social Development, *Arab Human Development Report 2002.* New York, NY: UN, 2002.

Uzair, Mohammad. *Interest-Free Banking.* New Delhi, India: Kitab Bhavan, 2000.

Vatikiotis, P. J. *The History of Modern Egypt: From Muhammad Ali to Mubarak.* 4th ed. Baltimore, MD: Johns Hopkins University, 1991.

Vikør, Knut. *Between God and the Sultan: A History of Islamic Law.* Oxford, UK: Oxford University, 2005.

Vogel, Frank E. and Samuel L. Hayes. *Islamic Law and Finance: Religion, Risk, and Return.* The Hague: Kluwer Law International, 1998.

Walls, Andrew F. *The Missionary Movement in Christian History: Studies in the Transmission of Faith.* Maryknoll, NY: Orbis, 1996.

Warde, Ibrahim. *Islamic Finance in the Global Economy.* 2d ed. Edinburgh, UK: Edinburgh University, 2010.

Watt, W. Montgomery. *Bell's Introduction to the Qur'an.* Edinburgh, UK: Edinburgh University, 1970.

_____. *The Formative Period of Islamic Thought.* Oxford, UK: Oneworld, 1998.

_____. *Islamic Philosophy and Theology: An Extended Survey.* 2nd ed. Edinburgh, UK: Edinburgh University, 1985.

_____. *Muhammad at Mecca.* London, UK: Oxford University, 1960.

_____. *Muhammad at Medina.* London, UK: Oxford University, 1956.

Weber, Max. *Economy and Society: An Outline of Interpretive Sociology.* Vol. 1. Edited by Guenther Roth and Claus Wittich, translated by Ephraim Fischoff and others. Berkeley, CA: University of California, 1978.

White, James R. *What Every Christian Needs to Know About the Qur'an.* Bloomington, MN: Bethany House, 2013.

Wiet, G., V. Elisséeff and Ph. Wolff. "The Development of Techniques in the Medieval Muslim World." In *Manufacturing and Labor.* Edited by Michael G. Morony, 3-32. Hampshire, UK: Ashgate, 2003.

Wilson, J. Christy. *Today's Tentmakers: Self-Support—An Alternative Model for Worldwide Witness.* Wheaton, IL: Tyndale House, 1979.

Wilson, Rodney. *Banking and Finance in the Arab Middle East.* New York, NY: St. Martin's, 1983.

———. "The Development of Islamic Economics: Theory and Practice." In *Islamic Thought in the Twentieth Century.* Edited by Suha Taji-Farouki and Basheer M. Nafi, 195-222. London, UK: I. B. Tauris, 2004.

———. "Islam and Economic Development." In *Islam in the Modern World.* Edited by Denis MacEoin and Ahmed Al-Shahi, 119-131. New York, NY: St. Martin's, 1983.

———. "Making Development Assistance Sustainable Through Islamic Microfinance." In *Shari'a-compliant Microfinance.* Edited by S. Nazim Ali, 63-75. London, UK: Routledge, 2012.

Winter, Michael. "Ottoman Egypt, 1525-1609." In *Modern Egypt, from 1517 to the End of the Twentieth Century.* Vol. 2. Edited by M. W. Daly, The Cambridge History of Egypt, 1-33. Cambridge, UK: Cambridge University, 1998.

Wismer, Ron. "Business is Mission: An Integrated Model." *Evangelical Missions Quarterly* 51 (July 2015): 268-275.

Wolf, Eric R. "The Social Organization of Mecca and the Origins of Islam." *Southwestern Journal of Anthropology* 7, no. 4 (Winter, 1951): 329-356.

Woodberry, J. Dudley. "Contextualization Among Muslims: Reusing Common Pillars." In *The Word Among Us: Contextualizing Theology for Mission Today.* Edited by Dean S. Gilliland, 282-312. Eugene, OR: Wipf and Stock, 1989.

Yamamori, Tetsunao. *God's New Envoys: A Bold Strategy for Penetrating "Closed Countries."* Portland, OR: Multnomah, 1987.

Yoder, Richard A., Calvin W. Redekop and Vernon E. Jantzi. *Development to a Different Drummer:*

Anabaptist/Mennonite Experience and Perspectives. Intercourse, PA: Good Books, 2004.

Yunus, Muhammad. *Banker to the Poor: Micro-Lending and the Battle Against World Poverty.* New York, NY: Public Affairs, 2003.

Yusoff, Nik Mohamed Affandi bin Nik. *Islam and Business.* Edited by Ismail Noor. Selangor, Malaysia: Pelanduk, 2002.

⸻. *Islam and Wealth: The Balanced Approach to Wealth Creation, Accumulation and Distribution.* Selangor, Malaysia: Pelanduk, 2001.

Zaman, S. M. Hasanuz. *Economic Functions of an Islamic State: The Early Experience.* Rvd. ed. Leicester, UK: The Islamic Foundation, 1991.

Zeitlin, Irving M. *The Historical Muhammad.* Cambridge, UK: Polity, 2007.

www.ingramcontent.com/pod-product-compliance
Lightning Source LLC
Chambersburg PA
CBHW052140300426
44115CB00011B/1453